International Joint Ventures

International Joint Ventures

An Interplay of Cooperative and Noncooperative Games Under Incomplete Information

By Ursula F. Ott

© Ursula F. Ott 2006

First published 2006 by
PALGRAVE MACMILLAN
Houndmills, Basingstoke, Hampshire RG21 6XS and
175 Fifth Avenue, New York, N. Y. 10010
Companies and representatives throughout the world

PALGRAVE MACMILLAN is the global academic imprint of the Palgrave Macmillan division of St. Martin's Press, LLC and of Palgrave Macmillan Ltd. Macmillan® is a registered trademark in the United States, United Kingdom and other countries. Palgrave is a registered trademark in the European Union and other countries.

ISBN-13: 978–0–333–96896–3   hardback
ISBN-10: 0–333–96896–4   hardback

This book is printed on paper suitable for recycling and made from fully managed and sustained forest sources.

A catalogue record for this book is available from the British Library.

Library of Congress Cataloging-in-Publication Data
Ott, Ursula F., 1965-
    International joint ventures : an interplay of cooperative and
    noncooperative games under incomplete information / by Ursula F. Ott.
        p. cm.
    Includes bibliographical references and index.
    ISBN 0–333–96896–4 (cloth)
    1. Joint ventures. 2. International business enterprises–Decision making.
3. Strategic alliances (Business) 4. Game theory. I. Title.

HD62.47.O885 2006
338.8′8–dc22   2005044518

10   9   8   7   6   5   4   3   2   1
15   14   13   12   11   10   09   08   07   06

Printed and bound in Great Britain by
Antony Rowe Ltd, Chippenham and Eastbourne

To Marek and Anna Tereza,
my real life international joint venture

Contents

List of Tables

List of Figures

Acknowledgement

Firstly, I would like to thank the editor Jacky Kippenberger for her patience, encouragement and understanding in the long phase of finishing the monograph which was marked by childbirth and other complications.

Secondly, thanks to the Austrian Science Fund for the financial support in the form of two grants, Erwin-Schroedinger-Grant and Charlotte-Buehler-Grant, and the British Academy, Small Research Grant.

Numerous discussions with colleagues and friends helped to develop ideas and offered insights during the writing of the book. Thanks to the comments of participants at seminars at the London School of Economics (LSE) and the Judge Institute at Cambridge University, participants at the First World Congress of the Game Theory Society, and participants at conferences of the Academy of International Business (AIB) and the European International Business Academy. I am indebted for stimulating discussions and valuable comments of Sudipto Bhattacharya, Trevor Buck, Mark Casson, Paul Dobson, Joern Rothe, Ursula Schneider and Bernhard von Stengel.

Special thanks goes to Joerg Borrmann, without his constant challenging thoughts, intellectual support and encouragement, this book would have never been possible to be published.

I am indebted to Marek, for his important encouragement to finish the book. The biggest thanks goes to Anna Tereza, my little daughter, who had to wait for my attention while I was writing the book.

1
Introduction

BEATRICE: (*off stage*) Thank you, Truffaldino.
TRUFFALDINO: (*shouting off L.*) Everything all right, sir?
FLORINDO: (*off stage*) Thank you, Truffaldino, that was delicious.
TRUFFALDINO: (*to audience*) I've done it. Served two masters at the same time and neither of them knows the other exists. And now for me pudden. (He goes to pudding and takes off cloth, tying it round his neck like a napkin. To pudding.)

Carlo Goldoni, *A Servant of Two Masters*

Introduction

The big questions in international business are related to transactions and negotiations crossing national and cultural borders. Managerial decisions transferred to an international level have to tackle uncertainties about the impact of geographical and cultural distance. It can be regarded as a special dimension which creates tension between the players. Thus, international business research needs to address these problems and to emphasize solution concepts on an abstract level in order to show the mechanisms at work. This research monograph considers international business as a field which should combine various theoretical concepts from other well-established disciplines to provide a robust tool for real life problems and their solutions. The author wants to encourage the reader to start a journey into the abstract world of economic theory with the aim to disentangle complex real life scenarios. It is, therefore, important to draw attention to an attractive way of dealing with problems by playing games. Games were, historically, a miniature of life, take monopoly or chess. A complex decision-making scenario, such as in business or war, transferred to an abstract level, empowers the players to analyze an inherent mechanism. These games offer the possibility to tackle difficult problems and find solutions in a playful and entertaining way. Focusing on chess, the strategist thinks in terms of plan rather than in single moves. He can decide how he would like his position to improve over the next few moves, he sets sub-goals, then begins to think about how to reach those end points. The art of planning ahead to obtain those positions where the tactics will be likely to decide matters in one's favor. The analogy of such a strategic game translates well into the strategic decision-making of international business. Though we can assume that the rules of the game are clear to every player, the uncertainties about crucial features determined by incomplete knowledge about specific factors need to be addressed. Thus, another analogy from the opening play of chess can be taken to the international business setting. Each separate opening should be looked upon as a plan for the development of the pieces. Within the broad framework of that plan, there is always room for flexibility, for innovation and improvization. The naming of chess openings is a colorful area. Some are named after their inventors or popularizers and others after their countries or cities of origin (English opening, Dutch opening, Sicilian Defence, Vienna Game etc.). Uncertainties about strategic behavior in the international context could be analyzed by using game theoretical reasoning with regards to opening the black box of decision-making on an international level. The appropriate example is an international equity joint venture which combines resources from firms across borders. The success and failure depends on strategic factors and the ability to anticipate risks and opportunities. A compact way of analyzing this is based on the strong tool of a game theoretic perspective.

What is an international joint venture?

Compared to domestic joint ventures, international joint ventures are formed with the intention to facilitate the penetration in new markets and to reduce risks of cross-border transactions. Another distinction between the two types is that the latter consists of a small number of parent firms with different sizes and a less balanced distribution of equity (Valdes Llaneza and Garcia-Canal, 1998).

Reducing risks and getting access to new markets are major goals of international co-operations such as mergers, strategic alliances, contractual forms of co-operation and international joint ventures (IJVs).

Table 1.1   Domestic versus International Joint Ventures

Domestic Joint Venture	International Joint Venture
To seek collusive practices,	To facilitate the penetration in new markets,
To get access to the know-how of the others,	To develop a new product and/or production process,
To penetrate new sectors	To reduce risks of cross-border transactions,
More than one partner	Small number of partners
Partners have similar size	Partners have different sizes
Greater predominance of equal equity	Less balanced distribution of equity in IJVs – particularly in LDCs

Source: Valdes Llaneza and Garcia-Canal, 1998

To focus on equity IJV, this special type of a multinational enterprise is a company being formed by two or more firms in two or more countries (Beamish et al, 1994; Kogut, 1988a). The entry rationale of this endeavor lies in acquiring technical know-how, raw materials access, production equipment, distribution facilities and/or capital endowment furthermore in developing a new product or production process (McConnell and Nantell, 1985). Since different cultures, management techniques, legal systems and logistic issues occur in an IJV, the complexity of such a company dealing with asymmetries between the parent firms was investigated by lots of empirical studies.

The international management and business literature captures various definitions of international joint ventures (IJVs). Shenkar and Zeira (1987) pointed out that a clear definition has not been found until the late eighties and they came up with the following definition (p. 547): 'An IJV is a separate legal organizational entity representing the partial holdings of two or more parent firms, in which the headquarters of at least one is located outside the country of operation of the joint venture. This entity is subject to the joint control of its parent firms, each of which is economically and legally independent of the other'. The authors developed their definition by elaborating on the notion of 'parents'. This notion is essential in characterizing IJVs, since parent firms feature 'both the independence of the JV as a separate legal entity as well as its partial dependence on those parties for raw materials, know-how, capital, trademarks, resources, markets, political support or personnel' (p. 547).

An International Joint Venture (IJV) can be defined as a newly formed company by two or more enterprises in two or more countries.

The purpose of an IJV is to acquire technical know-how, production equipment, distribution facilities and/or capital endowment as well as to develop a new product or manufacturing process (Beamish, Killing, Lecraw and Morrison, 1994; Kogut, 1988a; McConnell and Nantell, 1985).

IJVs and game theory

Why is it important to apply game theory to the IJV? How can we translate IJV characteristics into the game theoretical notation and terminology? Which games can be or will be played in an IJV? These problems will be handled in two steps by the general definition of game theory and by the application to the IJV situation in particular. Firstly, game theory provides solution concepts for situations of co-operation and conflict. Under the assumption that human behavior is rational, the players' actions and their pay-offs lead to a description of multi-person decision-making. We can distinguish between 'non-cooperative' strategies, which means that the players' choices are only based on their self-interest and 'co-operative' behavior, which develops axioms to capture the idea of self-interest, fairness and binding agreements (Fudenberg and Tirole, 1991). Secondly, in game theory special rules are used to describe a game. The description of a game should include at least the players, the strategies and the pay-offs. Essential elements are the information structure, outcomes, equilibria and the time structure. Thirdly, there are two ways of presenting game theory: the extensive form (a game tree as an equivalent to a decision tree) and the strategic or normal form which shows the pay-offs in a matrix (Gardner, 1995; Gibbons, 1992; McMillan, 1992; Myerson, 1991; Rasmusen, 1994).

The two classic games are chess and poker. The rules of chess are, for instance, relatively simple, yet the complexity of the game is derived from the contingencies of strategic reasoning which leads to a game of alternating moves represented best in a game tree. The structure of the game contains different openings, middle games and endgames. Thus, the link to the life cycle of an IJV can easily be drawn. The game can be solved by following the path which leads to find out who wins and how. As far as games of complete and incomplete information are concerned, there is either common knowledge or uncertainty about the player's preferences or pay-offs. Games under incomplete information such as poker are characterized by introducing nature, which is a dummy player and draws the type of player randomly. The types can have different features with respect to the special stage of the game. Since an IJV has to deal with strategic reasoning in the various stages of the life cycle like in the foundation, the management and the termination period, game theoretical reasoning offers a tool to multi-person decision-making processes. Furthermore, like in poker, several situations in an IJV occur in which the information is incomplete, or the players are lying or embezzling. Depending on the setting of the IJV, the firms play certain games. The problems are either related to finding out the right strategies or to disclosing hidden information and action. In the following chapters, the IJV scenarios are analyzed following the assumption that parent firms have to anticipate co-operation and conflict of the players involved during the life cycle. The underlying concept can be seen as a framework for multi-person decision-making in an IJV.

Ghemawat (1997) pointed out several problems for the use of game theory in business strategy and divided it in supply and demand side of the critique. On the supply side, the amazement that 'despite the works of Von Neumann and Morgenstern (1944), Schelling (1960), and their successors, the sorts of "strategic" (self-consciously interactive) considerations emphasized by game theory have not resonated more with strategists who must anticipate business competitors' moves'.

On the demand side, Ghemawat (1997) refers to Rumelt, Schendel and Teece (1991, pp. 18–22) in which several specific problems were cited:

a) Knowledge about the strategic phenomena to be studied is outside the scope of game theory and game theorists are (asserted to be) generally unwilling to learn much about business, leaving a leading role for scholars (presumed to be strategists rather than economists) who identify phenomena worth studying.
b) Game-theoretic analyses focus on explaining the possible existence of interactive effects rather than assaying their practical importance, which hurts predictive power.
c) Game-theorists model strategic phenomena piecemeal, in a way that focuses on a minimal number of economic variables to the exclusion of others – psychology, political, organizational, technological, and even economic – which limits both scientific testability and practical utility.
d) Game-theoretic equilibrium may be an unreasonable outcome to expect to observe in practice because of the information and the degree of rationality required to get there.

e) While game-theoretic models of industrial organization focus on external interactions, the roots of competitive advantage may be internal.

While there are these valid problems, it is important to point out that game theory offers a prescriptive approach to managerial problems. Myerson (1991) states that the range of applicability of expected-utility maximization in real decision-making is important. Thus, 'we must remember that any model of decision-making can be used either descriptively or prescriptively. That is, we may use a model to try to describe and predict what people will do, or we may use a model as a guide to apply to our own (or our client's) decisions. The predictive validity of a model can be tested by experimental or empirical data.' (Myerson, 1991, p. 22). The next step of a theoretical perspective is the testing of the hypothesis derived from the propositions tackled on the abstract level.

The abstraction of a problem can lead to solutions which would otherwise either not be seen or discussed away. Especially, the dismal view of the economics perspective in game theory can help to avoid a rosy picture shown by other disciplines which lack rigor. Thus, a robust way of analyzing and tackling problems in complex business settings not only helps to find the needle in the haystack, but also helps to strengthen a discipline which would otherwise end up in the muddy waters of illogical waffling.

This monograph provides an abstract approach towards the complex management of an IJV and it uses game theory for real life problems. Since the IJV literature and the international business material was thoroughly studied the critics of game theory mentioned in (a) can not be applied in this respect. Furthermore, the variables chosen are based on the IJV problems and applied to the specific context – a richer approach towards pay-offs could be found. Overall, this monograph wants to develop a robust analysis to complex problems in IJVs by looking at the static and the dynamic nature of a co-operative venture during the life cycle. This can only be tackled in a compact outlet and therefore the monograph was chosen over a journal article. Even though, journal articles are now much more popular to disseminate knowledge, there is a need to publish research monograph in order to generate knowledge for complex phenomena which need to be embedded in the relevant literature of the theory and the particular strategic subject. Thus, the conclusion deals with the theoretical contribution and the managerial implications.

MNEs and foreign alliances – the 'co-opetition' perspective

The combination of co-operation and competition in International Business was already used in a monograph written by Luo (2004) who investigates 'co-opetition' of multinational enterprises (MNEs) and their stake holders among them foreign alliances. This leads to the study of international alliances which contains equity joint ventures and collaborative agreements. The term 'co-opetition' shows the inter-play between co-operative and competitive strategies between the players. Therefore, it seems important to contrast Luo's monograph to this research monograph.

Luo's monograph deals with MNEs and its alliance partner in the co-opetition sense of an institutional approach. His understanding of control (used as competition in this context) and co-operation is a coupling between these two notions. He views them as 'two simulta-neously existing and mutually interactive processes embedded in repeated economic exchanges between alliance partners' (p. 102). Luo dissects control into private and collective control. Thus, the chapter deals with private and collective control in combination with co-operation. The outcome is a framework of typologies which should lead to better understanding of questions such as what are typical conditions or features shared by each typology identifier, what are strategic responses from alliance partners under each typology iden-tity that can yield highest possible unilateral or joint gains and how relational characteristics influence the control-cooperation dualism. The chapter is concluded by a case study of the alliance between DAEWOO and General Motors.

Compared to Luo's monograph, this research monograph uses co-operation and competition in the game theoretical sense of coalitions and non-cooperative games. The author wants to emphasize that the control types are, furthermore, endogenously given and considered as strategic archetypes of parental control within an IJV. The co-operative arrangements, therefore, take shared management, dominant and independent IJVs into account. Control mechanisms are critical to both majority and minority owners. Equity control is a crucial mecha-nism of exercising managerial control. Another managerial control mechanism can be seen as occupying key functional management and controlling key technological resources. These co-operative arrange-ments include IJV configurations such as R&D laboratories, joint pro-duction development, co-production, joint marketing and shared distribution services. The typology aims at the combination of strategic archetypes with IJV configurations. This should help to design games and develop contracts for each type.

The following chapters are structured in the way that the co-operative and non-cooperative games being played in an IJV can be tackled on an abstract level and prescriptions for managerial problems can be found. Since information economics (adverse selection, moral hazard and signaling) deals with incomplete information or behavior under uncertainty, the structure of the chapters shows the static and the dynamic approach towards information asymmetries. It is more important whether the players (firms) play games with each other than what kind of structure and control mechanism they show. Thus, this monograph takes the notion of 'co-opetition' further and shows games being played in an IJV.

The structure of the book

The book is about the strategic relationship of foreign firm, local firm and IJV management in a collaborative international joint venture. It is embedded in a theoretical analytical tool – game theory and its application – to offer a means of analysis which is compact and connects various stages of an IJV with information asymmetries. With regards to theoretical underpinning, the uncertainties between the players in the periods of an IJV are analyzed and solutions are offered to avoid conflict.

The first chapter of the book is an introduction into IJVs and game theory. The game theoretic perspective and its applications are the focus of chapter two. This part should give the reader the opportunity to position game theory in the context of economics, management and international business. The assumption is that game theory is not just the Prisoner's Dilemma, but also a useful tool to tackle information asymmetries. The applications of game theory are far-reaching and normally not covered in an in-depth analysis in International Business. Therefore, a monograph offers a unique possibility to use a complex theoretical tool to analyze a complex business phenomenon.

The third chapter uses the rules of the game as a structure to research the literature on IJVs and position players, their actions and strategies, the pay-offs and the timing of the game.

The fourth chapter is designed to introduce the notation of the later chapters and the general framework of an IJV life cycle theory based on game theoretic reasoning. Various criteria to structure IJVs are shown. This should help to position IJVs in terms of strategic interaction and the combinations of IJV configurations.

The fifth chapter deals with the static common agency problem which was already derived in the theoretical underpinning chapter. The start of the chapter gives an introduction into the typology of IJVs used in the rest of the monograph. The static view of an adverse selection and moral hazard problem in IJVs is used to show the games which can be played due to information asymmetries during the set-up phase of an IJV. It is important that the assumption that the players have private knowledge about the quality of their contribution affects their behavior in the next stages. It is, therefore, important to analyze the information asymmetries about knowledge and effort in the IJV management. Since the IJV management is a combination of representatives of both parents (foreign and local firm), the uncertainty about the quality of the management has an impact on the duration of an IJV. This chapter analyzes the contingencies of uncertainties, offers pay-offs for the games being played and the order of the play in these games. Thus, the theoretical approach helps to visualize the problems of co-operation and conflict in IJVs. The adverse selection problem is generally known as the 'lemon problem' and derived from the 'uncertainties in the used car market'. It is important that contracts are offered ex ante to enhance truth-telling. In a moral hazard context, the players are considered to cheat after the signing of the contract and this problem finds practical relevance in the insurance industry.

The sixth chapter deals with the dynamic perspective on the adverse selection scenario and the possibility to signal the type of the player. The signaling is considered a dynamic process since it implies that the other players can update their beliefs about the type of the informed agent.

The seventh chapter provides another dynamic common agency approach – the repeated game. This time it is the moral hazard problem which is analyzed in a dynamic context as the repeated moral hazard. Besides this dynamic approach, the termination scenarios in IJVs are used to show the possibilities of planned and unplanned terminations, the friendly and unfriendly relationship of the parents in this respect and finally, the cheating or co-operating behavior of the agent. The termination scenarios are leading to the typology of the IJV and the repeated moral hazard problem. Therefore, we have covered the uncertainty about knowledge and effort over the duration of an IJV.

The conclusion provides theoretical contributions and managerial implications to show the robustness of the findings in the monograph. This was the first time that the complex phenomenon of IJVs was embedded in a rigorous way of analysis to show the importance of tackling uncertainty about ability and effort in cross-national collaborative enterprises. The monograph, though, a more and more unpopular means of disseminating knowledge was chosen to look at the problems of complexity, uncertainty and duration in an IJV.

The mathematical appendix provides the models for the mathematically interested reader. The monograph is intended for international business scholars and uses therefore a mathematical appendix to provide the strength of the theoretical tool.

2
Theoretical Underpinning

Game theory

In order to position the monograph's contents, game theory and its solution concepts are based on the works of Von Neumann and Morgenstern (1944), Nash (1950, 1951, 1953), Selten (1965) and Harsanyi (1967–68). These game theorists represent the various perspectives and solution concepts. Based on their equilibrium concept, solutions could be derived.

Applications of game theory can be found in different directions of economics: (1) Microeconomics and Game Theory (2) Information Economics – Incomplete Information Solution Concepts, Asymmetric Information (3) Personnel Economics – Incentive Theory, Team Theory (4) Regulation Economics – Cost and Pricing Mechanisms (5) Industrial Organization. In the field of Management, game theoretical reasoning can be found in Finance and Accounting, Strategic Management and Management Science (operations research). Compared to its economics applications, game theory is not widely used in management, let alone in International Business. Thus, it is important to outline the theoretical background and its potential in this chapter.

In game theory special rules are used to describe a game. The description of a game should include at least the number of players, the strategies and actions as well as the pay-offs. Additionally, the information and time structure has to be considered. Secondly, there are several ways of presenting game theory such as the extensive form (a game tree as an equivalent to a decision tree), the strategic or normal form which shows the pay-offs in a matrix and the Bayesian form (Gardner, 1995; Gibbons, 1992; McMillan, 1992; Myerson, 1991; Rasmusen, 1994). Thirdly, it can be distinguished in general between co-operative and non-cooperative game theory. The word 'non-cooperative' means that the players' choices are based only on their self-interest, in contrast to 'co-operative' behavior, which develops axioms to capture the idea of fairness and binding agreements (Fudenberg and Tirole, 1991).

In the case of dynamic games presented in extensive form, there is a difference between strategies and actions (occurring only in dynamic games). A strategy for a player is any rule determining a move at every possible information state in the game. Each player can choose between two or more actions (left or right, bottom or top) whereas a strategy is a complete plan of actions (Myerson, 1991; Rasmusen, 1994). Related to an underlying extensive-form game, an action for a player in a Bayesian game may represent a plan that specifies a move for every contingency being considered as possible after learning the player's type. For this reason, a strategy for player i in the game under incomplete information is defined to be a function from his set of types T_i into his set of actions C_i.

Concerning the information structure of an IJV, information is a source of bargaining strength, and the information set is a player's knowledge at a particular time of the values of different variables. The elements of an information set are the different possible values and the actions being taken previously. The information set can change over time. Information is common knowledge if it is known to all the players, if each player knows that all the players know it, if each player knows that all the players know that all the players know it, and so on (Rasmusen, 1994). As far as a player knows all previous moves of the opponent, and this is true for all players then there exists a game of perfect information like chess. Imperfect information occurs when certain moves or actions of a player cannot be observed by other players. It is important to show that imperfect information is not incomplete information. In games of perfect and imperfect information players know all relevant characteristics of their opponents and nobody has private information about special individual features. These games are called games with complete information. The games with incomplete information occur in the case of unobservable preferences, endowment or features of a player. We can describe this situation as hidden information. A game with incomplete information can be transformed in a game of imperfect information through the moves of nature (dummy player). This requires to show a precise description of all possible combinations of types of players as well as the specification of their subjective probabilities (Harsanyi, 1967/68; Holler and Illing, 1996; Rasmusen, 1994).

Games and their equilibrium concepts

With regards to the earlier mentioned solution concepts, game theory should be explained in the context of static and dynamic game theory and game theory of complete and incomplete information. The relevant solution concepts can be named as Nash equilibrium, Sub-game perfect Nash equilibrium, Bayesian Nash equilibrium, perfect Bayesian equilibrium. The following table combines these strands of game theory and the monograph can be positioned in the column of incomplete information (marked grey therefore).

Table 2.1 Solution Concepts in Game Theory

Games	Complete Information	Incomplete Information
Static Games	Nash Equilibrium	Bayesian Nash Equilibrium
Dynamic Games	Subgame Perfect Equilibrium	Perfect Bayesian Equilibrium

Games of incomplete information

Dealing with information asymmetries and uncertainties, it can be stated that this issue has been addressed by various disciplines. Thus, in order to give a consistent background the focus lies on the game theoretical development and its applications in economic theory. Therefore, the theoretical underpinning is based on the seminal work of Harsanyi (1968), which can be seen as the introduction to information economics which focuses on problems of adverse selection, signaling and moral hazard. This shows the bridge between the early days of game theory and modern economic theory, especially information economics. Since international business can be considered as a hybrid of economics and management, it might be worth to derive methods from tools based on a well-established discipline and apply it to real life problems in international business. The advantage of such a procedure lies in gaining insights about the mechanism on an abstract level and finding solutions for managerial issues.

Harsanyi (1967–68) developed the games of incomplete information (with static games and dynamic games). The game theoretical applications which are useful for the underlying monograph are information economics, agency theory and common agency theory as a particular application for multi-principal-agent theory. The following table shows

the applications and some authors in the field as well as the contents
of the theoretical concept.

Table 2.2   Applications of Games of Incomplete Information

Information Economics	Agency Theory	Common Agency Theory
Akerlof, 1970; Mirrlees, 1971; Spence, 1973	Jensen and Meckling, 1976; Holmstrom, 1979; Myerson, 1982; Guesnerie and Laffont, 1984	Bernheim and Whinston, 1986; Martimort, 1996; Stole, 1990; Mezzetti, 1997; Gal-Or, 1991
Adverse Selection (uncertainty about the ability of a player, quality of a business transaction) Moral Hazard (uncertainty about the effort induced) Signaling (uncertainty about the ability and quality, yet the informed player sends a signal at the beginning)	Contractual Relationship: (Principal is the uninformed player and Agent is informed player) Control Hierarchy	Co-operative and non-cooperative game theory (two principals and one agent) Contractual relationship: (Principals are the uninformed players and Agent is informed player; different possibilities of co-operation) Control and hierarchy

In the past two decades, key issues like partner characteristics, formation motives, performance and control have dominated the theoretical
and empirical research of international joint ventures (IJV) in a variety of
academic disciplines (Parkhe, 1996). Especially, the international business literature contains empirical research on these topics. Nevertheless,
the theoretical aspects and the application of theoretical tools to the
special organizational form of an IJV still seem to be a challenging
endeavor.

Geringer and Woodcock (1995) developed a principal-agent contractual model (Jensen and Meckling, 1976; Holmstrom, 1979; Myerson,
1982; Guesnerie and Laffont, 1984) for IJVs. They used agency theory
in order to combine a contractual approach with a socio-psychological
perspective. This was the first time that agency theory was applied to
analyze joint ventures and to study cross-cultural behavior in the international business literature. The authors examined whether the total
number of partners participating in a joint venture or the cross-cultural
divergence among these partners have an impact on the subsequent

performance of the IJV. The principal-agent model was developed to show the efficient structure of joint ventures. Although this paper generated insights about the inherent structure of the IJV, the authors missed to derive the nature of this specific business endeavor. Geringer and Woodcock stressed the presence of two contracts and two principals, yet their focus was on the nature of the contracts involved instead of the multiple hidden information and communication problems.

In general, the relationship between the parties of an IJV is described as a 'contract' which reflects the efficient organization of information and risk bearing according to Jensen and Meckling (1976). The role model of a principal-agent relationship shows that one party delegates work to the other who performs that work. The focus of the theory is on the contingent entity influenced by the principal and agent's self-interest, bounded rationality and risk-aversion. Furthermore, factors like goal conflicts and information asymmetry have an impact on the efficiency and effectiveness of the contract. Geringer and Woodcock distinguished between behaviorally based and outcome-based contracts depending on the capability to monitor the behavior of the agent and on the measurability of the outcome. As far as the authors introduced agency theory to the IJV issue, an important tool was applied to analyze hidden information, Ott (2000a) pointed out the special nature of IJVs in a common agency approach (two principals and one agent).

The common agency literature

The special common agency problem can be found in situations where an agent serves several principals (Bernheim and Whinston, 1986; Gal-Or, 1991; Martimort, 1992, 1995a and 1995b, 1996; Stole, 1990). Martimort (1996) and Stole (1990) have developed a theory of common agency or a multi-principal-agent theory. This means that each principal offers a contract to the agent. The agent announces his type to the principal, given the other principal's contract and the agent's optimal reaction to contract offers, which maximizes her expected payoff. With two principals, if the agent does not announce her type truthfully to principal i, she may also lie to principal j, and perhaps in a different way.

Bernheim and Whinston (1986) developed the first step towards a coherent, abstract framework for analyzing common agency situations. They extended the bilateral principal-agent model to situations in which a number of risk-neutral principals independently attempt to influence the decision of a common agent. The authors have shown that aggregate equilibrium incentive schemes are always efficient in the sense that the equilibrium action is implemented at minimum cost. Furthermore, they have proved that whenever collusion among the principals could achieve the first best solution, strong Nash equilibria exist and induce the efficient outcome. Where collusion could not achieve the first best, non-cooperative interaction will not give the second-best solution. The non-cooperative and the collusive (second-best) solutions were compared for a special case. Bernheim and Whinston could show that the distribution of net rewards among the principals is, in general, indeterminant.

Gal-Or (1991) looked at common agency in oligopolies. The author showed that if the agent has private information about the costs, forming a common agency in a oligopoly may induce both advantageous and disadvantageous implications on the profits of the firms. Facilitating better coordination of production and pricing decisions, a common agency could limit the firm's options in extracting the informational rents of their agents. Gal-Or proved that contracting with independent agents arises as equilibrium behavior, when the prior uncertainty about the agent's cost or when the degree of correlation among the costs of different agents are significant.

Martimort (1996) developed the multi-principal-agent theory for the case of exclusive dealing. The article deals with the provision of incentives in a setting of competing manufacturer-retailer hierarchies under adverse selection. It studies the competition between hierarchies under the assumption of secret wholesale contracts and analyzes the choice of retailing channels between rival manufacturers. Martimort (1995b) envisaged furthermore the role of governmental bodies as a multi-principal-agent problem.

Adverse selection – common agency

Cross-border ventures have to tackle problems inherent to the international business scenario with regards to information asymmetries, attitudes towards risks and the proneness to dishonesty. Given two firms in two countries intending to form an IJV, the set-up phase is characterized by the uncertainty concerning the quality of each contribution and expertise. According to Akerlof (1970), one of the more important aspects of uncertainty is the difficulty of distinguishing good quality from bad quality in the business world. The famous 'lemon model' was applied to the 'used car market' in the case of merchants. In general, the author mentioned its applicability for the production process in which the skill to identify the quality of inputs and to certify the quality of outputs is necessary. Especially, the latter scenario leads to consider an adverse selection problem in IJVs because of the complementary resources provided by the parents. Combining the difficulty of distinguishing good quality from bad quality in the production process with the uncertainties two parents of an IJV have to face by forming a joint enterprise, the development of a model of uncertainty about the quality of an IJV management seems to be appropriate.

Akerlof (1970) stated in his seminal paper that 'dishonesty in business is a serious problem in underdeveloped countries' and the model 'gives a possible structure to this statement and delineates the nature of the external economies involved'. The author showed that dishonesty or misrepresentation of the quality of automobiles costs $\frac{1}{2}$ unit of utility per automobile and reduces the size the used care market from N to 0 which was subsumed as costs of dishonesty, in general. Although Akerlof indicates that there is considerable evidence that quality variation is greater in 'underdeveloped' areas than in developed areas because of the need for quality control of exports (State Trading Corporations), the difficulty of distinguishing good from bad quality occurs especially in the case of either technological or marketing knowledge with regard to IJVs in developed and developing countries.

Balakrishnan and Koza (1993) mentioned in their paper on the differential advantages of joint ventures over acquisition in ex ante costs in the light of adverse selection that transactions governed by a joint venture will be efficient for three reasons. (1) The short-term gains from dishonesty may be outweighed by the threat of termination or the potential liquidation because of the resulting downstream inefficiencies, which reduce the incentives to misrepresent. (2) By way of shared ownership, the joint venture introduces limited formal and informal property rights and obligations for each parent. (3) The joint venture affords opportunities for learning and gathering new information about the value of the partner's assets. Concluding that the joint venture is not a costless mechanism for combining assets, disputes over sharing the gains are still possible because of the absence of a 'unity of command'. Furthermore, the costs of managing and controlling the joint venture occur due to shared control. Another difficulty arises because of re-negotiations which are also potentially expensive. Thus, the authors perceive that a 'joint venture is a compromise between a contract and a hierarchy'.

According to Killing (1982), there are only two shareholders in an IJV which means that we consider the shareholder as principal and thus the multi-principal nature of an IJV can be verified. The shareholders are the local and the foreign firm due to their ownership rights on the IJV. Depending on the control situation and the dominance of the parents, three archetype structures were developed. The partner firms constitute the third player by their own representatives. Another feature of the triangle situation occurs by adding the attitude toward risks to the principals and the agent. Assuming that the agent is the IJV management, we have two problems to consider: (a) an adverse selection problem of uncertainty concerning the quality of the IJV management from the local and the foreign parent's perspective and (b) a principal-agent relationship with hidden action problems which may occur during the production and distribution process. Thus, the presence of uncertainty in the case of an IJV leads to the difficulty of designing efficient, incentive compatible contracts.

Balakrishnan and Koza (1993) pointed out in their model that, based on the synergy effects of joint ventures, an IJV is formed to combine complementary assets from partners of dissimilar businesses. Special focus lies on the mechanism of the development of transactions and the re-negotiation of compensations for individual contributions. The information revelation may lessen the adverse selection problem. It occurs in the case of hidden information of one parent when contracting over specific issues, which stresses the asymmetric information structure between the two parties. Reuer and Koza (2000a) pointed out that parent firms combine two perspectives with both ex ante valuation uncertainties and ex post integration challenges when assembling their complementary resources. Reuer and Koza (2000b) strongly refer to the argument that asymmetric information speaks to inter-industry transactions and ex ante resource valuation problems. In general, the findings of the authors supported the asymmetric information perspective on resource combination through joint ventures. Nevertheless, the complexity of an IJV combining at least technological know-how of one parent with market knowledge of the other parent bears a problem of offering the right incentives to reveal the information necessary for the success of the joint enterprise.

Under the assumption that the IJV has private information about the quality of the management in terms of co-operation, the parents are interested to induce the agent to reveal his information about his ability by the contract he accepts. The two principals may offer their contracts independently or co-operatively. The representatives of the two principals are forming a coalition or the board of the IJV management. The agent has private information about the homogeneity of the group and can, therefore, invest more or less into the dynamics of the group in order to reduce the total costs or maximize the output or profit. The agent can use his private information to even imbalances within the group. With regards to the risk attitude of the IJV management, the principals are risk-neutral and want the manager to maximize expected profits, whereas the manager's consumption and utility depend almost on the payment for managing the firm. For this reason, the manager is risk-averse and his effort has a strong impact on the firm's profit (Campbell, 1997, p. 78). Another assumption can deal with a risk-neutral management which bears the risk through 'selling the store' contracts (Rasmusen, 1994).

The interrelated flow of information and communication triggers problems of information asymmetries. Since both parents provide the IJV with resources and have to create a set-up scenario, an important issue needs to be addressed by pointing to the common agency relationship (Bernheim and Whinston, 1985 and 1986; Gal-Or, 1991; Martimort, 1996). Geringer and Woodcock (1995) developed a principal-agent approach for IJVs and Ott (2000a) stressed that an IJV has the characteristics of common agency with adverse selection and moral hazard problems. Therefore, we can take the framework of a common agency game and apply incentive schemes to the particular case of adverse selection and moral hazard (Macho-Stadler and Perez-Castrillo, 2001; Rasmusen, 1994). The game-theoretic models of adverse selection and moral hazard were characterized by Myerson (1991, p. 263) as the need to give players an incentive to report information honestly and to implement recommended actions.

Moral hazard – common agency

Mezzetti (1997) developed a theory of incentives for a common agency game where an agent chooses his level of performance in two complementary tasks performed for different principals. The agent has private information about the difference in his productivity. Mezzetti showed that sharing a common agent is advantageous because it allows more surplus to be generated and the principal can use the situation that the agent is facing countervailing incentives to reduce his information rent. Depending on the type. Furthermore, Mezzetti analyzed that with comparable productivities a flat fee paid by both parents can be used, while dealing with large differences in productivities an incentive pay should be appropriate. Co-operation between the principals was suggested in order to extract more rent from the agent and delivers higher benefits to them especially when the agent has a substantial advantage in one of the tasks. The social costs of co-operation between the principals can be seen in a reduction of specialization. The agent will always lose from co-operating principals. Thus, the total surplus is higher under independent contracting. Mezzetti's analysis can be applied to IJVs in the context of research labs providing both parents with research projects or in marketing units with two brands.

Double moral hazard in joint ventures was observed by Chi (1996) who pointed out that the lack of performance verifiability might lead to a shirking problem. Dealing with the contributions of the parent firms, like technology of the foreign parent and local expertise of the local partner, the output of the venture is dependent on the actions of both firms involved. For this reason, Chi focused on a situation where both parents of such a contractual relationship are tempted to shirk their responsibilities. The author showed furthermore that a contract under which each party shares a fraction of the output is superior to a contract under which one of them is paid only a flat fee. For this reason, the mechanism design of an IJV seems to be important for the actual management process and the behavior of all parties involved.

Another approach to tackle the moral hazard problem in joint ventures was developed by Dasgupta and Tao (1999). The authors showed the importance of sharing equity instead of output because of its ex ante verifiability in order to avoid contractual incompleteness. Like Chi the two authors pointed out the double moral hazard nature of this special business unit.

The above-mentioned publications developed the reasoning based on problems of either contractual completeness or incompleteness. The IJV-literature itself did not focus on these topics, though the problem of performance verifiability occurs in all major articles of this stream of literature. Besides the article of Geringer and Woodcock (1995), Winfrey and Austin (1996) and Ott (2000a), there could not be found a body of research dealing with agency problems in the IJV-literature and even further it did not really lead to a formal or theoretical discussion in the international business literature. For this reason, the following section will stress the impact of principal-agent relationships in equity IJVs. This monograph introduces a formal framework to problems in an IJV.

Considering the tension between these firms, the focus lies on the managers involved and this leads to a much more complicated setting which was dealt with in a multiple-party approach (Osland and Cavusgil, 1998). The general assumption of this multiple-party approach deals with the objectives and perceptions of all kinds of managers involved in the IJV business, such as the manager of the local and the foreign firm as well as the local representative and the foreign expatriate in the IJV. The authors focused on US-China joint ventures and showed that it is important to seek information from all parties to joint venture. According to the findings of the in-depth interviews, each of the four groups of managers involved has a varying set of criteria they use in evaluating the joint venture. The authors found evidence of foreign parent companies not acting in the best interest of the IJV by selling components and materials to the IJV at high prices and local parents were interested in increasing worker productivity to increase the dividends that they received from the IJV. Insights gained show that US parent company managers are more likely to use return on investment or internal rate of return, while Chinese parent company managers focus on dividends or dividends plus taxes. The short-term perspective on profit of Chinese parent firms triggers a different approach of US IJV directors towards managing the IJV. Thus, the objectives of each managerial group differ and the outcome of the joint venture depends on the proneness to co-operate.

Another way of looking at the tensions derived in an IJV is based on role theory. Shenkar and Zeira (1992) examined the organizational and personal correlates of role conflict and role ambiguity of CEOs. Their findings were that the role conflict was lower when the number of parent firms was higher and when the CEO had spent more years with the organization, furthermore the role ambiguity was lower when the CEO had more years of education. The result that there exists a lower level of role conflict in the case of a larger number of parents points to a phenomenon in role theory. Its explanation was derived from the fact that the more parents are involved, the easier the CEO can maneuver among them and pursuing its own objectives rather than follow the directives of the parents. Thus, when there are two parents, it is more likely that they struggle for dominance, send conflicting messages and limit the ability of the CEO to reach decisions of its own interest. According to this study the international operations are characterized by frequent failures to decode, understand and interpret communicated information, and such information problems are considered to be a major source of role ambiguity for the CEOs. It was difficult to determine whether messages were intentionally or unintentionally obscure. Not only the chief executive officers can be subsumed under the notation A_{IJV}, but also different employee groups of the IJV may lead to the general notion of an agent. Shenkar and Zeira (1987) considered in an earlier paper human resource management issues, which can be used to specify the players. There are three main groups of employees in an IJV: the foreign parents expatriates (managers to the IJV), the host parent transferees (employed by the local firm and transferred to the IJV) and host country nationals (directly hired by the IJV). Additionally, the literature considers third country expatriates of the foreign parent, the local parent and the IJV. The authors mention two other groups such as the foreign headquarters executives and the host headquarters executives who play major roles in the headquarters of the parents or as board members of the IJV. The latter personnel groups can be distinguished as principals when being in charge at the headquarters. Depending on the ownership structure and the control rights of the IJV, the presence of two parent firms in the management process could create a special principal-agent relationship. Although the human resource perspective can be seen as an additional complication of the underlying problem, it is necessary to point out the different reference groups within the organization of an IJV. Furthermore, the above-mentioned conflicts in communication and difficulties can be materialized by defining the various players in an IJV. Another aspect of disaggregating the complexities of the IJV organization lies in the clarification of different perceptions about performance and objectives of the employee groups.

To predict behavior in a multiple-party decision-making scenario, it is advisable to use the empirical insights gained over the past decades as a starting point and to develop an abstract reasoning in order to predict future behavior. The complexity of signing contracts, negotiating and managing in international joint ventures can be analyzed in this context. Based on a game-theoretical framework, the moral hazard problems of the organizational design of an IJV are interrelated and various solution concepts are introduced to handle difficulties in this static common agency scenarios.

Signaling – dynamic common agency

Having considered the double adverse selection problem in an IJV as an uncertainty about the quality of the management due to combining two firms and creating a third player, another approach to deal with this problem is the signaling of skills from the agent. Thus, the timing could be almost similar to the adverse selection section apart from the agent giving signals about his ability to the principals. This is the first time that signaling is applied to the common agency literature and, therefore, the usual perspective of the job market will be changed into the IJV problem.

In general, skills are not observable ex ante. Thus, contracts have to be offered to get a true revelation of the quality of their skills. Several ways of moving are possible which might result in screening or signaling (Spence, 1973; Riley, 2001). Signaling takes place when the agent knows his ability and offers his skills first. In case the parents move first and offer their contracts, there we have a screening scenario. The signaling comprises a vast literature in economic theory over the last twenty-five years. Besides the pioneer papers of Vickrey (1961), Mirrlees (1971) and Akerlof (1970), Spence (1973) set the stage for unprecedented papers in 'job market signaling' and research in labor markets. Spence explored the implications under the assumption that it is the informed agent who must move first. In a signaling game, firms are seeking to hire a new type of technology consultant who may be of high or low quality. The author used education as a signal. Signaling, therefore, occurs in situations in which one of the parties to a contract is interested in signaling some characteristics before the contract is signed (Campbell, 1997; Macho-Stadler and Perez-Castrillo, 2001). We apply, therefore, the theoretical concepts of common agency and signaling to the situation of contracting in IJVs in order to get revelation about the quality of the IJV management.

The signaling literature was developed in the early seventies based on Akerlof (1970), Mirrlees (1971) and Spence (1973). These theoretical foundations of information asymmetries and the design of incentive schemes indicate that a principal has an incentive to offer a set of alternative schemes that single out agents with different characteristics. This was reflected in several cases on the job market in which a higher type agent chooses a high-powered incentive scheme even so he has to pay higher taxes. Mirrlees (1971) studied optimal incentive schemes, whereas Spence (1973) and Akerlof (1970) studied equilibrium incentive schemes. These papers created a vast literature on signaling, however there is a theoretical controversy about the characterization of conditions under which equilibrium incentive schemes exist.

Taking the classic example of job market signaling as a basis for analyzing problems in an asymmetric information setting in international business, the existence of private information influences a contract's format in IJVs, too. In this chapter, situations will be analyzed in which one of the parties to an IJV contract is interested in signaling some characteristics before the contract is signed. Like in the previous chapter we have to deal with the quality of the IJV management and its influence on the parties involved as well as the impact on the future co-operation between the players. Thus, a special theoretical concept for IJVs needs to be based on the mathematical tool of game theory and on the influence of various contracts derived from the incentive theory. Additionally, aspects of common agency as a combination of both theoretical concepts need to be applied to the problems in IJVs. Therefore, solution concepts with a rigorous theoretical background should provide means of tackling information asymmetries and its consequences in IJVs.

During the life cycle of an international joint venture (IJV) uncertainties especially arise in connection with the quality of the IJV management and the effort level invested into the production process and the marketing of the new product. Incomplete information about the success and failure of the international business project occur in the beginning of each joint venture and can be related to the information asymmetries between the players – the local and foreign parent firms as well as the IJV management itself. Shenkar and Zeira (1987) distinguished between three groups of employees in an IJV. The foreign parent expatriates (nationals of the country in which the headquarters (HQ) of the foreign parent is located, and who are assigned by that parent as expatriate managers), host parent transferees (host country nationals who are employed by the host parent and transferred to the IJV from headquarters or from one of the subsidiaries of that parent), host country nationals (nationals of the host country who are hired directly by the IJV and employed in it).

The complexity of decision-making in an IJV can be derived from the multiplicity of independent organizations in the IJV system with connected conflicting expectations. There needs to be a synchronization of different objectives, beliefs and attitudes (Shenkar and Zeira, 1987). Additionally, since an IJV might operate within a defined time horizon, the parent firms could have the intention to terminate the enterprise after having gained enough knowledge about the management or technological issues in order to pursue their own businesses. This creates uncertainty about the quality of the personnel transferred, the actions taken during the life cycle or about the splitting of the outcome and other operational factors derived from the learning perspective of one side.

Focusing on the players' information asymmetries, local knowledge was one of the major advantages domestic firms can possess compared to the foreign parent, which leaves the latter in a situation of uncertainty about the preferences of the other player. Apart from the case of the two players bargaining under incomplete information, the IJV management has more information about the actual operational performance of the newly founded enterprise (Shenkar and Zeira, 1992). For this reason, there are either both parents knowing less of the joint firm or one of the partners has more information about the IJV business depending on the different influence and control levels in combination with reports from the IJV management.

Having shown the problems of asymmetric information with respect to the quality of the management, several steps need to be considered to work on the problem. First, we have to develop a framework, which captures the special strategic constellation. Secondly, the information asymmetries need to be addressed and appropriate concepts should combine this with the first step. Additionally, incentive schemes should be offered to get revelation about the hidden information. Therefore, the starting point is the theoretical framework of common agency, followed by the signaling game concept, which provides a tool for offering incentives.

Endgames

The last two decades were characterized by an explosive growth of international cross border co-operations. Several joint ventures and international alliances have come to a mature stage of their life cycle or even considered the termination of the alliance. To focus on the case of equity-based IJVs, the issue of exit shows the importance of preparation for this scenario. In the case of a joint business entity run and owned by a local and a foreign firm, the reputation between the parents influence the process of a long-term business relationship. Furthermore, the different strategies and actions taken during the actual management period have an impact on the endgame scenario. Serapio and Cascio (1996) showed examples of 'divorces' in the international business setting. Besides the reasons of termination, the scenarios in dealing with the process were mentioned such as planned/ unplanned, friendly/unfriendly and both agree/one partner refuses. This raises the issue of the development in a long-term business relationship and the importance of reputation and re-negotiation in a repeated game.

A case of planned termination was for instance the joint venture between General Motors and Toyota, called New United Motor Manufacturing, Inc. (NUMMI) which had a limited duration of twelve years (Weiss, 1987). The influence of antitrust bodies (FTC) on the negotiation process determined this outcome of the formation process. Besides the deliberate finite game structure of the above-mentioned NUMMI joint venture, the stability of joint ventures was raised as an important issue in the literature. Special ways of termination and restructuring occur in the dynamic process of an organization. Concerning the long-term relationship of IJV players, structural changes and reconfigurations (Yan and Gray, 1994) have to be considered over time for several reasons. Firstly, as far as IJVs serve as a means of entering into foreign markets, the initial reason of founding an IJV, e.g. avoiding host country prohibitions of whole foreign ownership, may be obsolete and a wholly owned affiliate might be the result. Secondly, the IJV's importance to the parents may diminish and the joint venture can be phased out. Thirdly, when the substantial learning process of one parent devalues the other's expertise such as the accumulation of technological know-how or management and production techniques. Another reason for restructuring might be the change of bargaining power between the parents. Although the intention to reconfigure the IJV can be seen as a co-operative strategy in the business relationship, the issue of cheating or punishing in the last round of a repeated game should not be undervalued. To show the different forms of termination, the endgame scenarios such as termination by acquisition, termination by dissolution and termination by reorganization or restructuring can be considered.

General endgame problems need to be considered and their influence on the divorce contract might be analyzed, too. Several questions occur in this context such as whether the endgame problems could be avoided by designing an appropriate first contract or which strategies the players should choose in the last stages of the game.

To study the strategic setting of the termination stage, the players may have the choice to co-operate or to cheat. For this, the strategy to choose cheating for the last stage would be a so-called Grim strategy (Rasmusen, 1994). Since the repeated game character provides the possibility to consider a change in behavior from one stage to the other, different theoretical concepts were applied to show various types of reasoning behind the supergame, e.g. the repeated Prisoner's Dilemma and the Chainstore Paradoxon (Selten, 1978). Starting with a 'source game' (Selten, 1978) such as the Prisoner's Dilemma, the repetition of strategic behavior should lead to the outcome of the supergame. Different theoretical approaches were applied to show the rationality behind the solution paths, such as induction theory, co-operation theory and/or benevolence theory which were applied to the Chainstore game by Selten.

Repeated games

To study the strategic setting of the termination stage, the model of a repeated game examines the logic of long-term interaction. The players have to take into account the effect of their current behavior on the other players' future behavior, which explains co-operation, revenge, cheating and threats. Osborne and Rubinstein (1994) mentioned as primary achievement of the theory the isolation of types of strategies that support mutually desirable outcomes in any game. The repeated interaction of individuals gives insights into the structure of behavior in terms of 'social norms'. This means that in order to sustain mutually desirable outcomes each player needs to punish any player whose behavior is undesirable.

The endgame effect shows that game theoretic reasoning leads to the result that it would not pay anything to co-operate in the last stage of the game. For this, the strategy to choose cheating for the last stage would be a so-called Grim strategy (Rasmusen, 1994). Since the repeated game character provides the possibility to consider a change in behavior from one stage to the other, different theoretical concepts were applied to show the various reasonings behind the supergame, e.g. the repeated Prisoner's Dilemma and the Chainstore Paradoxon (Selten, 1978). Starting with a 'source game' (Selten, 1978) such as the Prisoner's Dilemma, the repetition of strategic behavior should lead to the outcome of the supergame. Different theoretical approaches were applied to show the rationality behind the solution paths, such as induction theory, co-operation theory and/or benevolence theory which were applied to the Chainstore game by Selten.

Reputation

Campbell (1997) looked at the reputation effect in terms of competition between producers and the relationship of producers and consumers. The effect of reputation on behavior, in general, has an impact on relationships and can be studied in a short-run or long-term decision-making scenario. The term 'reputation' in economics comprises situations in which there is a hidden characteristic, and one or more players have something to learn about the type (characteristic) of other players. Reputation effects occur in situations in which the rivals know that they will face each other repeatedly, under similar conditions, and may regret actions that enhance their utility in the short run at great cost to their rivals. With respect to the importance of reputation in a dynamic game, we can consider reputation as the record of a player's performance in the past.

Repeated moral hazard

The moral hazard problem will continue to exist in an IJV, since managerial incentive problems are closely tied to learning about managerial capability. Rogerson (1985) studies a repeated moral hazard case with a risk-neutral principal and a risk-averse agent. The principal can borrow and save at a fixed interest rate and the agent discounts future consumption. It could be shown that memory plays an important role in every Pareto-optimal contract. Additionally, the restriction of the agent's access to credit is necessary to achieve a Pareto-optimal outcome and the agent would choose to save some of his wage if he could.

Fudenberg, Holmstrom and Milgrom (1990) analyzed lifelong and single period contracts as well as moderate term contracts such as employment contracts. Their results suggest that the benefits of extending contract length are positively related to the length and extent of the information lag. Contracts can, therefore, be designed to balance the gains from incorporating all the information relevant to the current contract period against the costs of lengthening the contract term. The employee turnover in jobs that do not exhibit substantial information lags is higher than in jobs that do. In general, managerial workers are paid differently compared to factory workers or salesmen because of the information conditions of their work. Managerial activities contribute directly to future production in ways, which are not reflected in current performance measures. Long-term contracts, dependent on the arrival of additional information on current activities, are important in managerial contracting. Fudenberg, Holmstrom and Milgrom considered adverse selection and moral hazard cases in their analysis.

Fudenberg and Tirole (1990) studied a principal-agent problem with moral hazard under re-negotiation. The contract can be re-negotiated after the agent's choice of action and before the observation of the action's consequences. The model has two implications for executive compensation. Firstly, a CEO who has made important long-run decisions will be able to choose from a menu of contracts, such as some offering a fairly certain payment and some offering a riskier, performance-related payment. Secondly, an executive compensation may be insensitive to how well the firm performs after he retires, even if this performance conveys important information about the executive's actions. There will be a distribution of contracts, some of which depend on post-retirement performance. There are three items in executive compensation consistent with the theory: salary (fairly independent of performance), earnings-related items (bonus and performance plans) and stock-related items (stock appreciation rights and phantom stock plans). Fudenberg and Tirole (1990, p. 1280) analyzed the re-negotiation problem the following way: 'First, the parties meet and sign an original or ex-ante contract c1 which specifies the agent's monetary compensation as a function of the realized outcome. Then the agent chooses an effort level e. This effort generates a probability distribution p(e) over outcomes; the principal will observe the realized outcome but not the agent's choice of e. After the effort is chosen, but before the outcome is realized, the parties have the opportunity to re-negotiate, replacing c1 by another contract c2. Here we must specify the way in which re-negotiation proceeds. We examine the case in which the principal is able to implement the optimal mechanism at the re-negotiation stage, which will typically involve the principal offering the agent a menu of contracts, one for each level of effort that the agent may have chosen. This specification is comparatively simple because the principal has no private information. The results on the informed principal problem show that the same conclusions are obtained if the agent is the one who proposes contracts during the re-negotiation and one requires the contract to be "strongly renegotiation-proof"'.

Chiappori et al (1994) consider the dynamic dimension in moral hazard models. According to the authors, two conditions are necessary for the optimal long-term contract to be implementable via spot contracts. Firstly, the long-term optimum should be renegotiation-proof. Secondly, spot contracts should provide efficient consumption smoothing. The analysis contains as well the effect of the availability of credit to the agent. The repetition of the moral hazard problem generates, furthermore, hidden information at the recontracting dates. Thus, the renegotiation-proof contract implements the minimum effort level.

Holmstrom (1999) argued that it is not possible to consider moral hazard problems disappearing in the long-run and that contracts will clearly play an important role in that context. The question is now what kind of contracts and how to approach the dynamic common agency problem in an IJV.

Repeated common agency

Common agency relationships are in general an enlargement of the simple principal-agent relationship to the case in which one agent contracts with several principals (Bernheim and Whinston, 1985 and 1986; Gal-Or, 1991; Martimort, 1996). In a dynamic common agency setting

(Olsen and Torsvik, 1995; Bergemann and Valimaki, 1998), several issues are considered. Olsen and Torsvik (1995) focused on decentralization and the ratchet effect of centralization. The authors showed that in a dynamic framework without commitment there are cases where it is never optimal to completely centralize the provision of incentives. The authors found some interesting results about how the optimum degree of centralization varies with other parameters, especially the importance of the future relative to the current period. It is, therefore, optimal to make incentive provision highly centralized if the future is of either very high or very low importance, whereas in the intermediate case the optimum degree of delegation increases as the weight attached to the future increases. Bergemann and Valimaki (1998) considered a dynamic common agency situation with symmetric information. The authors focused on the existence of a marginal contribution equilibrium where each principal receives her contribution to the coalition of the agent and remaining principals. The structure of the intertemporal pay-offs is analyzed in terms of the flow marginal contribution. The model was restricted to a symmetric information environment, which is in an IJV case not realistic. Thus, the intertemporal model of Olsen and Torsvik (1995) might be a better basis, yet there is the lack of commitment involved. However, the authors addressed a couple of interesting questions, which can be related to the IJV problem.

The repeated game solution concept considers time aspects and enables to build on a static game in order to obtain insights into behavioral issues over a time period. Dynamic games of incomplete information are the underlying framework for the endgame chapter. For this reason, we have to look at the perfect Bayesian equilibrium concepts. Gradually advancing from dynamic games under incomplete information over dynamic moral hazard to dynamic common agency, the dynamic double moral hazard problem in an IJV shows a combination of theoretical solution concepts and real life termination scenarios. Therefore, we start to develop the problem, show the timing of the game and the model with the solution concepts.

Suppose the situation of a three player IJV-model (i = foreign firm, local firm and IJV), the impact of their different utility functions ($u_i = u_{foreign}$, u_{local}, u_{IJV}) on the management and the efforts of the IJV-board of directors may lead to success or failure of the business endeavor. The actions ($c_i = c_{foreign}$, c_{local} and c_{IJV}) chosen to contribute to the success or failure of the IJV have to be considered too. Different strategic behavior occurs in the long run of an IJV. Developing a reputation over the special stages and considering learning of the players, the co-operative aspect of the joint enterprise in the beginning of the endgame scenario has to be taken as a prerequisite of the game. Apart from focusing on the several reasons, which may lead to the difficulties in managing the joint venture, the abstraction of the problem might provide solution concepts.

3
The Rules of the IJV Games

The literature review is already structured in the rules of the game, which might be in other circumstances unusual, yet it serves the purpose of guiding the reader through the literature and defining the elements of an IJV game in relation to its life cycle. The life cycle of an IJV is related to the timing of the games involved. Thus, the duration of an IJV is split into parts which can be modeled as games.

Introduction

To focus on the design of an international joint venture, it is important to consider the studies being conducted by international business scholars, management scientists and economists with different perspectives of IJVs. Various approaches in the management and the economic literature intended to develop research on the theory of joint venture and on the tools for managing this important means of international business. A lot of empirical research investigated issues like motives, performance measures, success factors, stability or partner nationalities by applying various statistical methods. Some authors developed eclectic frameworks for further analysis (Kogut, 1988a; Datta, 1988; Inkpen and Beamish, 1997). Nevertheless, literature overviews stressed the problem of 'messy' research (Parkhe, 1993a: 227) and 'significant conceptual and methodological gaps' in the international joint venture literature (Parkhe, 1996: 429). Parkhe concluded that 'research on JVs has tended to gravitate toward four major topics: motives for JV formation, partner selection/characteristics, control/conflict and JV stability/performance. While each topic is individually important, there has been little effort to reintegrate the insights into a higher-order theory of JVs' (1996: 451).

International joint ventures being regarded as complex business units possess a lot of variables and features to apply different theoretical approaches. This monograph is intended to stress on the development of a theoretical perspective of IJVs. For this reason, the already existing theoretical applications to problems of IJVs show the various attempts to capture its special nature. For instance, the transaction cost theory (Hennart, 1988 and 1991; Kogut, 1988a; Geringer and Hebert, 1989) emphasizes on minimizing the sum of production and transaction costs. The strategic behavior theory (Kogut, 1988a) postulates, furthermore, that firms transact by the mode which maximizes profits through improving a firm's competitive position compared with its rivals. Both transaction cost theory and strategic behavior theory were seen as complementary in the case of international joint ventures. Kogut (1988a) and Inkpen (1995) developed the organizational learning approach, which views joint ventures as a means by which firms learn or seek to retain their capabilities. The role conflict and role ambiguity theory (Shenkar and Zeira, 1992) was applied to personnel and organizational issues of international joint ventures. The central problem is the role conflict of CEOs in international joint ventures connected with the number of parent firms involved and with the experiences gained in the organization. The application of the agency theory (Veugelers and Kesteloot, 1994; Chi, 1996; Balakrishnan and Koza, 1993) focuses on the problem of information asymmetries and agency costs in combination with joint ventures. The internalization theory (Casson, 1990; Buckley and Casson, 1996; etc.) deals with the rationale that allows both partners to acquire some of the benefits of internalizing knowledge flow without incurring the full set-up costs of a merger. Buckley and Casson (2000) looked at the typology and strategy set of IJVs. They found that there are not only many configurations but also many contractual alternatives to each of these, such as mergers and licensing agreements which were analyzed together with IJVs. They suggested that an important advantage of the IJV is that it allows the partner firms to benefit from internalizing knowledge without the full set-up costs of a merger. They showed that in an IJV with technology and marketing contributions, IJVs could have joint research, joint production and joint marketing units as well as separate distribution units. In the following chapter, the economic model of IJVs is considered as a basis and will be used in connection with strategic implications for IJVs. Since strategic configurations and game theoretical reasoning can be combined, it is important to emphasize on the applicability of a robust concept to show co-operation and self-interest of a complex organizational venture.

Apart from game theoretic models in the industrial organization literature, in the agency theory literature and the bargaining literature, there is no exposition of the abstract principles of an IJV in connection with game theory. Parkhe postulated the development of a coherent body of work with an underlying theoretical structure. This chapter intends to show the special game theoretical structure of IJVs by introducing the rules of the game on the basis of condensing the existing empirical IJV literature and applying them to the life cycle of an IJV. The intention of this general game theoretical design is that IJV research may use the guidelines of such a game and play the parts of the players by anticipating the other players moves as well as by looking forward and reasoning backwards. Since the complexity of an IJV offers more than one game and has an inherent conflicting and co-operative structure, the games IJVs play can be analyzed by applying the rules developed in the next two sections.

The elements of an international joint venture game

The game theoretic problems will be handled in two steps by offering the general definition of game theory and by the application to the IJV situation in particular. Firstly, game theory provides solution concepts for situations of co-operation and conflict. The word 'non-cooperative' means that the players' choices are based only on their self-interest, in contrast to 'co-operative' behavior, which develops axioms to capture the idea of fairness and binding agreements (Fudenberg and Tirole, 1991). Secondly, in game theory special rules are used to describe a game. The description of a game should include at least the players, the strategies and the pay-offs. Essential elements are the information structure, outcomes, equilibria and the time structure. Thirdly, there are two ways of presenting game theory: the extensive form (a game tree as an equivalent to a decision tree) and the strategic or normal form which shows the pay-offs in a matrix (Gardner, 1995; Gibbons, 1992; McMillan, 1992; Myerson, 1991; Rasmusen, 1994). The game tree would be too complex for games being played in the IJVs and will, therefore, be replaced by the time lines and the order of the play (see in the 'Common Agency' chapters).

As far as there are different forms of presentation like extensive and strategic form games, the elements can be developed out of the core ingredients of the IJV defined above. To develop different games we can use the notation and find appropriate solution concepts. The three general types of games are the following (Myerson, 1991):

Strategic or normal form game Γ is $\Gamma = (N, (C_i)_{i \in N}, (u_i)_{i \in N})$ where N is a nonempty set of and for each i in N, C_i is a nonempty set of strategies available to each player i and u_i is a function from $X_{j \in N} C_j$ into a set of real numbers **R**.

An extensive form game Γ^e is a dynamic model and a rooted tree together with functions that assign labels to every node and branch, with the following conditions $\Gamma^e = (N, (C_i)_{i \in N}, (u_i)_{i \in N})$ is the normal representation of Γ^e, whereas C_i is the set of actions and $u_i(c)$ is the expected utility pay-off to player i in Γ^e $u_i(c) = \sum_{x \in \Omega^*} P(x|c)w_i(x)$.

The Bayesian game Γ^b is a game with incomplete information using the type of player T_i as set of all possible profiles or combinations of types that the players have in the game. The probability function p_i must be a function from T_i. For this reason, we can specify the Bayesian game as $\Gamma^b = (N, (C_i)_{i \in N}, (T_i)_{i \in N}, (p_i)_{i \in N}, (u_i)_{i \in N})$.

Modeling an IJV situation means transferring the characteristics of the joint enterprise into rules of the game. The determination of the number of players, their strategies and pay-offs will be important for all possible combinations of moves by the players. Since the different presentation of game theory contain players (N), strategies $(C_i)_{i \in N}$ and pay-offs $(u_i)_{i \in N}$ as core components, the following paragraphs focus on the translation of IJV key issues into this terminology. Furthermore, the information structure and the timing will be analyzed as additional game theoretical elements.

Players

An IJV is a complex business entity in which the involved firms act in co-operation or competition concerning their self-interest. Depending on the stage of the life cycle, more than two players and their relationship have to be considered. The simple case of two parent firms negotiating over the set-up of the third player, the IJV itself, occurs only in the formation period of the new enterprise. For this reason, the phase of the IJV foundation deals with a local and a foreign firm. The interaction of the various players differs from one stage to the other of an IJV life cycle. The next step considers the IJV management as third player. Chief executive officers acting in charge of or being responsible for the IJV are important players in the game. However, a forth player needs to get attention because of the influential power. Government bodies and antitrust institutions of supranational level play an important role during the whole life cycle of an IJV. In this monograph, the forth player only affects the IJV indirectly in the dominant parent IJV. It should be mentioned that governmental issues need to be looked at in IJVs in a separate way, since this would complicate the problems even more.

The newly formed enterprise contains resources from both parents. The special contributions of the local and foreign firms can be seen in the following table. The IJV itself will be made up by these inputs and this leads to the functional configurations of IJVs which play an important part in the typology of IJVs developed in this monograph.

Some examples of newly found companies and with their parent firms are pointed out in the following table.

Research focusing on partner choice and partner selection criteria (Geringer, 1991; Burton and Saelens, 1982) was conducted to lay stress on successful partner relationships when forming an IJV without having former business experience. Furthermore, scholars were interested in partner asymmetries (Harrigan, 1988), partner contributions (Blodgett, 1991) and knowledge acquisition from parents (Berg and Hoekman, 1988; Lyles and Salk, 1996).

Partner asymmetries caused from different cultural, economic, technological, and legal backgrounds occur in nearly every co-operative form of international business. Harrigan (1988) argues that joint ventures are more likely to succeed when partners possess complementary missions, resource capabilities, managerial capabilities and other attributes that create a strategic fit. Similar cultures, asset sizes, venturing experience level and related activities have a positive impact on the duration of a venture. The bargaining power and the possible domi-

Table 3.1 IJVs and the Resources

Local Firm	Foreign Firm
Market Entrance	Management Techniques and Expertise
Market Knowledge	Technological Know-how
Local Bureaucracy	Capital Endowment
Production Facilities	Marketing Experience
Raw Material and other Resources (Capital Endowment, Human Resources)	

International Joint Venture (IJV)
Research Laboratory
Production Unit
Marketing Unit
Combination

Table 3.2   Examples of IJVs

Local Firm(s)	Foreign Firm(s)	International Joint Venture (IJV)
General Motors	Toyota	NUMMI (terminated in1998)
China Electronics Import and Export Corporation	Hewlett-Packard	Hewlett-Packard China Ltd.
China Trade Omni-Development Center China Youth Travel	Ramada	Ramada Renaissance Guilin
Hubei Province Bureau of Animal Husbandry	Pig Improvement Company Oxford	Hubei Pig Improvement
Aerospatiale, DASA	British Aerospace, CASA	Airbus

nance of a potential parent affect furthermore the structure of a joint venture. The strength of a partner could be the result of his competitive advantage in technology, market position and location. Geringer (1991) showed the importance of selecting a partner who can supply the complementary skills or capabilities by introducing a typology of selection criteria. For this reason, he distinguished between task and partner-related dimensions. Task-related criteria refer to those variables being related to the viability of a proposed venture's operation and include patents or technological know-how, financial resources, experienced managerial personnel and access to marketing and distribution systems. Whereas partner-related criteria refer to those variables like the partner's national or corporate culture, the degree of favorable past association between the partners, compatibility of management teams and organizational size and structure of the partner.

Parkhe (1993a) examined whether the performance and the game theoretic structure of strategic alliances are significantly related and whether this relationship is moderated by partner nationality. Although the study focused on strategic alliances, the results are particularly interesting for the relationship between partners in an international business co-operation setting. Parkhe's typology links each dimension of inter-firm diversity (societal culture, national context, corporate culture, strategic direction and management practice) with the components of the alliance structure. The differences in perception, in home government policies, in national industry structure and in institutions and the differences in the strategic interests of partners as well as the differences in the management styles and in the organizational structure of parent firms are determining factors in international alliances.

Having mentioned the partner nationality as a special feature, the fact that at least two different cultures work together in an enterprise leads to problems related to multinationality in comparison to the domestic joint venture. Buckley and Casson stated that the obstacles to IJVs are cultural distance leading to misunderstanding and distrust (Buckley and Casson, 1996). Many studies were conducted to analyze the cultural characteristics of the IJV-partner firms (Burton and Saelens, 1982; Dasgupta and Siddharthan, 1985; Gomes-Casseres, 1988; Harrigan, 1988; Kogut and Singh, 1988; Pan, 1996; Parkhe, 1993a; Richter and Vettel, 1995; Schaan and Beamish, 1988; Shenkar and Zeira, 1992; Shenkar, 1990; Sheridan, 1993; Svenjar and Smith, 1984; Terpsta and Simonin, 1993; Turpin, 1993; Webster, 1989; Yan and Gray, 1994). All these studies show the impact of partner nationalities on IJV success, stability and human resource issues. Furthermore, some authors distinguished between IJVs with partners of developed and developing countries. Differing basic objectives of the two firms are an obvious source of problems (Miller, Glen, Jaspersen and Karmokolias, 1996). The developing country firm may be quite large by local standards, but not in comparison with the partner of a developed country. Business perspectives of the two firms can vary substantially, not only because of their cultural differences but also because of the differences in sizes.

Concerning the size of the parents, large and small firms can be distinguished. Doz (1988) and Harrigan (1988) stated for instance that international co-operations offer large firms a channel to tap into the innovative and entrepreneurial potential of smaller companies as well as to overcome some of their own rigidities. Smaller firms perform research and development for the larger firm and/or transfer innovations to them. Larger firms offer smaller firms the possibility of getting access to world markets without having built an infrastructure, to negotiate complex agreements without multiple agents and to experience volume manufacturing. For this reason, parent firms with different sizes are a major characteristic of IJVs and lead to dissimilarities in this respect.

Apart from partner differences and partner selection criteria, the partner contributions based on the expertise of the parent firms have to be considered as one of the driving forces to set up an IJV. Blodgett (1991) observed ownership patterns associated with combinations of partner expertise in IJVs. The partner contributions were technology, knowledge of the local environment and/or marketing staff and government suasion. The combinations were furthermore: technology-government suasion, technology-local knowledge, local knowledge-technology, and technology-technology. Local knowledge was the contribution most consistently associated with a minority share of equity in the original agreement, and supplying technology does not allow a firm to dictate terms in the face of host-country policies. In general, government restrictions tend to give the local entity an important advantage.

Depending on the four basic purposes (Beamish et al, 1994) of the IJV – strengthening the firm's existing business, entering new markets with existing products, obtaining new products for existing markets and diversifying into new business – firms have different concerns and are looking for different partner characteristics. In protecting existing businesses, IJVs are used to give their parents economies of scale and can be formed as raw material/component supply joint ventures, research and development joint ventures as well as marketing and distribution joint ventures. Besides the co-operation in functional areas, the partner firms may be horizontally or vertically integrated in the joint venture with the intention to benefit from an internalization advantage. According to Buckley and Casson (1996), the rationale of a joint venture is that it allows both parent firms to obtain an advantage from internalizing knowledge flows without incurring the full set-up costs of a merger. Referring to the already mentioned R&D joint venture as the simplest case of collaboration, the practical difficulty is the sharing of the results. Competition between the products exploiting the same technology can dissipate partner's rents and encourages collusion in the marketing of the final product. Other problems may occur when both firms contribute technology but only one of them contributes marketing expertise. This scenario can arise when a new technology has to be adapted to local production conditions and customer requirements. The situation of new technology generating a new product that requires a distinctive approach to retailing may lead to the contribution of marketing expertise of both firms, whereas only one firm contributes technology.

As far as the two parent firms form an IJV, a triangle of interaction results from this constellation. Shenkar and Zeira (1992) examined the organizational and personal correlation of the role conflict and the role ambiguity of chief executive officers in international joint ventures. The results show that role conflict was lower for CEOs with more years in service, while role ambiguity was significantly lower for CEOs with more years of education. Furthermore, the role conflict was positively correlated with differences in ownership, with size differential and with objectives gap, and inversely correlated with autonomy and education. An interesting finding was that the higher the number of parents, the lesser the role conflicts. This leads to the situation that the more parents, the freer the CEO is to maneuver among them and that the IJV may pursue its own objectives rather than follow the directives of the parents. The international operations can be characterized by frequent failures to decode, understand and interpret communicated information. Cultural distance among parent firms and between them and the IJVs should be taken into account in partner selection and during the management process. The results, furthermore, show that certain cultural differences may be regarded as complementary rather than conflicting assets (Shenkar and Zeira, 1992; Schaan and Beamish, 1988). The paragraphs of the section 'Strategies' and 'Pay-offs' will elaborate on the role of the third player focusing on the different control and performance issues in connection with the constellation of parents and the IJV. Since information asymmetries are already mentioned the figure below contains the various players transferred into the terminology of principals and agents, whereas the latter has an information advantage which needs to be revealed through appropriate incentives. Coalitions of players show the co-operative effect of multi-person decision-making in the IJV itself, although the interaction between the partner firms is characterized by both co-operation and self-interest.

Shenkar and Zeira (1987) found nine subject areas related to personnel issues such as staffing, promotion, loyalty, delegation, decision-making, unfamiliarity, communication, information and compensation. Focusing on those areas which can be related to game theoretical reasoning, we look at staffing, promotion, delegation, decision-making, communication, information and compensation. Staffing: A gap between the actual and desired composition of the work force of IJVs is mentioned for several groups of employees: (a) foreign and host parent managers in HQ responsible for staff selection; (b) foreign parent expatriates transferred by the foreign parent to work in the IJV; (c) host parent transferees (i.e. host parent(s)' employees transferred from host parent HQ to the IJV) and (d) host country nationals employed by the IJV. Promotion: Those host country nationals directly recruited by the IJV face the problems of blocked promotion of host country nationals in IJVs and restrictions on transfers from the IJV to HQ of the host and foreign parent firms. Top positions are usually reserved for foreign expatriates or for host parent transferees. Delegation: There is tendency among the parent firm to limit the delegation of authority to the IJV staff. Sources of disagreement between parents are the desired extent of autonomy sought by the venture, the frequency of expatriates' consultation with their HQ, or the frequency of participation of foreign parents' representatives in board meetings of the venture. Decision-making: The complexity of decision-making in an IJV occur because of cultural differences and the multiplicity of independent organizations in the IJV system with connected conflicting expectations. Thus, there needs to be a synchronization of different objectives, beliefs and attitudes. Communication: Communication difficulties occurred between the IJV and the HQs, yet informal channels could be found to overcome these problems. Information: The difficulty of receiving exact information poses problems for foreign parent expatriates in the IJV. Some reasons for screening information are suspicion regarding the latent intention of the other parent and the protection of technological knowledge. Compensation: Dissatisfaction with compensation gaps is a major problem for host country nationals due to the existence of more reference groups. Related to this problem are the difficulties to assess performance of the IJV because of different procedures and performance standards.

Shenkar and Zeira (1987) distinguished between three groups of employees in an IJV. The foreign parent expatriates (nationals of the country in which the HQ of the foreign parent is located, and who are assigned by that parent as expatriate managers), host parent transferees (host country nationals who are employed by the host parent and transferred to the IJV from headquarters or from one of the subsidiaries of that parent), host country nationals (nationals of the host country who are hired directly by the IJV and employed in it). Third country expatriates can be employed by the parents or the IJV itself as additional group.

Shenkar (1990) raised a couple of managerial problems for IJVs in the PRC, in particular. Yet, some of these issues can be applied to other countries too. Thus, we would like to stress these four mentioned problems: foreign exchange, controlling the board, managing the venture and managing human resources. In all IJVs the Board of Directors is very important because of the multiplicity of parents headquarters and their frequently conflicting objectives. The Board 'takes over' various managerial functions and serves as a 'buffer' to these conflicting demands. The Board decision-making process is often a problem due to the strength between the local and the foreign participants, which might be of little concern in the case of decision-making by consensus. With respect to the limited duration of an IJV (see dynamic common agency), the foreign parent may be reluctant to provide a broader range of data and training to the host managers beyond what is explicitly in the contract or for day-to-day management. Though the Joint Ventures Law specifies the senior positions filled by the local and the foreign representatives, disagreement might be 'developed around the period time the foreign expatriates remain in the venture before being replaced by PRC people' (p. 86). Furthermore, the parents might tend to minimize the autonomy it grants to the managerial team when there are conflicting objectives of the parents. Interesting cases of moral hazard and adverse selection – though not discovered as such in the paper – were found in Shenkar's article. The problem of surplus workers was stated as particularly severe in IJVs which took over operating plants from the Chinese parent. 'The US manager of Babcock and Wilcox's IJV in Beijing was surprised to find 600 beds in the factory, where employees would nap during working hours. He estimated that out of 3,600 employees, 1,200 were working while 2,400 were loafing' (p. 86). Another example was found in Cardio-Pace, where the 'US parent of a Baoji-based IJV, found the Chinese wanted to staff the venture with a few dozen excess assistant managers and workers' (p. 86). Though it is easier to intervene in an early stage, it could be difficult to tackle such problems in the case of state enterprises or other situations related to legal restrictions and obligations. Especially, in the Chinese bureaucratic and political environment human resource management has to deal with discipline and attendance. On a managerial level, indoctrination and tradition of centrally-planned economy created a pool of passive, untrained managers, with little motivation and initiative (Shenkar, 1990). Even when skilled staff is available, the local or foreign parent might be reluctant to transfer it to the IJV and might prefer to send superfluous and less qualified personnel. This problem can be found in many IJVs in which 'dead wood' was transferred.

The forth 'player' in the game is the aggregation of external authorities such as antitrust bodies and institutions of the host government. According to Datta (1988), the host government part focuses on aiming at increased local employment, import substitution, conservation of foreign exchange, technology transfer and the minimization of foreign control of local industry. Concerning antitrust bodies like the Federal Trade Commission or the European Commission, the role as a player in the IJV game occurs in the initial stage of a joint venture or in the bargaining over the IJV formation. Furthermore, trade unions of the host country have as well bargaining power in the negotiation process of the IJV formation with regard to the local workforce (Weiss, 1987). The importance of key stakeholders in international joint venture negotiations may occur as well in connection with partners of Central and Eastern European transitional countries (Brouthers and Bamossy, 1997).

Figure 3.1 shows the relationship and the interaction of the various players in an IJV. The rules of the IJV game need a foreign firm and a local firm as partners and each of them is sending their representatives – or called agents – to the board of management of the IJV. For this reason the third player contains at least two different types of employees which have an impact on the management process. The local player and the foreign player have besides their self-interest a co-operative result as objective of the joint enterprise. Co-operation and conflict arise because of the nature of the IJV as a triangle of three firms which have a strong incentive to maximize the benefits of the joint endeavor. Furthermore, at least two external players have to be considered from the point of view that there exists an influence through antitrust bodies and governmental institutions of the host country. The strategic setting of the external player may lead to further games in connection with the various firms involved in an IJV, though it is not relevant in this monograph.

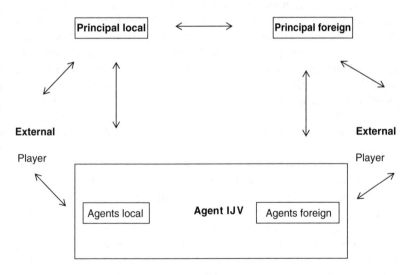

Coalitions and subgroups

Figure 3.1   Players and their Relationship in an IJV

Having mentioned the players and their interactions, the next step is to look at another component of the rules of the game – the strategies and actions each player may choose in order to obtain the intended pay-offs. For this reason the arrows in the figure above are indicators of this scenario.

Strategies

In game theory, strategies are, unlike actions, unobservable and only mental (Rasmusen, 1994). This chapter deals firstly with the strategies of each parent, secondly with the strategic situation of the three players, such as parent firms and IJV, and thirdly, with the strategic set of the external authorities in some stages of an IJV. Nevertheless, the actions each player can take are to be seen as essential for the games being played in an IJV.

To begin with the strategies of the two players, the simple case shows strategies with conflicting and co-operative elements in the negotiation period of an IJV. On the basis of either long standing business experiences or new initial contacts, the two players have a different bargaining behavior in the negotiation stage. The strategies both parents are pursuing derive from their different cultural backgrounds, objectives and competitive situation. The results are shown in the terms of the contract, as well as ownership and control patterns, and may be dependent on the contributions of each player. The strategies of the parent firms in the bargaining stage are ownership strategies, production strategies, technology-transfer strategies, marketing strategies, and financial strategies. In detail, the following parental strategies occur in an IJV-like growth in domestic and international markets, access to new markets, diversification, acquiring brand names and trademarks (Afriyie, 1988; Gomes-Casseres, 1988), learning of management or production techniques and acquisition of technological know-how (see NUMMI).

Buckley and Casson (1996) showed in their economic model of international joint venture strategy the impact of key explanatory factors on strategic choice. They developed their model for IJVs in high-technology industries compared to mergers and licensing agreements on the basis of the internalization theory. For the formation of an IJV the results generate predictions about the variations within industries, between industries, across countries and over time. Factors like technology uncertainty are firm specific and explain why firms in the same industry adopt different strategies. The pace of technological change can be seen as industry-specific and explain differences in frequency of

IJVs in special industries. Cultural distance is specific to pair wise combinations of countries and explains differences in international distributions of IJVs within an industry. The explanatory factors were listed as followed: market size, pace of technological change, rate of interest, cultural distance, protection of independence, missing patent rights, economies of scope and technological uncertainty. Buckley and Casson determined that not just economic factors appear in the model but also variables of technology, culture, and psychology.

The three archetypes of IJVs developed by Killing (1982) are the dominant parent venture, the shared management enterprise and the independent joint venture. These categories were used to describe control. Contractor and Lorange (1988) and Datta (1988) advanced frameworks for IJVs using these archetypes to show different strategic decisions based on the control types. Barden, Steensma and Lyles (2005) studied the influence of parent control structure on parent conflict in Vietnamese IJVs and used the dominant and shared control perspective. Though the particular case of Vietnamese IJVs was the application of the framework, the much more interesting part of this paper was the investigation into the control and conflict in IJVs based on the parental strategic configuration. The authors proposed that the control structure-conflict relationship is contingent upon parent contributions of proprietary assets and knowledge and parents' capabilities to effectively monitor the value-creating processes of the IJV. An important statement in this context is that 'conflict in a cooperative relationship results from perceived discrepancies, incompatible wishes, or irreconcilable desires' (p. 158). The empirical part showed that numerous multinational corporations try to create value by bringing financial resources, proprietary technologies and modern capitalist management practices to outmoded state-owned enterprises and local companies. The local partner contributes land, insights into the local culture and markets and in many cases legal legitimacy with local governmental bodies. The partners are dependent on each other in terms of control over technical/operations aspects and financial or local matters. Barden, Steensma and Lyles (2005) furthermore suggested that inter-partner conflict is contingent on the partners' control over the IJV, their contributions to the IJV, and their abilities to understand and monitor the IJV operations

Whatever strategic and control structure is considered in an IJV, it has implications on the strategies the players can choose. Since these relationships are determined by partner contributions to the IJV, these are looked at closer in the following paragraphs. The parental contributions have an impact on the relationship between the parents, the players in the IJV, organizational behaviors and the actions taken with regards to asymmetric information and communication in the IJV. Yan and Gray (1994) found that the technological resources – such as manufacturing knowledge, product knowledge and capital equipment – that the partners provide influence the outcome of the IJV bargaining process. Thus, this perspective leads to the strength and weaknesses in the IJV decision-making procedures or the bargaining power in the IJV control and strategic structure. Especially, the study of transitional IJVs (IJVs in developing, transactional economies) offer an ideal context for observing the role of resource contributions in the relationship between control-structure and inter-parent conflict. However, in developing economies technology and technological know-how are generally the most scarce, proprietary and firm-specific resources. Contributions of less firm-specific resources, such as financial resources, legal legitimacy or local market knowledge are expected to be less influential (Barden, Steensma and Lyles, 2005).

The dominant parent strategy is connected to the concept of a wholly owned subsidiary with the dominant partner. The board of directors consisting of executives from each parent plays a subordinate role, the IJV's strategic and operational decisions are made by the executives of the dominant partner. This is appropriate in response to the pressures from the host government or to a passive partner seeking purely financial investment with an acceptable rate of return. Lorange and Probst (1987) stated that this strategy type shows a self-organizing system consisting of a dominant parent together with a joint venture adapting to be consistent with its parent future strategic interests. Splitting the value-creating functions between the dominant partner and the IJV organization, it often may be difficult to establish a sufficiently simple division of labor. Accepting changes in roles between the two players should lead to redefine the execution of the IJV's strategies.

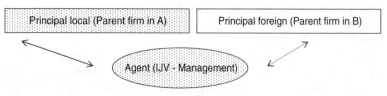

Figure 3.2   Dominant Parent IJV

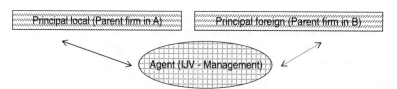

Figure 3.3   Shared Management IJV

The shared management venture is more common in manufacturing processes where one partner supplies the technological know-how and the other firm provides the enterprise with knowledge of the local market. Both partners play an active role (Datta, 1988). Each of the parents continues to have an active interest in the same type of business. This leads to the assumption of having two inter-related self-organizing systems as far as the relationship between firm A and the IJV and between firm B and the IJV is concerned. Both parents and the IJV are involved in the value-creating process. Given potentially diverging perspectives may lead to the result of compromises. Created conflicts may be hard to resolve if one parent attempts to shift more autonomy over to the joint venture organization at a faster rate, while the other tries to hold back (Lorange and Probst, 1987).

The independent joint venture is relatively free from parental interference and is relatively rare. For Lorange and Probst (1987) the free standing joint venture shows the situation that none of the parents have a strong direct operating future strategic interest in the strategy that the joint venture is pursuing. The structuring of the various tasks in the value-creating process can be done like in an independent company. It is up to the parents to equip the joint venture with a degree of redundancy for having the necessary capacity to be flexible. Datta (1988) points out that numerous interdependencies inevitably exist between the joint venture and the parent enterprises. Furthermore, parents are generally reluctant in giving joint ventures the autonomy and freedom to develop independently.

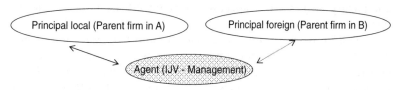

Figure 3.4   Independent IJV

The actions players can pursue are dependent on their strategic interest. For instance, in the negotiation stage one parent may offer a split of the equity pie depending on the contribution or on the host government policy and the other parent may either accept or reject it, which shows a simple game theoretical behavior in bargaining or contracting. In the management stage of the life cycle, the parents may offer incentive schemes and the management of the IJV may as well either accept or reject it. Furthermore, the third player can now decide either to embezzle or to co-operate. Another possibility of behavior could be that a high or low effort will be put into the joint enterprise depending on the self-interest of the parent firms or on the considered gains of the IJV. Furthermore, the players can learn during their period in the IJV and for this reason they have to re-negotiate contract terms or make a decision to quit the IJV. Another set of actions can occur in the last stages of the cycle when the players have the possibility to co-operate or to cheat, to reward or to punish. Since the game theoretical terminology is dependent on an abstract view of a given situation, a neuralgic point in this approach occurs because of a clash of interests between the complexities of management perspectives versus the elegance of mathematical reasoning by finding simple solutions. The art of combining those antipodes lies in each game itself and how the players fill the methodological setting with the contents of the management practice.

The strategic implications between the parents and the IJV have been introduced to give a theoretical structure to an IJV organization. Furthermore we could introduce another level of abstraction by combining these archetypes with the complexities of IJVs strategies (Buckley and Casson, 1996). Buckley and Casson emphasized on the parent's contribution of marketing and technology, which is consistent with the underlying approach towards IJV theory, and the joint unit in either parent country or a third country. This joint enterprise was distinguished in research laboratories, production units, marketing units and distribution units depending on the IJV's purpose and the parent's objectives. Thus, the author wants to combine both strategic approaches to capture the complexity of IJVs with respect to the parent-IJV relationship and the internal strategic scenario.

Choi and Beamish (2004) developed another type of strategic configuration of management control in IJVs. They found that a split control management type performs better than dominant or shared managements in IJVs. The new category was tested on IJVs in Korea. Choi and Beamish distinguished between MNE-partner-dominant IJV, a local-partner-dominant IJV, a shared control IJV and a split control IJV. The development of a control-partitioning framework was based on the need to adjust to JV structures in emerging markets in which the partners agree to control distinct functional activities, such as an MNE and a local partner contributing technology and local knowledge related skills. The firm-specific advantage is important in this context and transferred to the joint venture. The MNE partners have been shown to contribute to IJVs in emerging markets, product and process technology, brand name/trade mark and international marketing support. The local partners' firm-specific advantage was found to be local marketing, local personnel management or management of local government relations. For emerging markets, it is an important possibility to consider a split-control management. It is as well not in the scope of the monograph to investigate whether other countries might use this concept as well.

Besides these strategic configurations and control structures, the importance of contracts as relationships between the players needs to be emphasized. Geringer and Woodcock (1995) developed a principal-agent contractual model (Jensen and Meckling, 1976; Holmstrom, 1979; Myerson, 1982; Guesnerie and Laffont, 1984) for IJVs. They used agency theory in order to combine a contractual approach with a socio-psychological perspective. This was the first time that agency theory was applied to analyze joint ventures and to study cross-cultural behavior in the international business literature. The authors examined whether the total number of partners participating in a joint venture or the cross-cultural divergence among these partners have an impact on the subsequent performance of the IJV. The principal-agent model was developed to show the efficient structure of joint ventures. Although this paper generated insights about the inherent structure of the IJV, the authors missed to derive the nature of this specific business endeavor. Geringer and Woodcock stressed the presence of two contracts and two principals, yet their focus was on the nature of the contracts involved instead of the multiple hidden information and communication problems. Thus, the strategic implications of the configurations for offering contracts and developing relationships based on offers and counteroffers of contracts are crucial for the communication and information process in an IJV. Luo (2004) pointed out that international managers should realize the importance of coupling contractual completeness with environmental conditions and transactional dynamics. Therefore, the author concluded that the optimal level of contractual completeness depends on a transaction's characteristics as well as on the institutional environments facing the IJV. Furthermore, it can be suggested that managers must ensure that an IJV contract delineates situational flexibility in areas that are critical but under the influence of an uncertain environment. The strategic choice in an IJV to offer a contract and incentive schemes is based on the strategic configuration between the parents and their IJV management and on the control structure between the parent firms and the IJV. The co-operative and the competitive relationship under incomplete information between the players will be considered.

Pay-offs, outcome, performance

In the IJV literature some studies examine performance issues, performance measures, the relation of performance and control and the performance and output sharing (Osland and Cavusgil, 1996; Chi, 1996; Geringer and Hebert, 1989 and 1991; Anderson, 1990; Dussauge and Garrette, 1995; Kogut, 1988b; Parkhe, 1996). The performance verifiability is one of the major difficulties which have to be tackled in the IJV.

Performance outcomes in terms of managerial satisfaction, financial results, change in ownership shares, technology transfer and level of exports were analyzed for US-Sino joint ventures by Osland and Cavusgil (1996). Using subjective measures like satisfaction may be difficult in order to get objective data and on the other hand profits are not directly comparable across different industries and stages of IJV life cycle. The profitability of a parent firm is not only based on the IJV's profit, but also on transfer prices, royalties and management fees. Financial returns may also be generated through mechanisms other than dividends, including supply contracts. Geringer and Hebert (1989) propose a model of IJV performance as a function of the fit between the international strategy of the parents, the IJV strategy and the parameters of control. Some measures of performance are profitability, cost efficiency, perceptual measure of satisfaction, instability (change in ownership structure), survival, composite index including financial, non-financial and industry-oriented measures.

Furthermore, Geringer and Hebert (1991) examined the reliability of and the correlation between various IJV performance measures. There was a strong correlation between the three objective performance measures (survival, stability, duration) and the subjective assessments of overall satisfaction with IJV performance as well as the individual dimensions assessing overall performance (sales level, market share, profitability). In turn, the results of the correlation between more specific individual dimensions (quality control, cost control, labor productivity, and customer service) and the objective measures were less strong. Apparently, the IJV's perceptions of one parent's satisfaction were closely related to the other parent's perception of this parent's satisfaction.

Anderson (1990) stated that the assessment of performance is because of its amorphous purposes and its 'uncertain, risky settings' extremely difficult. Performance evaluation incorporates different views, at least those from each parent and the joint venture. Anderson classifies the measures in an 'input-output continuum corresponding with long-short-term orientation'. The state of the organization as an input result measure includes a lot of qualitative criteria such as harmony among partners, moral, adaptiveness and innovativeness. More quantitative-oriented inputs are productivity and financial resource indicators. According to Anderson, the purpose of some joint ventures is learning something like unfamiliar markets, technology or management technique. Learning may contribute to future or current performance. The next step in the input-output continuum occurs with marketing intermediate variables such as relative product quality and relative price. Finally, Anderson divides between marketing measures of performance and financial measures of performance. Specifying both measure groups on the one hand in market share and customer satisfaction and on the other hand in profit rate and cash flow. The assessment of outputs by appropriate inputs depends on criteria such as the maturity of the joint venture, familiarity of markets and products, mode of manufacturing, competition and entry barriers, standardization of goals.

McGee et al (1995) investigated the relationship between performance and the experience of a new venture's management team, its choice of competitive strategy and the use of co-operative arrangements. The findings point into the direction of Anderson's statements about the maturity of the joint venture. For marketing and manufacturing co-operative activities, joint ventures with experienced managers benefit more than new ones, although inexperienced managers do not necessarily harm the performance of joint ventures. In the case of high-technology industries inexperience in technology may actually lead to damage the performance.

Difficulties in the context of performance measurement are the verifiability and the output sharing in joint ventures. Chi (1996) examined the mechanisms of arbitration and output sharing. Under imperfect performance verifiability, it is important how the residual output of the joint venture is borne by the two partner firms. It was proven that the total pay-off of the venture is higher if the residual output is borne by the party with the input contributions being less verifiable (ceteris paribus), more productive or subject to lower opportunity costs (Chi, 1996). Another possibility to overcome the problems of performance verifiability was shown by Dasgupta and Tao (1999). The authors showed the importance of sharing equity instead of output because of its ex ante verifiability in order to avoid contractual incompleteness.

Osland and Cavusgil (1998) developed an interesting and for the evaluation of performance important 'multiple party' approach which was investigated in the context of US-China joint ventures. Although only eight large IJVs were subject of this study, 40 managers were interviewed and delivered the perspective that there are different perceptions and objectives about performance concerning the various participants in the IJV like the US parent, the Chinese (or PRC) parent, the US IJV manager and the PRC IJV manager. The findings uncovered that US parent company managers are more likely to use return on investment or internal rate of return as performance measure, while Chinese parent company managers focused on dividends, and short-term profits. Rather than concentrating on long-term profitability and market share, some US IJV managers reported that they had to produce high annual dividends in order to keep the Chinese parent satisfied. The Chinese parent company managers heavily relied on an economic development model of performance and for this reason technology transfer and foreign exchange earnings were important performance criteria. The US partner management evaluated the IJV on enterprise-level dimensions. The Chinese IJV management used a wider set of firm output measures than the manager of the Chinese parent firm, whereas the US IJV managers employed the most extensive set of different enterprise level measures such as product quality, total costs and product scope. Different perceptions about the satisfaction over the performance of the IJV can be shown in the Chinese managers' view that the joint venture lead to an exchange of cultures, technology and management skills and, in contrast, the US managers seem to be content when they are in control of the IJV. For this reason, several US managers related their dissatisfaction about their IJVs to the lack of control over pricing, hiring and firing and foreign exchange. Dissimilar objectives occur as well between Chinese parent managers which aim to get technology transferred to China and Chinese IJV managers intending to improve product quality. Although the investigation was merely based on the US-Chinese IJV perspective, it could be shown that the complexity of an IJV involves not only three organizations but also four sets of managers and for this reason different performance criteria. The following types of performances were developed for this investigation and cover the variety of pay-offs: profits, sales, product quality, market share, productivity, production level, total costs, product scope, technology transfer, management skill transfer, foreign exchange, competition in country A or B, co-operation as internal process.

Luo and Park (2004) found 13 objectives for the parents in IJVs and pointed out the goal differences. The objectives are profitability, taking advantage of investment incentives by the host government, local market expansion, technology transfer, developing R&D capabilities, cost reduction, global market expansion, export growth, access to monetary resources, risk reduction, opportunity to join forces with competitors, learning management and production skills and opportunity to employ skilled personnel. They suggested that IJV performance depends on co-operation not only between the partners but also with the IJV management. The so-called tripartite co-operation in their study comprises co-operation between foreign parent and local parent (horizontal co-operation), between local parent and venture management (vertical co-operation for local partners) and between foreign parent and IJV management (vertical co-operation for foreign partners). The authors showed in an empirical study the strong positive impact of co-operation between partners on performance.

Dhanaraj et al (2004) investigated relational embeddedness between the foreign partner's and the IJV managers and its impact on tacit and explicit knowledge transfer in IJVs. The results show the influence of tacit and explicit knowledge on IJV performance. Tacit knowledge is abstract and in IJVs, it is managerial and marketing expertise which can be considered as tacit. Whereas, quantifiable technologies and processes are more explicit and easily transferred. The relational embeddedness plays an important role in the transfer of tacit knowledge in an IJV, especially in a mature stage of an IJV life cycle. Thus, the knowledge transfer in IJVs has an impact on learning, on information asymmetries, on control issues and on communication in the IJV management process.

Information structure

As far as complete and incomplete information are concerned, each player's pay-off function can either be common knowledge or uncertain.

Games under incomplete information are developed by introducing Nature – a dummy player. This means choosing the type of player randomly.

In the initial stage of an IJV the two players have different information about their strategies and private values about their objectives. During the life cycle of an IJV further uncertainties occur concerning the performance, the effort level invested into the production process and the marketing of the new product as well as about other operational issues of the joint business. Incomplete information about the success and failure of the project arises in the beginning of each joint venture and can be connected to the verifiability of the performance. Considering an IJV as a company with a defined time horizon, the parent firms could have the intention to terminate the enterprise after having gained enough knowledge about the management or technological issues in order to pursue their own businesses. This creates uncertainty about the actions taken during the life cycle or about the splitting of the outcome and other operational factors derived from the learning perspective of one side. Since the firms have to protect their reputation, their behavior will lead to conclusions about their ability to co-operate or their proneness to cheat. Incomplete information leads to a dummy player called nature and to the randomization of events to happen.

Focusing on the players' information asymmetries, local knowledge was one of the major advantages domestic firms can possess compared to the foreign parent, which leaves the latter in a situation of uncertainty about the preferences of the other player. Different perceptions about the level of technological skills, management experience and cultural behavior form information asymmetries and occur in the beginning of the joint venture process (Harrigan, 1988). Apart from the case of the two players bargaining under incomplete information, the IJV management has more information about the actual operational performance of the newly found enterprise (Shenkar and Zeira, 1992). For this reason, there are either both parents knowing less of the joint firm or one of the partners has more information about the IJV business depending on the different influence and control levels in combination with reports from the IJV management. In the case of the interactions with the host government and its strategies, the information structure can be generated to a more complex phenomenon.

Balakrishnan and Koza (1993) pointed out in their model, that based on the synergy effects of joint ventures, IJVs are formed to combine complementary assets from partners of dissimilar businesses. Special focus lies on the mechanism of the development of transactions and the re-negotiation of compensations for individual contributions. There exists the possibility of repeated contracting as well as the termination which can be translated into repeated games and endgames. The information revelation may reduce the adverse selection problem. It occurs in the case of hidden information of one parent when contracting over specific issues, which stresses the asymmetric information structure between the two parties. Balakrishnan and Koza show in their article the perspective of a joint venture in a relatively balanced setting such as the introduction of limited formal and informal property rights and obligations concerning shared ownership. For this reason, the members of the governing board collectively make the decisions of the policies pursuit in the joint venture. The absence of the 'unity of command' and shared control lead to higher administrative costs of managing and controlling. The shareholders of the parent companies being involved in the joint ventures obtained significantly larger extra returns, when these companies were engaged in businesses which were further apart in a technological and a managerial sense. Although value was created in all joint ventures, joint ventures between parents in dissimilar businesses were favored by shareholders (Balakrishnan and Koza, 1993). The simple case of R&D joint ventures with technology contribution from either sides show that both parents are interested in aiming at disclosure of technological knowledge either through flat fee contracts or sharing of output (Bhattacharya, Glazer and Sappington, 1992). The complexity of IJVs combining at least technological know-how with market knowledge bears a problem of offering the right incentives to reveal the information necessary for the success of the joint enterprise.

Time structure

The more IJVs mature (Serapio and Cascio, 1996), the issue of exit or endgame scenarios will be more important and the time structure is considered to be an important factor in designing IJV games. Some studies examined the life cycle of a joint venture. Parkhe (1996) suggests furthermore to develop IJV theory on the basis of the joint venture life cycle and Kogut (1988a) states that joint ventures undergo a cycle of creation, institutionalization and termination. According to Eisele (1995), there are several stages in an IJV such as initiation stage, negotiation stage, implementation stage, management stage and termination stage. There are different modes to structure the IJV's life cycle and the complexity of the organization needs special emphasis on the inherent multi-person decision-making procedure. The phenomenon of an IJV lies in the competitive conditions that motivate the formation of a joint venture, that occur during its management stage and may finally lead to the termination. For this reason, creation and termination are major issues in this section.

Concerning the long-term relationship of IJV players, structural changes and reconfigurations (Yan and Gray, 1994) have to be considered over time for several reasons. Firstly, as far as IJVs serve as means of entering into foreign markets, the initial reason of founding an IJV, is avoiding host country prohibitions of whole foreign ownership, during the management stage this may be obsolete and a wholly owned affiliate might be the result. Secondly, the IJV's importance to the parents may diminish and the joint venture can be phased out. Thirdly, when the substantial learning process of one parent devalues the other's expertise such as the accumulation of technological know-how or management and production techniques. Another reason for restructuring might be the change of bargaining power between the parents. Although the intention to reconfigure the IJV can be seen as a co-operative strategy in the business relationship, the issue of cheating or punishing in the last round of a repeated game should not be undervalued. To show the different forms of termination, the endgame scenarios such as termination by acquisition, termination by dissolution and termination by reorganization or restructuring have to be considered. In general, four major scenarios with the possible actions taken are to be distinguished as the unplanned/friendly, unplanned/unfriendly, planned/friendly and planned/unfriendly termination of the IJV.

Another issue in connection with repeated games addresses the reputational effect. Garvey (1995) investigated this effect in a model where two parties make non-contractable contributions to an economic undertaking. Although the paper investigates joint venture agreements and subcontracting in Japanese automobile part industry, it could be pointed out that repeated investment decision and low discount rates favor such forms of co-operation in the long-term perspective. The optimal allocation of ownership between the parties is more similar in a repeated than in a one shot version. Since IJVs have the properties of repeated games because of its equity basis, ownership structure, purpose of endeavor and the intentional learning perspective of the parents, the players' behavior creates a long-term relationship with effects of reputation in this respect.

Lin and Germain (1998) dealt with a crucial variable – the length of time that an IJV has endured (or the age of the IJV). Therefore, the longer an IJV relationship has existed, the more likely it is that problem-solving behavior will be relied upon. IJV age results in familiarity which not only produces an open, problem-solving approach to conflict resolution, but also a greater willingness to push for a partner's desired course of action. Another reason for positive effect of age according to the authors was that the longer an IJV has existed, the less likely partners are to rely on written agreements in conflict resolution. Though the paper gives some insights into the conflicts and problem-solving mechanism, the authors were keen to mention that limitations exist due to the selection of the countries (US-Chinese), the exclusion of failed IJVs and the inclusion of only on-site IJV managers. The authors stated therefore an important characteristic of an IJV that you get a different picture when observing on-site IJV managers and parent company managers.

Meschi (1997) explores in his article the extent to which the longevity of an international joint venture affects the intensity of its cultural differences (in a sample of 51 international joint venture set up in Hungary). In the center of interest lies the cross-cultural issue of joint management. The chronic instability and a record level of failure can be related to the problems which trace back to cultural factors such as mutually incompatible social or organizational models. Since an IJV is an independent organization that federates the operations of two or more parents, individual and collective frictions can arise between the local professionals and expatriates working in the IJV. The success of the IJV is dependent on the congruence between the different cultures involved. Thus, the search for a culturally-compatible partner needs to be emphasized and can be shown by Meschi's statement 'When two or more companies start working together, their respective cultures come into contact: the local employee must deal with a different, sometimes unknown, foreign cultural environment, and likewise for the expatriate employee. The cultures represented in the international joint venture may collide and produce culture shock, disrupting the entire operation of the newly-formed company. Although relatively little is known about the means by which cultural differences actually influence international joint ventures, even less is known about the effectiveness of different managerial approaches used to handle cultural (national and organizational) issues in such ventures' (p. 214). Meschi emphasized in his study that the partners must develop a joint strategy of cultural integration. For culturally-incompatible partners to become compatible, the cultural transformation is a time-consuming, incremental and evolutionary process and therefore determined by time and learning. Compared to transferring large numbers of expatriate or local employees from existing operations of respective partners, the option to hire new employees offers an opportunity to facilitate the integration into another culture since the new recruits are less rooted in a given organizational culture. Meschi postulates that IJVs must create and develop a specific culture shared by the partners and referred to a set of conditions required for the ultimate success of the integration process. First, sufficient time to control and harmonize the entity's cultural differences must be granted and secondly during that period integration measures should be undertaken.

Yan and Zeng (1999) postulate the reconceptualization of instability in IJVs. The authors redefine instability as 'the extent to which the IJV alters its strategic directions, re-negotiates its contract/agreements, reconfigures its ownership and/or management structures, or changes the relationship with its parents or the relationship between the parents that may have a significant effect on the venture's performance'.

Zhang and Rajagopalan (2002) examined the inter-partner credible threat in IJVs by using an infinitely repeated prisoner's dilemma. The authors showed that inter-partner credible threat can address appropriation concerns and coordination cost concerns simultaneously. 'Coordination costs in IJVs stem from the organizational complexity of decomposing tasks among partners along with ongoing coordination of activities to be completed jointly or individually across organizational boundaries and the related extent of communication and decisions that would be necessary' (p. 458). Having focused on the appropriation concerns, the authors found that when firms anticipate high appropriation concerns, they are likely to organize alliances with more hierarchical contracts. Because more hierarchical contracts provide stronger control mechanisms such as increased monitoring and better incentive alignment than less hierarchical contracts (p. 459). The authors reviewed the role of equity ownership and control in this respect and found that they are two conceptually different constructs. Equity ownership is but one input to the process of defining control of the IJV. The second type is partners' management control or overall control of the IJV. Partners might exercise control through having one's own staff members in key positions in the IJV and having regular meetings to prevent sudden complications in operations. The third type is partners' control over specific operational activities in the IJV. The authors, furthermore, investigated the coordination costs concerns. The role of the partners in IJVs is different to shareholders, since parents are visible and powerful. Managers in IJVs face multiple sets of expectations and must simultaneously accommodate the interests of all partners. Additionally, managers often face subordinates who have allegiance to different partners and perceive their future promotion to be dependent on supervisors in their partner firms instead of those in the IJV. Inter-partner credible threat was considered as dynamic and though exogenous forces could affect inter-partner credible threat, the authors discuss the effect of two forces – organizational life cycle and learning. Thus, IJVs at different stages of their organizational life cycle need different expertise. Most local partners in developing countries contribute to the formation via facilitating local government relation, registering the ventures, renting lands and recruiting workers. After the formation period, these contributions are sunk costs and have no effect on the partnership. In this stage, business expertise such as technology and access to marketing channels is a credible threat. If the local partner does not have expertise, it is likely to be held up by the foreign partner who will generate the most rents from the IJV. If the main contribution of the foreign partner is technology transfer and over time the IJV does not depend on the foreign partner's continuous supply of technology, the foreign partner could be held up and the local partner will appropriate the most rent from the IJV. As mentioned before, partner learning creates a credible threat, since IJV/alliances have been described as a tool to facilitate learning of the parents. Partner learning can change inter-partner credible threat in the way that the partner that learns faster will be free from the other partner's threat sooner. It was argued that foreign partners' acquisition of local knowledge will shift the relative bargaining power between the foreign and local parents and can affect the stability and duration of the IJV. The study suggested that if partners have credible threat, they do not have to control the IJV to protect their positions. The authors suggest that a majority of IJV failure is caused because partners do not consider credible threat and its evolution over time before entering an IJV. Thus, if a firm lacks credible threat, it should not enter an IJV and should choose flexible collaboration forms without equity ownership. Furthermore, it is important to consider learning effects over time, which is particularly important for local partners in developing countries because they lack international collaboration experiences.

The next section connects the above-mentioned elements of a game and the structure of an IJV by specifying the rules and the order of the play.

Like chess or poker, an IJV game needs to have clear guidelines in order to play the different versions and to get different results. Since the real life situation of IJVs can be characterized by heterogeneous settings, the outcome of the particular game is up to the individual circumstance and is uncertain right from the beginning. The provision of such a game theoretical perspective is not only intended as an academic exercise but also as a framework for actual solution concepts.

The structure of an IJV and its game theoretical potential – the rules and the timing

An IJV game Γ^{IJV} is a combination of different elements being derived from the literature condensation. The following table aggregates the rules of the game and gives an idea of the different possibilities in playing this game.

Table 3.3 The Rules of an IJV Game

Game-theoretical Elements	Rules in an IJV Game
Players (N)	Two-player model: negotiation of P_L and P_F Three-player model: $P_i = (P_{Loc}, P_{For}, P_{IJV})$ IJV model
Types of Players (T_i) uncertainty about	Contribution to the enterprise, experience level, ability and effort level of the IJV management
Strategies of parents in IJV (C_{IJV})	Dominant parent strategies, shared management strategies, independent joint venture strategy
Pay-offs (u_i)	Profits, change in ownership shares and market share, marketing results (sales, customer satisfaction, quality control) and financial results (ROI, ROE), labor productivity, technology transfer, learning, level of exports, cost efficiency and cost control, stability, survival.
Information structure – incomplete information	Uncertainties about the preferences of the players determined by the type
Information structure – asymmetric information	Contracting between the parents and the parents and IJV itself, asymmetric information about the cost function and about the ability and effort level, control issue about effort and report of the other player or players
Time structure	Set-up Period, Management Period and Termination Stage

Source: Ott (2003)

A coherent concept of an IJV life cycle has to consider not only the rules of the game, but also the timing of an IJV game. The following table develops the several stages of an IJV in connection with the players, their crucial actions and the outcome. Since the methodology offers different games played by the parent firms, the IJV management and external players, the game theoretical application is intended to provide insights into strategic problems and cases for individual purposes. The path to win or lose a particular game can be traced back by the means of this theoretical tool.

The order of the play of an IJV game shows the combination of different stages from the formation until the termination of the enterprise. The periods can be aggregated to a bargaining game, a contracting game and a repeated game. Indicators of these games are the negotiation over the ownership shares, the development of incentives and finally the learning of the parents as a sign of a repeated game. Nevertheless, the abstraction of the problem gives only a glimpse of an idea how to proceed in the different settings. Not only the asymmetries of both parents in the set-up phase of the joint venture matter, but also problems of coalitions in the IJV and

Table 3.4   Stages, Players, Actions and Game Theoretic Perspectives

Stage in IJV Life Cycle	Players and their Actions	Game Theoretic Perspectives
Negotiation stage	Parent foreign and parent local negotiate over ownership shares	Bargaining, Common agency games (adverse selection, signaling)
Set-up stage	IJV is founded	Common agency starts
Set-up stage	Parents offer incentives	Common agency (moral hazard)
Management	IJV manager reports	Common agency (moral hazard)
Management	Players co-operate or cheat	Repeated games (moral hazard)
Management	Players learn	Repeated games (re-negotiation, reputation)
Termination	Success or failure of the IJV	Endgame problems
Termination	Termination scenarios	Endgame problems

the players' reporting behavior as well as the incentives to co-operate or to cheat occur during the managerial process of this endeavor. Furthermore, repeated cheating or learning will lead to punishment and reward scenarios and has an impact on the success and the failure of an IJV. Finally, the termination scenarios are to be considered as a consequence of the co-operative and conflictive behavior during the life cycle of an IJV. Game theoretical reasoning can be applied over the whole time horizon, since the intention of the monograph is to show that the various periods contain games being played by the parents and by the IJV management.

The logic of an IJV situation can be understood by showing the game theoretical structure of this particular form of international transaction. In the first stage, we have at least two players from two countries, the local and the foreign firm. Focusing on the parent firms, there are some types or combinations of characteristics which have an impact on their moves. Apart from the market size, the cultural implications are important for the negotiation behavior of the parents, and the functional contributions like marketing, technological and financial knowledge may lead to the development of special strategies in order to perform well or get satisfying pay-offs for each parent firm and the IJV itself. The second stage deals with the revelation of hidden information and action of the players. The management period is characterized by information asymmetries between the parent firms and the IJV depending again on the chosen strategic setting. Finally, in the termination stage of an IJV the parent firms may pursue strategies of co-operation and competition to get their appropriate outcome. Besides learning issues, the reputational effect of the behavior matters in the endgame too. The specific structure of an IJV links its properties with the rules of the play, and the application of game theory to the life cycle can be seen as an analytical tool to analyze multi-person decision-making processes with co-operative and conflicting components.

Having developed the rules of the game, it is now important to look at the notation, the game theoretical framework of IJVs and the mechanism in the various IJVs. The following chapter is designing the conceptual basis for the analysis of games of incomplete information in IJVs.

4
A General Framework for Multi-Person Decision-Making

Introduction

This chapter can be seen as the source for the next chapters. Notation, configuration, and mechanisms are explained and will be used in the adverse selection, moral hazard, signaling and endgame chapters to provide consistency throughout. Regarding an IJV as an international enterprise dealing with multi-person decision-making processes, the information structure between the parent firms and the management bodies is furthermore of special interest. How to handle a decision-making process? Is it a poker or chess situation? Which strategies do we and our counterparts use or how to reveal the hidden information? What about signals? As far as game theory provides solution concepts for bargaining situations, principal-agent relationships and other problems of multi-person decision-making, the application of this mathematical tool might be appropriate, although the formal level will be kept on a minimum in this part.

The elements of an IJV game

Introduction to the game theoretical elements

Modeling an IJV situation means transferring the characteristics of the business unit into the rules of the game. Based on the previous chapter, the players, strategies, pay-offs, timing and information structure can now be connected into a game theoretical framework.

Players

To begin with two players, this simple case occurs when two parents p_{Loc} and p_{For} (local and foreign firm) bargain over the formation of an IJV.

Adding an additional internal player (two parents and the joint venture p_{IJV}) is important in the implementation stage of an IJV, and adding external players p_E (government and/or antitrust body) to the different stages of the IJV's life cycle leads to at least four players involved in an IJV life cycle. Let us specify the number of players as

$$N = \{P_i\}, \ (i = 1,...,n)$$

As a first step in the modeling of an IJV game, there are two players as parent firms. For notation reasons, player I is called the local firm p_{Loc} and player II will be the foreign firm p_{For}. The two-player model $P_i = (p_{Loc}, p_{For})$ occurs in the first period of an IJV.

Describing the players in the different settings the next step to figure out is the involvement of a third player in the game of an IJV. To diversify the two three-player models

- $P_i = (p_{Loc}, p_{For}, p_{IJV})$ IJV model

The internal three-player model shows the interaction between the parents and the IJV management (Manager assigned by the parents, board members, business development managers).

This part of the book is designed to develop the notation and the mechanism of IJV games. Mechanism in this context means the relationship between the players, their strategies, the pay-offs and the information structure over a given period – the duration of the IJV in this context. Starting with the parent firms as the two basic players, the parent firms could be configured in various ways. For empirical and theoretical purposes, the development of the features of the parents should lead to an elegant structure in an IJV life-cycle model.

Concerning the two-player IJV-model under incomplete information, the types of players have to be specified:

- according to the size (large and small firms),
- according to the industry (aerospace, automobile, food processing, communication, paper, chemicals, rubber, metal, machinery, electrical and electronic equipment, utilities, etc.),
- according to the countries (developed, less developed, developing countries; industrialized and developing countries; USA, Canada, Japan, Western or Eastern European, Asian countries, Latin American and African countries),

- according to the functional contributions (supplier of raw material, production skills, marketing know-how, managerial capabilities, financial contributions, R&D).

Describing the features of the players, pairwise combinations for the case of two players pertain to the nature of the game. To start with the analysis of the different size combinations, large (s_L) and small (s_S) firms are to be considered. Regarding the case of player 1 as local firm and player 2 as foreign firm in an ordered pair, the order is important to show later on the set of problems and strategies connected with each player. The following can be written:

$$P_{Size} (P_{Loc}, P_{For}) = \{(s_L, s_L), (s_L, s_S), (s_S, s_S), (s_S, s_L)\}$$

Table 4.1 Players According to their Size

Local Firm	Foreign Firm	
	Large Foreign Firm	Small Foreign Firm
Large local firm	(s_L, s_L)	(s_L, s_S)
Small local firm	(s_S, s_L)	(s_S, s_S)

Both parents could be large firms (s_L, s_L), which is the case of IJVs between two multinationals for instance Toyota and General Motors forming NUMMI. On the other side, both parents could be small firms (s_S, s_S), which is a very unlikely case and only possible in technology intensive industries. For the sake of simplicity, we consider this as a very rare scenario. This leads to the two other cases of a large local firm and a small foreign firm as parents of an IJV and small local firm setting up a joint venture with a large foreign firm. Theoretically, all four cases could be possible. Yet, it is important to connect the size with the countries of origin in order to get a bigger picture.

Considering the country combinations of an IJV, the two players may come from a developing (c_{ding}) or a developed (c_{dd}) country in the simplest case. Different cultural backgrounds influence the bargaining procedures. Interactions between the players of various cultures may have an impact on the time structure and their chosen strategies. For this reason, the combinations between players are characterized in the following way:

$$P_{country} (P_{Loc}, P_{For}) = \{(c_{dd}, c_{dd}), (c_{dd}, c_{ding}), (c_{ding}, c_{ding}), (c_{ding}, c_{dd})\}$$

Table 4.2   Players According to the Status of their Country

Local Firm	Foreign Firm	
	Developed Country	Developing Country
Developed country	(c_{dd}, c_{dd})	(c_{dd}, c_{ding})
Developing country	(c_{ding}, c_{dd})	(c_{ding}, c_{ding})

With regard to the distinction between developed and developing countries, refinements about the impact of culture on bargaining behavior should be given. On the basis of several IJV studies conducted in countries like USA, Japan, the Far East and special European countries (Britain, France, Germany, Italy, and Russia, Sweden) cultural aspects in the life cycle of an IJV have proven to be important. Furthermore, it might be interesting to model on Latin American, Arab and African countries and their strategies in bargaining.

$$P_{Culture} (P_{Loc}, P_{For}) = \{(c_{USA}, c_{EU}), (c_{USA}, c_{JAP}), (c_{EU}, c_{USA}), (c_{EU}, c_{EU}), (c_{EU}, c_{JAP}), (c_{JAP}, c_{USA}), (c_{JAP}, c_{EU}), (c_X, c_{USA}), (c_X, c_{EU}), (c_X, c_{JAP})\}$$

Table 4.3   Players According to their Country of Origin

Local Firm	Foreign Firm (HQ)		
	USA	Europe	Japan
USA	Domestic	(c_{USA}, c_{EU})	(c_{USA}, c_{JAP})
Europe	(c_{EU}, c_{USA})	(c_{EU}, c_{EU})	(c_{EU}, c_{JAP})
Japan	(c_{JAP}, c_{USA})	(c_{JAP}, c_{EU})	Domestic
Emerging markets (China, Arab countries, etc.)	(c_X, c_{USA})	(c_X, c_{EU})	(c_X, c_{JAP})

This part of the configuration between the parents marks an important step into clustering the foreign partner as headquarter (HQ) and the local partner as host in relation to the countries where the parents have their cultural background. Thus, the general classification in US, European and Japanese based foreign parents leads to important implications with regards to contributions, staffing and information asymmetries. Joint ventures between both parents coming from USA and

Japan are considered as domestic, whereas both parents having their firms based in Europe does not necessarily lead to a domestic joint venture.

Considering the contributions to the IJV, Buckley and Casson (1996) analyzed that the parents can contribute either technology or marketing or both. In this context the configuration of the parents could look like the following matrix:

$$P_{Contribution} (P_{Loc}, P_{For}) = \{(c_T, c_T), (c_T, c_M), (c_T, c_F), (c_M, c_T), (c_M, c_M), (c_M, c_F), (c_F, c_T), (c_F, c_M), (c_F, c_F)\}$$

Table 4.4   Players According to their Contributions

Local Firms	Foreign Firm		
	Technology	Marketing	Finance
Technology	(c_T, c_T)	(c_T, c_M)	(c_T, c_F)
Marketing	(c_M, c_T)	(c_M, c_M)	(c_M, c_F)
Finance	(c_F, c_T)	(c_F, c_M)	(c_F, c_F)

The contributions of the parents are important because of the impact on ownership ratios, bargaining power, return on investment and the strategic configuration of the IJV itself which will be dealt with in the later section of this chapter. The local and the foreign parent could both contribute technology (research lab), marketing (marketing units, distribution jv) or finance (contractual IJV and not relevant in this set-up). The financial contributions could lead to a particular strategic configuration in which one parent just intends to get an ROI back, whereas the other one contributes to the value-adding process. Important configuration with regards to the distribution of power are IJVs in which one parent contributes technology and the other one marketing.

Another way of distinguishing parental roles is based on the functions and the experience of the managers sent to the IJV.

The contributions of the two partners can be combined by joining together expert power of special functional areas. Special knowledge in marketing (f_M), production (f_P), finance (f_F), R&D ($f_{R\&D}$) as well as provision of raw materials (f_S) may lead to cross border joint ventures to overcome weaknesses. Functional expertise of the two players is not only an important factor as the feature of the parent firm or the contribution to the IJV, but it has also an impact on the strategies of the partners for instance in the bargaining over ownership shares.

Similar to the above-mentioned combinations, pairings of different functions can be outlined, although some of the below-mentioned combinations would not occur in reality, it will be shown to provide an abstract level of contribution pairings:

$$P_{Function} (P_{Loc}, P_{For}) = \{(f_S, f_S), (f_S, f_M), (f_S, f_P), (f_S, f_F), (f_S, f_{R\&D}); (f_M, f_S),$$
$$(f_M, f_M), (f_M, f_P), (f_M, f_F), (f_M, f_{R\&D}); (f_P, f_S),$$
$$(f_P, f_M), (f_P, f_P), (f_P, f_F), (f_P, f_{R\&D}); (f_F, f_S), (f_F, f_M),$$
$$(f_F, f_P), (f_F, f_F), (f_F, f_{R\&D}); (f_{R\&D}, f_S), (f_{R\&D}, f_M),$$
$$(f_{R\&D}, f_P), (f_{R\&D}, f_F), (f_{R\&D}, f_{R\&D})\}$$

Table 4.5   Players According to their Functional Contribution

Local Firms	Foreign Firm				
	Supply	Production	Marketing	Finance	R&D
Supply	(f_S, f_S)	(f_S, f_P),	(f_S, f_M)	(f_S, f_F)	(f_S, f_{RD})
Production	(f_P, f_S)	(f_P, f_P),	(f_P, f_M)	(f_P, f_F)	(f_P, f_{RD})
Marketing	(f_M, f_S)	$f_M, f_P)$	(f_M, f_M)	(f_M, f_F)	(f_M, f_{RD})
Finance	(f_F, f_S),	(f_F, f_P)	(f_F, f_M)	(f_F, f_F)	(f_F, f_{RD})
R&D	(f_{RD}, f_S)	(f_{RD}, f_P)	(f_{RD}, f_M)	(f_{RD}, f_F),	(f_{RD}, f_{RD})

Another possibility of diversification is connected to experience, and it can be distinguished between inexperienced (i) and experienced (e) chief executives in the parent firms.

$$P_{Experience} (P_{Loc}, P_{For}) = \{(e, e), (e, i), (i, e), (i, i)\}$$

Strategies and actions

The game theoretical element 'strategy' can be developed for the two players in the negotiation stage and for the parent firm and the IJV in the management period as well as for the external players. Strategies are rules that tell the player which action to choose at which moment of the game. In a two-player model, strategies of each player may be: growth in domestic and international markets, access to new markets, diversification, acquiring brand names and trademarks, transfer of technology, transfer pricing. Factors influencing the strategies are market size, pace of technology change, rate of interest, cultural distance, protection of independence, missing patent rights, economies of scope. Like in the case of functional expertise, the contributions of the parent firms to the IJV may have an impact on the strategies. The pure strategy outcome space can be enlarged by probabilities and result in mixed strategies.

Strategies of the parent firms and the IJV, like dominant parent strategy, shared management strategy, independent joint venture strategy (Contractor and Lorange, 1988; Datta, 1988, Killing, 1982), may reflect the shares or contributions of the partner firms and the strength of the players. Furthermore, strategies of the external authorities occur as host government strategies (regulations, expropriation, blocking of profit repatriation) and strategies of antitrust bodies. Let us specify the strategies for player i in the strategy set or strategy space

$$C_i = \{c_i\}, \ (i = 1,...,n) \tag{4.1}$$

we can now specify the strategies of the parent firms in general as

$$C_i = (c_{Loc}, c_{For}) \tag{4.2}$$

the strategies pursued in the IJV itself as

$$C_{IJV} = (c_{dom}, c_{shar}, c_{in}) \tag{4.3}$$

in relation to the dominant, the shared and the independent management, and those strategies of the external players as C_E.

The strategy profile is an ordered set of one strategy for each of the n players in the game

$$C = (c_1, ..., c_n) \tag{4.4}$$

The two-player structure can now be enlarged to a three-player scenario in which the strength between the three players needs to be emphasised.

Taking the independent, shared management and the dominant parent IJV archetypes as a basis, the above-mentioned categories and combinations of parental firms can already be used to show the configurations.

The three archetypes of IJVs developed by Killing (1982) are the dominant parent venture, the shared management enterprise and the independent joint venture. These categories were used to describe control.

Datta (1988) and Lorange and Probst (1987) advanced frameworks for IJVs using these archetypes to show different strategic decisions being based on the control types.

The dominant parent strategy is connected to the concept of a wholly owned subsidiary with the dominant partner. The executives from each parent compose the board of directors which plays a subordinate role, whereas the executives of the dominant partner are responsible for the IJVs strategic and operational decisions. This is an appropriate response to the pressures from the host government or to a passive partner seeking solely a financial investment with an acceptable rate of return. Lorange and Probst (1987) stated that this strategy type shows a self-organizing system consisting of a dominant parent together with a joint venture adapting to its parent future strategic interests. Splitting the value-creating functions between the dominant partner and the IJV organization, it often may be difficult to establish a sufficiently simple division of labor. Accepting changes in roles between the two players should lead to a redefinition of the execution of the IJVs' strategies. The concept of a dominant parent strategy can be found in IJVs having a parent from a developing country and the other one from a developed country. Because of the legal restriction in the host country it might only be possible to have major control rights in the hands of the local partner, whereas the foreign firm will contribute technological and/or management expertise or financial resources.

The shared management venture is more common in manufacturing processes where one partner supplies the technological know-how and the other firm provides the enterprise with knowledge of the local market. Both partners play an active role (Datta, 1988). Each of the parents continues to have an active interest in the same type of business. This leads to the second archetype of having two inter-related self-organizing systems as far as the relationship between firm A and the IJV and between firm B and the IJV are concerned. Focusing on the value-creating process, both parents and the IJV are involved and play an active role by contributing their resources. Given potentially diverging perspectives, this may lead to conflicts, co-operation or compromises. If one parent, for instance, attempts to shift over more autonomy to the joint venture organization, while the other tries to hold back, the strength of the parents and the bargaining power have an impact on the control scenario of the IJV (Lorange and Probst, 1987).

The independent joint venture is relatively free from parental interference and is relatively rare. For Lorange and Probst (1987) the free standing joint venture shows the situation that none of the parents have a strong direct operating future strategic interest in the strategy that the joint venture is pursuing. The structuring of the various tasks in the value-creating process can be done like in an independent company. It is up to the parents to equip the joint venture with a degree of redundancy for having the necessary capacity to be flexible. Datta (1988) points out that numerous interdependencies inevitably exist between the joint venture and the parent enterprises. Furthermore, parents are generally reluctant to give joint ventures the autonomy and freedom to develop independently.

Buckley and Casson (1998) showed in their paper on foreign market entry that IJVs are owned 50:50 by the two firms, could have various forms of joint ownership such as the production or distribution plant can be jointly owned. They assumed that the partner is always the local rival. Furthermore, they proposed if both production and distribution are jointly owned, then the market in intermediate output is internalized within the IJV. The IJV is assumed to be a 'buy in' by the entrant to the local firm. Greenfield IJVs' complexity increases considerably as a result. Another aspect is that the local rival contributes its facilities to the IJV, the IJV enjoys monopoly power in the same way that an acquisition does. When an IJV is linked to one of the entrant's wholly owned activities, the relevant intermediate product market is only partially internalized. Dependent on trust, the market can operate as though it was fully internal. Buckley and Casson (1998) developed a model on costs incurred for IJVs considering trust building, technology transfer, marketing expertise and intermediate output flow. Thus, the notation for the relevant costs for building trust are j_1 for technology transfer, j_2 for marketing expertise and j_3 for intermediate output flow. Learning costs m, adaptation costs a and trust-building costs j_i, q_i (i = 1,2,3) are once-and-for-all set up costs that are financed by borrowing at the given interest rate r. By contrast, the home location cost premium z and the transaction cost t_i (i = 1,2,3) are recurrent costs incurred each period. Where both entrant and rival possess production facilities with which to source an IJV distribution facility, they employ the IJV to maintain a monopoly price, but compete to supply it. The authors pointed out that the competition from the rival's production facility forces the entrant to supply the IJV itself. They suggest that if both entrant and rival possess distribution facilities able to draw upon an IJV production facility, then they can maintain a monopoly price by competing for a franchise to handle all the output. The entrant is forced to bid up the price for IJV output such that the profits are again shared with the rival through its stake in the IJV.

Buckley and Casson (1998) focused on twelve entry strategies and their variants. The authors distinguished between six strategies for joint ventures which will be shown in the following part: (1) *Integrated IJV* (entrant jointly owns an integrated set of production and distribution facilities $c_7 = rj_1 + rj_2 + ra$), (2) *JV in production* (entrant jointly owns foreign production, but uses an independent distribution facility $c_8 = rj_1 + rj_3 + ra$), (3) *JV in distribution* (entrant jointly owns foreign distribution, but subcontracts production to an independent facility $c_9 = t_1 + rj_2 + rj_3 + ra$), (4) *JV exporting* (entrant exports to a jointly owned distribution facility $c_{10} = z + rj_2 + rj_3 + s/2$), (5) *FDI/JV combination* (entrant owns foreign production and jointly owns foreign distribution facility $c_{11.1} = rj_2 + rj_3 + s/2$ and $c_{11.2} = rq_1 + rj_2 + rj_3 + ra$), (6) *JV/FDI combination* (entrant owns foreign distribution and jointly owns foreign production $c_{12.1} = rj_1 + rj_3 + ra + s/2 + sm$ and $c_{12.2} = rj_1 + rj_2 + rj_3 + ra$).

This monograph uses the basic idea of these strategic implications for IJVs and develops a typology for the combinations of joint research laboratories, production units, marketing and distribution units.

Showing the importance of the nature of the game in the different combinations of players according to their size, state of the country, cultural background, experience level of managers and their contributions to the IJV, there are some features leading to the characteristics of the Nature – choosing special types of probability distribution. There is a common a priori probability distribution – 'common priors'. Each player can assume the probability of his opponent being from a special type. These concepts can be applied in situations of incomplete information.

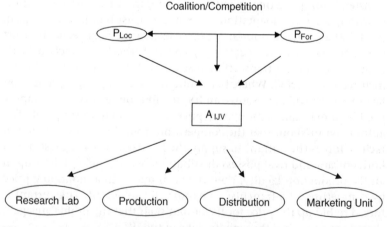

Figure 4.1   Strategic Interaction between Players

Table 4.6 Strategic Configuration Within an IJV

Agent IJV	Agent local	Agent foreign
1) Research Laboratory	Technological knowledge C(q)	Technological knowledge C(q)
2) Research Lab – Production Unit – Marketing (separate)	Technological knowledge C(q) Marketing knowledge R(q)	Technological knowledge C(q), Marketing knowledge R(q)
3) Production Unit + Marketing (joint and separate)	Technological knowledge Marketing knowledge R(q)	Technological knowledge C(q) Marketing knowledge R(q)
4) Distribution Unit	Marketing R(q)	Marketing R(q)

Pay-offs and performance measures

Regarding the performance as an element of the game, several measures of performance such as marketing or finance measures occur in an IJV. The performance of an IJV game can be considered for each player and the IJV itself. In general, performance might be profit, cash flow, cost efficiency, royalties, management fees, transfer prices, sales, market share, supply contracts for a parent firm and knowledge acquisition.

In strategic form games the number u_i (c) represents the expected utility pay-off that player i would get in this game if c were the combination of strategies implemented by the players. In general, it is assumed that all players choose their strategies simultaneously in a normal form game.

In extensive form games each terminal node has a label that specifies a vector of n numbers $(u_1,..., u_n) = (u_i)_{i \in N}$ and the number u_i is interpreted as the pay-off to player i when this node is the outcome of the game.

Luo and Park (2004) found 13 objectives for the parents in IJVs and pointed out the goal differences. The objectives are profitability, taking advantage of investment incentives by the host government, local market expansion, technology transfer, developing R&D capabilities, cost reduction, global market expansion, export growth, access to monetary resources, risk reduction, opportunity to join forces with competitors, learning management and production skills and opportunity to employ skilled personnel.

Information structure and time structure

Since the first section analyzed the different types of players, the information structure has to include incomplete information about the cultural background, the quality of contribution and the experience and effort level of the players. For this reason, nature as a dummy player has to choose which type to consider in the game. Incomplete information occurs at the beginning of the IJV formation in a situation of uncertainties between the parent firms and during the management period when it is uncertain whether players induce low or high effort into the performance of the IJV.

In reaching an agreement, the two players are facing hidden action and information about the contracting behavior of each other as an additional problem of asymmetric information. Furthermore, the two parties develop or form a third player – the IJV management – and another information problem called a multi-principal-agent or common agency situation. Both parents (principals) are interested to obtain knowledge about the effort of the IJV management, but the agent knows more about the actual costs and/or other factors of the management process. For this reason, the parents are interested in reports given by the management. The revelation principle deals with the truth-telling behavior of the agent towards the principals. Differences in the information structure within the triangle are predictable.

The time structure might be connected with the different stages of an IJV life cycle such as the formation, the management and the termination. For this reason, we may develop the different phases of a joint venture such as the negotiation stage, the contracting stage, the management stage and the termination stage. In each period we might apply game theory or its refinement such as bargaining theory, principal-agent theory, multi-principal-agent theory, contract theory or for the macro-perspective multi-stage games with communication or repeated games.

The following table shows the aggregate game theoretical elements in rows and the time structure of an IJV in columns. Strategies and pay-offs are put on an abstract level to diversify the assumptions in game theoretical models of IJVs.

The game-theoretical framework or mechanism of an IJV

Table 4.7 shows the inherent game theoretical structure of an IJV, whereas the actual moves and the order of the play are developed out of

Table 4.7 Game-theoretical Structure of an IJV

Stages Elements	Initiation Prerequisites	Management	Termination
Players	Player 1 Player 2 Nature	Player 1 Player 2 IJV-Management	Player 1 Player 2 IJV-Management
Strategies	Strategies of each parent in production, technology, marketing knowledge, acquisition	Strategies being derived from shared management, independent management, dominant parent	Ownership strategies, liquidation strategies
Pay-offs	Profits, financial and marketing results of each player	Profit, fees, dividends, financial and marketing results	Output shares, disposition of assets, survival as a firm
Information Symmetries	Incomplete information between parents	Multi-principal-agent situation	Asymmetric information between parents

the game. Depending on the players' common agency power, either the local or the foreign firm will start to negotiate over the contract terms of the joint venture. This pre-contractual common agency game under incomplete information might either result in an agreement or the rejection of the partnership. In the case of a contract, there are different asymmetric information situations to be considered. The actual management period of a joint venture will result in specific efforts, information structures as well as report strategies of the players involved. Since for these scenarios the moves and actions of the players are important steps in the game, the actual decision-making process and the order of the play is an elaborate contingency plan. Furthermore, the above-mentioned stages of the IJV game and the behavior of the players might be either aggregated into a multi-stage game with communication or focused in detail as common agency games and multi-principal-agent problems concerning special issues.

The logic of an IJV situation can be understood by showing the game theoretical structure of this particular form of international transaction. In the first stage, we have at least two players from two different countries with incomplete information about each other's bargaining behavior, preferences, contributions and experience

Period   Players, Interaction, Strategies, Information   Solution Concept

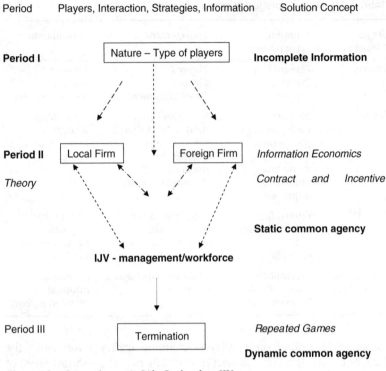

Figure 4.2   Game-theoretic Life Cycle of an IJV

levels. The market size and the cultural implications have an impact on the bargaining power and the negotiation behavior of the parents. The functional contributions like marketing, technological and financial knowledge may influence the ownership rights and lead to the strategies pursuit by each parent firm and the IJV itself in the management period. Additionally, the experience level of the parents matter. The second stage deals with the bargaining process of the two parents taking into consideration the different above-mentioned features. Thirdly, the influence of host governments and/or antitrust bodies (for instance FTC, EU as players) will determine the negotiation process over the formation of an IJV. The revelation of hidden information and action of the players is an important topic in the fourth stage of the IJV. It can be stated that in this period the two parent players as principals and the IJV management as agent may develop hidden information and action. So far, the management period is characterized by information asymmetries between the parent firms and the IJV depending on the different strategies, effort level and reporting behavior. Finally, in the termination stage of an IJV the parent firms may pursue again different strategies to get their appropriate outcome. Although an IJV is often intended as a finite game, conflicts between the parents may result in the dissolution of the enterprise in an early stage. Apart from co-operative and conflicting elements occurring in an IJV, incomplete information and dynamic processes have led to consider game theoretic solution concepts for the multi-person decision-making of an IJV.

The arrows show the flow of information, the strategies, the report and effort level as well as general interactions between the players.

For the different stages in an IJV, the problem of uncertainty occurs with a different focus. The following figure links the stages with the uncertainty and the basis of the contracts. Important uncertainty issues are quality of the management in terms of ability, cost structure, effort, performance, profit and failure and success. These uncertainties will be analyzed in the subsequent chapters on static and dynamic common agency.

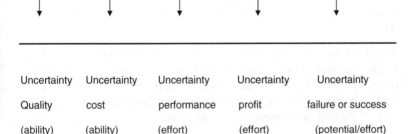

Stage 1	Stage 2	Stage 3	Stage 4	Stage 5
Uncertainty	Uncertainty	Uncertainty	Uncertainty	Uncertainty
Quality	cost	performance	profit	failure or success
(ability)	(ability)	(effort)	(effort)	(potential/effort)

Figure 4.3   Common Agency and Stage Contracting

To tackle the development of a theory of IJVs some basic assumptions have to be considered.

Assumption 1: Having shown the distinction between domestic and international joint ventures, the underlying problems are to be specified for International Joint Ventures (IJV) and thus for the special case of equity IJV which can be defined as special business entities.

Assumption 2: Since there are at least two parents involved in the creation of a new company, we assume that their contributions are complementary resources to yield a better fit of the IJV per se.

Assumption 3: From the economic, cultural and legal background of the parent firms there are combinations like developed country and developing country such as Western/Eastern partners.

a) Let there be a local firm from a developing country and the foreign firm of a developed country (MNE).

b) Let there be the local firm in a developed country and the foreign firm of a developing country.

Assumption 4: Besides the classical case of the developing/developed country combination, IJVs are found as well between parents of developed countries (famous examples are NUMMI and Airbus).

Assumption 5: From an ownership and control rights point of view, we consider the case of a dominant parent IJV. One parent plays a dominant role in the value-creating process, whereas the other partner contributes

a) financially or

b) technologically, but the host country's legal situation does not allow equality of the ownership.

Assumption 6: The value-creating process in the IJV will be shared according to the complementary contributions and the equal shares in ownership. For this reason, the IJV can be seen as shared management IJV.

Assumption 7: The rare form of an independent IJV can be considered in the scenario of two parents leaving the whole management process to the IJV itself without interference into the day to day business as well into major issues of the strategic setting. Both partners contribute financially and can be seen as shareholders.

Assumption 8: If the IJV is an independent IJV, then the players are risk-neutral and the contract is a selling-the-store (negative flat fee of principals).

Assumption 9: If the IJV is a dominant joint venture, the contracts are offered independently and one parent offers a flat fee contract (lower equity share) and the other an incentive contract.

Assumption 10: If the IJV is a shared IJV, both parents offer their contracts co-operatively with a special share ratio.

These general assumptions are important to set up the IJV games. Since each chapter and problem will deal with specific assumptions, the assumptions 1 to 7 are considered as fundamental and will be picked up explicitly for the different cases.

Besides the assumptions, the propositions for the different strategic types of IJVs need to be developed. They will be solved in the next chapters.

Independent IJV

Proposition 1: If we have an independent IJV, both parents transfer the power to make decisions to the IJV management, then we have negative flat fee contracts and the IJV management offers incentive contracts to the workforce.

Proposition 1a: If the IJV is set up as a research lab, then the contracts will be based on team work and the different tasks (technology and marketing).

Proposition 1b: If the IJV is set up as a research lab and joint production unit with separate marketing, then the contracts will encourage the joint work as team based on previous research and production contracts. The sales contract will be covered by the parents themselves.

Proposition 1c: If the IJV is set up as joint research, production and marketing unit, then the contracts will be offered according to their expertise in a team work approach.

Proposition 1d: If the IJV is set up as a joint research and distribution unit, yet the production will be dealt with independently, then the contracts will consider the marketing and technology skills whereas production processes will be dealt with separately.

Shared management IJV

Proposition 2: If we have a shared management IJV and the principals may offer their contracts co-operatively, then the joint venture management will receive a joint contract.

Proposition 2a: If the IJV is set up as a research lab with a shared management, then the contracts will be offered jointly and based on performance.

Proposition 2b: If the IJV is set up as a joint research lab and joint production unit with separate marketing in both countries, then the shared management structure will enforce co-operation using joint contracts for joint research and production and independent contracts for sales of the joint product.

Proposition 2c: If the IJV is set up as joint research, production and marketing unit, then the contracts will be offered co-operatively and according to their expertise (technology, production, sales).

Proposition 2d: If the IJV is set up as a joint research and distribution unit, yet the production will be dealt with independently, then the contracts will consider the sales and technology, whereas production processes will be dealt with separately.

Proposition 3: If we have shared management IJV and the principals offer contracts non-cooperatively, then the joint venture management will receive two contracts.

Dominant parent IJV

Proposition 4: If we have dominant parent IJV and the local parent is dominant, then the local firm offers the IJV management a contract based on their objective functions.

Proposition 4a: If the IJV is set up as a research lab with the local parent being dominant, then the contracts need to address the local and foreign employees separately. The contracts need to be based on technological know-how.

Proposition 4b: If the IJV is set up as a joint research lab and joint production unit with separate marketing in both countries, then the dominant parent will offer contracts for joint research and production and independent contracts for sales of the joint product. The foreign parent can offer a flat fee contract.

Proposition 4c: If the IJV is set up as joint research, production and marketing unit, then the contracts will be offered co-operatively and according to their expertise (technology, production, sales).

Proposition 4d: If the IJV is set up as joint research, production and marketing unit, then the contracts offered by the dominant parent need to enforce both employees to contribute to the performance, yet there will be a stronger focus on the foreign employees (technology and management expertise) since the local employees are easier to be monitored and controlled.

Proposition 4e: If the IJV is set up as a joint research and distribution unit, yet the production will be dealt with independently, then the contracts should encourage the joint research and sales. The dominant local parent will offer the own staff performance based contracts (sales contracts) for the production and cannot interfere in the other production.

Proposition 5: If we have dominant parent IJV and the foreign parent is dominant, then the foreign firm offers the IJV management a contract based on their objective functions.

Games of incomplete information

With the typology of IJVs based on the strategic and functional configurations as a starting point in the next chapter, the games of incomplete information are related to these particular features of the IJVs. Thus, it is important to introduce the uncertainties to the reader.

Adverse selection

Ex ante uncertainty about quality of management is the main issue in an adverse selection scenario in joint research laboratories, production units and distribution as well as marketing units. The typology of strategic archetypes and functional configurations in IJVs helps to structure the problem and to assign the ability levels to the IJV management. Ability is linked to the expertise of the agent (a combination of local and foreign representatives of the principals) and can be of high or low quality in this respect. The principals are not informed about the quality of the IJV management. Thus, it is possible to link the theory with real life problems. The contracts of parents (strategic interaction determines type of contracts) can be offered either co-operatively or independently. This is the strategic move of the parents. The contents of the contract is based on the objectives. Thus, it needs to consider the skills of the agent.

Moral hazard

Like in the adverse selection case, the moral hazard problem is applied to the typology of IJVs. The strategic interaction between the parents determines the way of offering the contracts and the functional configurations such as joint research lab, production, distribution and marketing unit shows the type of effort level (efforts with regards to technology, marketing and local knowledge, distribution and production). The contracts offered are therefore based on the efforts in technological knowledge input, sales marketing, managerial expertise or sales potential.

Signaling

To signal quality of the management in an IJV, the configuration of the IJV plays a determining role thus the number of research, production and sales contracts, can be used as a signal of experience. We can distinguish for the functional units: (a) Research lab (research contracts – size, volume, number) (b) Marketing/distribution unit (sales contracts – size, volume, number) (c) Production unit (production, research and sales contracts).

The following table shows possible contracts offered by the local principal I_{Loc}, the foreign principal I_{For} and the agent I_{IJV}. The incentive schemes are based on flat fees τ or incentive payments based on performance q or profit π.

To combine the strategic and control dynamics between the parents and the IJV configuration we are now able to develop a framework for game theoretical reasoning in a common agency context for adverse selection, moral hazard, signaling and endgame problems. The games being played between the parents and the IJV management (and workforce) reach from offering exclusive dealing contracts to co-operative and countervailing contracts.

Table 4.8   Three Player Strategic Structure and Incentive Schemes

Principal local	Principal foreign	Agent IJV
Independent IJV		
Principal local gets $I_{loc} = \tau_{loc}$	Principal foreign gets $I_{for} = \tau_{for}$	Agent offers $I_{IJV} = \tau_{loc} - \tau_{for}$ 'selling-the-store' contract
Dominant Management IJV one parent offers incentive contract and the other a flat fee contract		
Principal local offers	Principal foreign offers	Agent receives
$I_{loc} = \tau_{loc}$ Flat fee	$I_{for} = \tau_{for}$ Flat fee	$\tau_{loc} + \tau_{for}$
τ_{loc}	$\tau_{for}(q_{IJV})$ joint output	$\tau_{loc} + \tau_{for}(q_{IJV})$
$\tau_{loc}(q_{IJV})$	τ_{for}	$\tau_{loc}(q_{IJV}) + \tau_{for}$
$\tau_{loc}(q_{IJV})$	$\tau_{for}(q_{IJV})$	$\tau_{loc}(q_{IJV}) + \tau_{for}(q_{IJV})$
Or $\tau_{loc}(q_{For})$	$\tau_{for}(q_{loc})$	$\tau_{loc}(q_{For}) + \tau_{for}(q_{loc})$
Or profit dependent $\tau_{loc}(\pi)$	$\tau_{for}(\pi)$	$\tau_{loc}(\pi) + \tau_{for}(\pi)$
Shared management IJV jointly offered incentive schemes		
$\alpha \in [0, 1]$ $\alpha(\tau_{IJV})$	$(1 - \alpha)(\tau_{IJV})$	$\tau_{IJV}(\pi), \tau_{IJV}(q), \tau_{IJV}(R), \tau_{IJV}(C)$

5
Static Common Agency

Introduction

Considering an international joint venture as a game of three players with different tasks, capacities and strengths, the focus of this chapter lies on showing the theoretical background of the static common agency problem. As far as two parent firms located in two countries with special regulations are concerned, there exists at least one agent on the other side. The agent has hidden information of the joint venture enterprise. To reveal this information, incentive schemes and reporting methods could be applied. The theory of multi-principals describes how different incentive mechanisms compete with each other. Regarding the set of relationships between several parent firms and the joint venture, they regulate a set of competing contracts in which the control of the process is shared among these different participants. The design of control and communication channels is crucial to the underlying problem.

If the agent (management of the joint venture) knows something relevant to the performance, the contract of the principals (parent firms) needs to specify the terms of the contract to reduce informational disadvantages. Since the general assumption considers the IJV – an independent legal and business entity – as the agent, it is important to stress that the agent does not necessarily be a single person like in the conventional principal-agent theory. Thus, the underlying situation deals as well with problems of coalitions. For this reason, in common agency games we can find elements of co-operative and non-cooperative game theory. To start with the inherent problems of an IJV, the following questions are raised: How can hidden knowledge affect common agency problems in IJVs? Are there any possibilities of applying the revelation principle to the management of international joint ventures?

The author applies the principal-agent notions to the three archetypes of strategy and develops hidden knowledge as well as hidden action scenarios for the underlying cases. Furthermore, the order of the play and the timing of the adverse selection and moral hazard problems show the inherent game theoretical reasoning and replace the usual game tree due to the complexities of a real life situation. Furthermore, there exist two principals P_{Loc} and P_{For} and an agent who is the management of the international joint venture A_{IJV}. This management has special knowledge about the cost structure and other managerial details in the IJV. For this reason, the problem of asymmetric information between the parents and the IJV arises and the common agency framework provides the basis for incentive schemes. To get revelation of hidden information, the principals offer incentives to receive truthful reports from the management of the IJV about its efforts.

Before the common agency framework is applied to the IJV, the typology of IJVs needs to be developed and based on the mechanism of the previous sector the various strategic and functional configurations of IJVs are considered. This is important to design the right contracts and to get true revelation of the type of the agent.

Typology of IJVs

The development of a typology of common agency in IJVs is based on the strategic configuration between the three players which is built upon the three archetypes (a) independent IJV (b) shared management IJV (c) dominant parent IJV. This is the relationship between the parents and the IJV management. In order to have a compact typology of IJVs, the strategic configuration within an IJV matters, too. Therefore, the functional units are important to consider in a common agency structure. This should help to design contracts and mechanisms. Based on these functional units, the strategic configuration of joint research laboratories, joint marketing unit, joint production unit, joint distribution unit are connected to the strategic control types. This typology enables the author to analyze in a consistent manner the incomplete information games played by the players. Furthermore, the general critique of game theory to be positioned on an abstract level which does not encounter real life solutions can be dismissed and the applicability of game theory to problems in IJVs can be tackled in a useful way.

Table 5.1   Typology of IJVs

1) Independent IJV – selling-the-store contract:	2) Shared IJV – joint or independent contracts:	3) Dominant IJV – countervailing contracts:
a) Research Lab	a) Research Lab	a) Research Lab
b) Research Lab + Production Unit + Marketing in both countries separately	b) Research Lab + Production Unit + Marketing in both countries separately	b) Research Lab + Production Unit + Marketing in both countries separately
c) Research Lab + separate Production Units + joint Distribution	c) Research Lab + separate Production Units + joint Distribution	c) Research Lab + separate Production Units + joint Distribution
d) Research Lab + separate Production Unit + Marketing separate and joint	d) Research Lab + separate Production Unit + Marketing separate and joint	d) Research Lab + separate Production Unit + Marketing separate and joint
e) Research Lab + Production Unit + Marketing joint	e) Research Lab + Production Unit + Marketing joint	e) Research Lab + Production Unit + Marketing joint

Independent IJV – selling-the-store contract

This rare form of IJVs could be treated like a normal company, yet we have to realize that there are still parents playing a shareholder-like role by abstaining from managing the IJV. Nevertheless, the contributions to the IJV made by the parents could be seen in the configurations of the IJVs. The IJVs could still be distinguished into joint research labs, production, marketing and distribution units on a functional level

a) Research lab

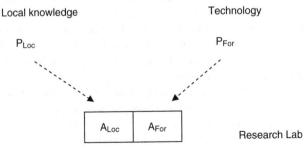

Figure 5.1   Independent IJV (Research Lab)

The location of parents, principal local might be in the USA, Japan, Europe and emerging markets, the notation is P_{Loc} (US, Europe, Japan, emerging markets) and the headquarters or the principal foreign can be located in the USA, Europe and Japan, respectively P_{For} (US, Europe, Japan). This gives the following country combinations of the principals $(P_{Loc}, P_{For}) = \{(c_{USA}, c_{EU}), (c_{USA}, c_{JAP}), (c_{EU}, c_{USA}), (c_{EU}, c_{EU}), (c_{EU}, c_{JAP}), (c_{JAP}, c_{USA}), (c_{JAP}, c_{EU}), (c_X, c_{USA}), (c_X, c_{EU}), (c_X, c_{JAP})\}$. Furthermore, the developing/developed country combination could look like $\{(c_{dd}, c_{dd}), (c_{ding}, c_{dd})\}$, such that both parents come from either developed countries or the local firm from a developing country and the foreign parent from a developed country. With regards to the contributions, the parents could set up the joint venture with their technological resources and their marketing know-how and financial endowments $(P_{Loc}, P_{For}) = \{(c_T, c_T), (c_M, c_T), (c_M, c_F)\}$. Both could provide the IJV with technology, the local player might provide market/local know-how and the foreign parent might contribute either technology or finance. Furthermore, functional contributions might reach from supply to R&D with the following possible combinations $(P_{Loc}, P_{For}) = \{(f_S, f_F), (f_S, f_{R\&D}); (f_M, f_F), (f_M, f_{R\&D}); (f_{R\&D}, f_{R\&D})\}$. Thus, the local player could contribute supply (raw material) and local knowledge, whereas the foreign player might only contribute R&D or finance.

The quality of the contribution is uncertain such as knowledge. To find out the level of technological knowledge, there needs to be an ex ante contracting scenario. Thus for the underlying adverse selection case, it is important to distinguish between tacit knowledge (local, marketing, management) and explicit knowledge (technology production) as well. The ability of the IJV management is linked to the knowledge provided and the joint research benefits from a high level of ability. In the ex post contracting stage, the moral hazard problem can be described in the way that the effort of the players for the IJV might be lower, since the intention to learn from the partner can be seen as an objective. In an independent IJV with a joint research lab the possibility to provide one's own ability and learn the other player's skills is connected to the nature of an IJV. Thus, it could be possible that one player uses the effort to learn from the other player instead of contributing to the joint enterprise.

This leads to the important aspects of uncertainty about the players' ability and effort level as well as their previous experience in IJVs or MNEs. The experience level can be seen as such that the IJV management is a combination of both parents' representative and both have experience in collaborative ventures $\{(e, e)\}$. In order to manage an independent research IJV, the representatives need to have experience. It could be possible that there is the following combination {(e, i), (i, e)}, that the local or the foreign part is inexperienced. The experience level can be based on the volume, number or size of research contracts previously managed. It is crucial that in independent IJVs with a joint research laboratory the quality of the manager can be measured by their experience level.

b) Research lab + production unit + marketing in both countries separately

Figure 5.2 Independent IJV (Research Lab, Production Unit, Marketing separately)

The location of parents can be written as P_{Loc} (US, Europe, Japan) and P_{For} (US, Europe, Japan) which leads to the following country combinations $\{(c_{USA}, c_{EU}), (c_{USA}, c_{JAP}), (c_{EU}, c_{USA}), (c_{EU}, c_{EU}), (c_{EU}, c_{JAP}), (c_{JAP}, c_{USA}), (c_{JAP}, c_{EU})\}$. Additionally, the developing/developed country combination could look like $\{(c_{dd}, c_{dd})\}$, since both parents come from developed countries.

Since the marketing is done in both firms separately, the contributions of both parents are $\{(c_T, c_T), (c_T, c_F), (c_F, c_T)\}$, they could provide the IJV with technology and/or finance. On a functional level the contributions might reach from supply to R&D in various combinations: $\{(f_S, f_S), (f_S, f_P), (f_S, f_F), (f_S, f_{R\&D}); (f_P, f_S), (f_P, f_P), (f_P, f_F), (f_P, f_{R\&D}); (f_F, f_S), (f_F, f_P), (f_F, f_F), (f_F, f_{R\&D}); (f_{R\&D}, f_S), (f_{R\&D}, f_P), (f_{R\&D}, f_F), (f_{R\&D}, f_{R\&D})\}$, yet without the marketing contribution.

As mentioned earlier, the experience level is especially important in independent IJVs and the combinations of both parents are either experienced or one is inexperienced and the other one has a high level of experience $\{(e, e), (e, u), (u, e)\}$. The experience level in an IJV should be that both agents have enough experience to successfully manage the joint enterprise. In order to reveal whether one player is inexperienced, there needs to be a contracting stage in which the agents show the level of experience, which will be used in the signaling game. The experience level can be based on contracts (research or production).

The adverse selection case considers the knowledge of production, technology, management. In the moral hazard scenario, cheating could occur in terms of low quality of contribution (production facilities, and technology) and like previously in a low effort level of technological expertise.

c) Research lab + separate production units + joint distribution

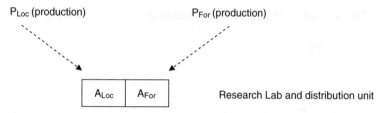

P_{Loc} (production) P_{For} (production)

| A_{Loc} | A_{For} | Research Lab and distribution unit |

Figure 5.3 Independent IJV (Research Lab, separate Production Units, joint Distribution)

In the same way as previously, both parents could have separate production units and joint research and distribution units managed as independent IJV. The location of parents could be in the USA, Europe and Japan and for the local parent additionally in emerging markets, called P_{Loc} (US, Europe, Japan, emerging markets) and P_{For} (US, Europe, Japan). The country combinations are again $\{(c_{USA}, c_{EU}), (c_{USA}, c_{JAP}), (c_{EU}, c_{USA}), (c_{EU}, c_{EU}), (c_{EU}, c_{JAP}), (c_{JAP}, c_{USA}), (c_{JAP}, c_{EU}), (c_X, c_{USA}), (c_X, c_{EU}), (c_X, c_{JAP})\}$. The developing/developed country combination could look like $\{(c_{dd}, c_{dd}), (c_{ding}, c_{dd})\}$.

The independent IJV has the following contributions from the parent firms $\{(c_T, c_T), (c_T, c_M), (c_T, c_F), (c_M, c_T), (c_M, c_M), (c_M, c_F), (c_F, c_T), (c_F, c_M), (c_F, c_F)\}$ and in terms of functional combinations, $\{(f_M, f_M), (f_M, f_F), (f_M, f_{R\&D}); (f_F, f_M), (f_F, f_{R\&D}); (f_{R\&D}, f_M), (f_{R\&D}, f_F), (f_{R\&D}, f_{R\&D})\}$.

For an independent IJV with joint research and distribution units, the management should have a high level of experience combined. Nevertheless, it could be possible that only one parent is experienced and the combinations look like $\{(e, e), (e, i), (i, e)\}$. The experience level could be measured with research contracts and sales contracts previously managed. For the adverse selection problem, the different ability levels can be identified as market access knowledge (tacit) and technological know-how. Both representatives could have private knowledge about the quality of their ability. Finally, the moral hazard case could have cheating in the form of embezzling and shirking (material and skills). The agent can induce a low effort level after signing the contract or even embezzle, since the IJV is dependent on the price mechanism and the independent IJV management has an entrepreneurial way of managing the venture.

d) Research lab + separate production unit + marketing separate and joint

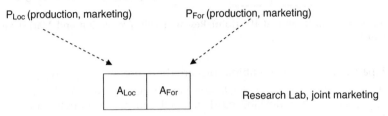

Figure 5.4 Independent IJV (Research Lab, separate Production Unit, Marketing separate/joint)

In the independent IJV with joint research and marketing, the location of parents can be P_{Loc} (US, Europe, Japan) and P_{For} (US, Europe, Japan). With regards to the country combinations, the elements of the previous cases can be identified $\{(c_{USA}, c_{EU}), (c_{USA}, c_{JAP}), (c_{EU}, c_{USA}), (c_{EU}, c_{EU}), (c_{EU}, c_{JAP}), (c_{JAP}, c_{USA}), (c_{JAP}, c_{EU})\}$. The developing/developed country combination could look like $\{(c_{dd}, c_{dd})\}$, since there are mostly developed countries involved.

Based on the possibility that either marketing is done separately or jointly, the marketing contribution is still considered $\{(c_T, c_T), (c_T, c_F), (c_M, c_T), (c_M, c_F), (c_F, c_T)\}$ and as well in terms of functional contributions $\{(f_M, f_M), f_M, f_F), (f_M, f_{R\&D}); (f_F, f_M), (f_F, f_{R\&D}); (f_{R\&D}, f_M), (f_{R\&D}, f_F), (f_{R\&D}, f_{R\&D})\}$.

In an independent IJV, the experience levels of both representatives could be $\{(e, e), (e, u), (u, e)\}$ and the measurement could be in research contracts and sales contracts. With regards to the quality of the ability to manage an IJV, there is uncertainty of tacit knowledge and the level of the quality of technical know-how. The moral hazard case can be focus on cheating after signing the contract and therefore low effort due to learning of technological or marketing skills of the other player is a possible scenario.

e) Research lab + production unit + marketing joint

Finally, like in the previous cases, the location of parents can be in the USA, Europe and Japan, P_{Loc} (US, Europe, Japan) and P_{For} (US, Europe,

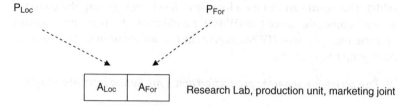

Figure 5.5 Independent IJV (Joint Research Lab, Production and Marketing Unit)

Japan). The country combinations are therefore $\{(c_{USA}, c_{EU}), (c_{USA}, c_{JAP}), (c_{EU}, c_{USA}), (c_{EU}, c_{EU}), (c_{EU}, c_{JAP}), (c_{JAP}, c_{USA}), (c_{JAP}, c_{EU}), (c_X, c_{USA}), (c_X, c_{EU}), (c_X, c_{JAP})\}$ and the developing/developed country combination could look like $\{(c_{dd}, c_{dd})\}$.

Ideally, the players might contribute their expertise in marketing and technology as well as a financial basis $\{(c_T, c_T), (c_T, c_M), (c_T, c_F), (c_M, c_T), (c_M, c_M), (c_M, c_F), (c_F, c_T), (c_F, c_M), (c_F, c_F)\}$ and the various combinations for the local and foreign agents' contributions cover supply (raw material), production facilities, marketing knowledge, finance and R&D $\{(f_S, f_S), (f_S, f_M), (f_S, f_P), (f_S, f_F), (f_S, f_{R\&D}); (f_M, f_S), (f_M, f_M), (f_M, f_P), (f_M, f_F), (f_M, f_{R\&D}); (f_P, f_S), (f_P, f_M), (f_P, f_P), (f_P, f_F), (f_P, f_{R\&D}); (f_F, f_S), (f_F, f_M), (f_F, f_P), (f_F, f_F), (f_F, f_{R\&D}); (f_{R\&D}, f_S), (f_{R\&D}, f_M), (f_{R\&D}, f_P), (f_{R\&D}, f_F), (f_{R\&D}, f_{R\&D})\}$. Thus, the parents can leave the IJV to its tasks, since the basic requirements are met.

Especially in an independent IJV which covers almost all functions (research, production and distribution/marketing) the experience level is important. Nevertheless, there are still the three combinations of experienced and inexperienced management $\{(e, e), (e, u), (u, e)\}$. The adverse selection problem focuses on the knowledge of production, marketing and technology. The uncertainty of the ability of the agent plays an important role. Yet, the independent IJV can always use a selling-the-store contract which reduces the risk for the parents. This is also possible for the moral hazard case in which embezzling and shirking (material and skills) might occur.

Shared IJV – joint or independent contracts

The classical understanding of a joint venture was already indicated in the article by Buckley and Casson (1998) of a 50:50 IJV which is found in the manufacturing industries. The parents share their responsibilities and outcome. They provide the IJV with complementary skills. The analysis of the entrant and incumbent like the competitive background of the parents' relationship could be considered in this context and the local parent can be seen as the rival of the foreign partner. Thus, the strategic configuration shows a different picture compared to the independent IJV.

a) Research lab

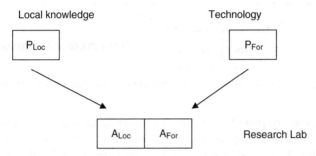

Figure 5.6 Shared IJV (Research Lab)

The shared IJV can have the location of parents in the USA, Europe, Japan and additionally the local player might have a wide range of countries from Eastern Europe, Asia, Africa and the Americas. Thus, the principal local P_{Loc} (US, Europe, Japan, Eastern European emerging markets, Arab countries, Asian countries, African and Latin American countries) and the principal foreign P_{For} (US, Europe, Japan) can have country combinations in the following way: $\{(c_{USA}, c_{EU}), (c_{USA}, c_{JAP}),$ $(c_{EU}, c_{USA}), (c_{EU}, c_{EU}), (c_{EU}, c_{JAP}), (c_{JAP}, c_{USA}), (c_{JAP}, c_{EU}), (c_X, c_{USA}), (c_X, c_{EU}),$ $(c_X, c_{JAP})\}$. The developing/developed country combination could look like $\{(c_{dd}, c_{dd}), (c_{ding}, c_{dd})\}$.

With regards to the contributions, the parents complementarily provide $\{(c_M, c_T), (c_M, c_F)\}$ and on a functional level $\{(f_M, f_S), (f_M, f_P),$ $(f_M, f_F), (f_M, f_{R\&D}); (f_P, f_{R\&D}); (f_{R\&D}, f_F), (f_{R\&D}, f_{R\&D})\}$. The local knowledge and marketing factor for the local parent are very strong and the technological contributions of the foreign parent are important to set up a research lab.

Both players are experienced in their own expertise $\{(e, i), (i, e)\}$ but lack the other's knowledge of the complementary skills. In the best case, they have a high level of experience in their respective fields of expertise. In the adverse selection scenario, local knowledge (tacit) is provided by the local representative and technology by the foreign player. The shared IJV management has the uncertainty of quality of contribution of the two rivals. The moral hazard problem considers cheating of both players (embezzling, sabotage, learning of competitors skills, shirking).

b) Research lab + production unit + marketing in both countries separately

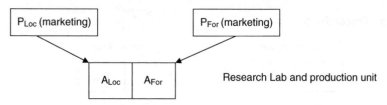

Figure 5.7   Shared IJV (Research Lab, Production Unit, Marketing separately)

The location of parents continues to be the same, like P_{Loc} (US, Europe, Japan, Eastern European emerging markets, Arab countries, Asian countries, African and Latin American countries) and P_{For} (US, Europe, Japan) as well as the country combinations $\{(c_{USA}, c_{EU}), (c_{USA}, c_{JAP}), (c_{EU}, c_{USA}), (c_{EU}, c_{EU}), (c_{EU}, c_{JAP}), (c_{JAP}, c_{USA}), (c_{JAP}, c_{EU}), (c_X, c_{USA}), (c_X, c_{EU}), (c_X, c_{JAP})\}$. The developing/developed country combination could look like $\{(c_{dd}, c_{dd}), (c_{ding}, c_{dd})\}$.

The contributions in the shared IJV with joint research and production are $\{(c_M, c_T), (c_M, c_F)\}$, since the contributions of the two players are complementary and are market knowledge or marketing for the local firm and technology or finance for the foreign agent. On the functional level, the contributions are $\{(f_P, f_S), (f_P, f_M), (f_P, f_F), (f_P, f_{R\&D}); (f_{R\&D}, f_P), (f_{R\&D}, f_F), (f_{R\&D}, f_{R\&D})\}$ which means that additionally to the R&D contributions of either player, there could well be production facilities and its knowledge as well as a financial basis for these IJV tasks.

Ideally, both players have experience in their respective fields $\{(e, e), (e, i), (i, e)\}$, it could be much more likely that the know-how is related to the complementary skills like above. Furthermore, the experience level can be measured using research and production contracts. In an adverse selection case, the low quality of production facilities, the tacit and explicit knowledge uncertainty are identified as ex ante incomplete information about the agent. In the ex post contracting stage, the moral hazard problem of cheating (embezzling and shirking, possibility of sabotage) occurs for all players.

c) Research lab + separate production units + joint distribution

In a shared IJV with separate production and joint research and distribution, the location of the parents can be like in the previous two cases.

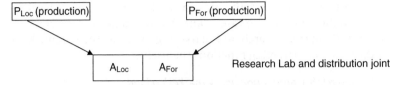

Figure 5.8 Shared IJV (Research Lab, separate Production Units, joint Distribution)

The contributions are vast $\{(c_T, c_T), (c_T, c_M), (c_T, c_F), (c_M, c_T), (c_M, c_M), (c_M, c_F), (c_F, c_T), (c_F, c_M), (c_F, c_F)\}$ and the functional combinations contain apart from supply and production the following combinations $\{(f_M, f_S), (f_M, f_M), (f_M, f_P), (f_M, f_F), (f_M, f_{R\&D}); (f_F, f_S), (f_F, f_M), (f_F, f_P), (f_F, f_F), (f_F, f_{R\&D}); (f_{R\&D}, f_S), (f_{R\&D}, f_M), (f_{R\&D}, f_P), (f_{R\&D}, f_F), (f_{R\&D}, f_{R\&D})\}$.

The experience level can be measured in previous research contracts and sales contracts $\{(e, e), (e, i), (i, e)\}$. The uncertainty about the tacit and explicit knowledge is in the ex ante stage and the ex post contracting stage shows the same possible cheating mechanisms as the previous cases. The effort levels can be low with regards to sales and technological input.

d) Research lab + separate production unit + marketing separate and joint

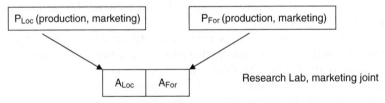

Figure 5.9 Shared IJV (Research Lab, separate Production Unit, Marketing separate/joint)

The shared IJV with joint research and marketing, but separate production and marketing could have the location of the parents in the following country combinations $\{(c_{USA}, c_{EU}), (c_{USA}, c_{JAP}), (c_{EU}, c_{USA}), (c_{EU}, c_{EU}), (c_{EU}, c_{JAP}), (c_{JAP}, c_{USA}), (c_{JAP}, c_{EU}), (c_X, c_{USA}), (c_X, c_{EU}), (c_X, c_{JAP})\}$. The developing/developed country combination could look like $\{(c_{dd}, c_{dd}), (c_{ding}, c_{dd})\}$.

Since the marketing can be either separate or joint, the contributions are $\{(c_T, c_M), (c_T, c_F), (c_M, c_T), (c_M, c_F),\}$ and functional combinations are $\{(f_M, f_F), (f_M, f_{R\&D}); (f_F, f_M), (f_F, f_{R\&D}); (f_{R\&D}, f_M), (f_{R\&D}, f_F), (f_{R\&D}, f_{R\&D})\}$. The ex ante and ex post contracting stage as well as the experience level are similar to the previous two cases. Note that the important difference is that the IJV shares research and marketing, whereas the parents have production and marketing functions themselves.

e) Research lab + production unit + marketing joint

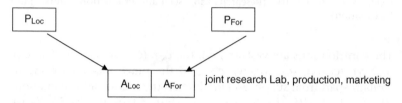

Figure 5.10   Shared IJV (Joint Research Lab, Production and Marketing Unit)

Finally, the shared IJV management in which research, production and marketing are jointly undertaken has the location of the parents, P_{Loc} (US, Europe, Japan, Eastern European emerging markets, Arab countries, Asian countries, African and Latin American countries), P_{For} (US, Europe, Japan). Respectively, the country combinations are $\{(c_{USA}, c_{EU}), (c_{USA}, c_{JAP}), (c_{EU}, c_{USA}), (c_{EU}, c_{EU}), (c_{EU}, c_{JAP}), (c_{JAP}, c_{USA}), (c_{JAP}, c_{EU}), (c_X, c_{USA}), (c_X, c_{EU}), (c_X, c_{JAP})\}$. The developing/developed country combination could look like $\{(c_{dd}, c_{dd}), (c_{ding}, c_{dd})\}$.

Both players endow the IJV with their expertise which is complementary and comprises knowledge about marketing and technology as well as production facilities $\{(c_T, c_M), (c_T, c_F), (c_M, c_T), (c_M, c_F), (c_F, c_T), (c_F, c_M)\}$. According to the complementary skills the functional contributions are as follows: $\{(f_S, f_M), (f_S, f_P), (f_S, f_F), (f_S, f_{R\&D}); (f_M, f_S), (f_M, f_P), (f_M, f_F), (f_M, f_{R\&D}); (f_P, f_S), (f_P, f_M), (f_P, f_F), (f_P, f_{R\&D}); (f_F, f_S), (f_F, f_M), (f_F, f_P), (f_F, f_F), (f_F, f_{R\&D}); (f_{R\&D}, f_S), (f_{R\&D}, f_M), (f_{R\&D}, f_P), (f_{R\&D}, f_F), (f_{R\&D}, f_{R\&D})\}$.

The experience level of the IJV management can vary between $\{(e, e), (e, u), (u, e)\}$ and can be based on previous experience such as research, production and sales contracts. The adverse selection problem is that the agent can provide a low quality of production facilities, local and marketing knowledge (tacit) as well as technology ex ante. Whereas the moral hazard problem in a shared IJV can have cheating in various forms (embezzling, shirking, sabotage, low effort of performance), since the issue of rivalry exists in this context.

Dominant IJV – countervailing contracts: local parent is dominant

The dominant parent strategy is connected to the concept of a wholly owned subsidiary with the dominant partner. The executives from each parent compose the board of directors which plays a subordinate role, whereas the executives of the dominant partner are responsible for the IJVs strategic and operational decisions. This is an appropriate response to the pressures from the host government or to a passive partner seeking solely a financial investment with an acceptable rate of return. The concept of a dominant parent strategy can be found in IJVs having a parent from a developing country and the other one from a developed country. Because of the legal restriction in the host country it might only be possible to have major control rights in the hands of the local partner, whereas the foreign firm will contribute technological and/or management expertise or financial resources.

a) Research lab

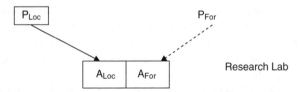

Figure 5.11   Dominant IJV (Research Lab)

The characteristic of the dominant IJV is that the location of parents is P_{Loc} (China, Eastern European emerging markets, Arab countries, Asian countries, African and Latin American countries), P_{For} (US, Europe, Japan) and country combinations are therefore limited to $\{(c_X, c_{USA}), (c_X, c_{EU}), (c_X, c_{JAP})\}$. The developing/developed country combination is clearly $\{(c_{ding}, c_{dd})\}$.

The contributions are local knowledge/marketing, and especially the dominance of the local side in this context occurs due to host government regulations. Thus, the following combinations might be possible in this setting $\{(c_M, c_T), (c_M, c_F), (c_F, c_T), (c_F, c_M)\}$ and $\{(f_S, f_{R\&D}); (f_M, f_{R\&D}); (f_P, f_{R\&D})\}$.

The experience level could be unevenly distributed, since the local player can have a lower experience level than the foreign part $\{(e, u), (u, e)\}$. Complementary expertise levels are important in this context. In the adverse selection stage, the local (host government) knowledge (tacit) and technological knowledge (explicit) are the source of uncertainty about contribution. The ex post contracting problem of moral hazard can occur when there are low R&D efforts, local corruption payments, bribe, shirking, sabotage.

b) *Research lab + production unit + marketing in both countries separately*

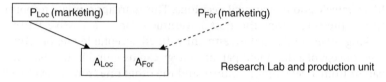

Figure 5.12 Dominant IJV (Research Lab, Production Unit, Marketing separately)

The location of parents remains the same as in the dominant IJV with research lab.: and country combinations are therefore $\{(c_X, c_{USA}),\ (c_X, c_{EU}),\ (c_X, c_{JAP})\}$. The developing/developed country combination should be $\{(c_{ding}, c_{dd})\}$.

The contributions contain technology, market knowledge and finance and occur in the following combinations $\{(c_T, c_M),\ (c_T, c_F),\ (c_M, c_T),\ (c_M, c_F)\}$. The functional expertise can be shown in the combinations $\{(f_S, f_F),\ (f_S, f_{R\&D});\ (f_M, f_F),\ (f_M, f_{R\&D});\ (f_P, f_F),\ (f_P, f_{R\&D});\ (f_F, f_P),\ (f_F, f_{R\&D}),\ (f_{R\&D}, f_F),\ (f_{R\&D}, f_{R\&D})\}$.

The experience level $\{(e, e),\ (e, i),\ (i, e)\}$ refers to market knowledge and technological know-how and can be measured in previous research and sales contracts. Both partners could have experience and either one could be inexperienced. In the adverse selection case, the ex ante uncertainty about the ability of the IJV plays a role in terms of technology and local knowledge as well as the quality of material and production facilities. With regards to moral hazard, cheating in game theoretical terms can occur in real life as corruption, low effort in production and R&D, embezzling, shirking, sabotage.

c) *Research lab + separate production units + joint distribution*

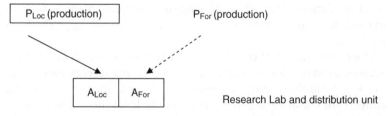

Figure 5.13 Dominant IJV (Research Lab, separate Production Units, joint Distribution)

The dominant parent and the representative are located in China, Eastern European emerging markets, Arab countries, Asian countries, African and Latin American countries, whereas the principal foreign can come from P_{For} (US, Europe, Japan) and the following country combinations are the outcome $\{(c_X, c_{USA}), (c_X, c_{EU}), (c_X, c_{JAP})\}$. Thus, there is only one developing/developed country combination possible $\{(c_{ding}, c_{dd})\}$.

The contributions of the players are $\{(c_M, c_T), (c_M, c_M), (c_M, c_F)\}$ and the functional expertise is provided in the following combinations $\{(f_M, f_M), (f_M, f_F), (f_M, f_{R\&D}); (f_F, f_M) (f_F, f_F), (f_F, f_{R\&D}); (f_{R\&D}, f_M), (f_{R\&D}, f_F), (f_{R\&D}, f_{R\&D})\}$.

Experience levels $\{(e, e), (e, u), (u, e)\}$ can vary dependent on the expertise (local knowledge, technological know-how) and can be distinguished in various ways according to complementary skills. Since the dominant IJV deals with joint research and distribution, the adverse selection problem considers the uncertainty about technical and marketing skills. In the ex post contracting stage, the moral hazard problem comprises corruption, embezzling, shirking, sabotage.

d) Research lab + separate production unit + marketing separate and joint

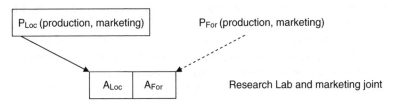

Figure 5.14 Dominant IJV (Research Lab, separate Production Unit, Marketing separate/joint)

In case of the dominant parent with joint research lab and marketing, the parents could still have their own production and marketing units. The location of parents remains the same and the country combinations are $\{(c_X, c_{USA}), (c_X, c_{EU}), (c_X, c_{JAP})\}$.

The players may contribute $\{(c_M, c_T), (c_M, c_F), (c_F, c_T), (c_F, c_M)\}$ and functional expertise $\{(f_M, f_M), (f_M, f_F), (f_M, f_{R\&D}); (f_F, f_{R\&D}); (f_{R\&D}, f_F), (f_{R\&D}, f_{R\&D})\}$.

As in the previous cases, it is possible to have both players experienced regarding their expertise or one experienced and the other one inexperienced $\{(e, e), (e, u), (u, e)\}$. In case both are inexperienced, this can be found out by offering appropriate incentive schemes. The uncertainty about technological, local and marketing skills can lead to the adverse selection problem of information asymmetries about the quality of the agent. In the moral hazard case, the dominant IJV has to tackle corruption, embezzling, shirking and sabotage ex post of the signing.

e) Research lab + production unit + marketing joint

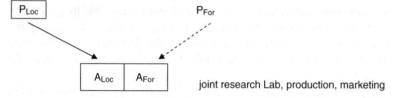

joint research Lab, production, marketing

Figure 5.15 Dominant IJV (joint Research Lab, Production and Marketing Unit)

Finally, the dominant IJV could have joint research, production and marketing. The location of parents is P_{Loc} (China, Eastern European emerging markets, Arab countries, Asian countries, African and Latin American countries) and P_{For} (US, Europe, Japan) which leads to the following country combinations $\{(c_X, c_{USA}), (c_X, c_{EU}), (c_X, c_{JAP})\}$. The developing/developed country combination could look like $\{(c_{ding}, c_{dd})\}$.

The contributions of the players are covering the combinations $\{(c_M, c_T), (c_M, c_M), (c_M, c_F), (c_F, c_T)\}$ and the functional expertise can occur in the following way $\{(f_S, f_M), (f_S, f_P), (f_S, f_F), (f_S, f_{R\&D}); (f_M, f_S), (f_M, f_M), (f_M, f_P), (f_M, f_F), (f_M, f_{R\&D}); (f_P, f_M), (f_P, f_P), (f_P, f_F), (f_P, f_{R\&D}); (f_F, f_S), (f_F, f_M), (f_F, f_P), (f_F, f_F), (f_F, f_{R\&D}); (f_{R\&D}, f_S), (f_{R\&D}, f_M), (f_{R\&D}, f_P), (f_{R\&D}, f_F), (f_{R\&D}, f_{R\&D})\}$.

If both are inexperienced, contracts need to be offered to reveal this situation in an appropriate way. The experience levels can be measured with previous research, production and sales contracts. The uncertain quality of production facilities, technological, managerial and marketing skills leads to contracts for the adverse selection problem and the uncertainty about the effort level leads to the moral hazard problems of corruption, embezzling, shirking and sabotage.

The following table shows examples for the above-mentioned types of IJVs. Due to the responsibility-ownership relationship, the interesting case of dominant parent IJVs for joint research/marketing unit and joint research/distribution unit was difficult to find. It might be a case for future research to look at them in an empirical investigation.

Table 5.2   Examples for the Typology of IJVs

	Independent IJV	Shared IJV	Dominant IJV
Research Lab (only) or Production Unit (only) or Marketing Unit/Distribution Unit (only)	Magyar Suzuki Com/Fiat (Suzuki Fiat) R&D only	Signant – (Ford, Renault, Peugeot) Hollographic Imaging LLC (Ford – UK DERA)	GM Nigeria (UAC Nigeria, GM) production only
Research Lab + Production Unit + Marketing in both countries separately	PATAC (Pan Asian Technical Automotive Centre Co) – SAIC Groups and GM	Shionogi – GSK (HIV neurology programs)	SEVEL (Societe Européenne de Vehicule Leger) of Fiat and Peugeot
Research Lab + separate Production Unit + Marketing separate and joint	Alcatel Shanghai Bell (develop and distribute GSM and CDMA mobile infrastructure)	UK-GM plant of GM and Renault	Difficult to find due to the responsibility-ownership relationship
Research Lab + separate Production Units + joint Distribution	EHP (Ericsson, HP) Telecommunications	Colgate Dental group (Nestle – Colgate Palmolive)	Difficult to find due to the particular responsibility-ownership relationship
Research Lab + Production Unit + Marketing joint	NUMMI (GM and Toyota)	Sony Ericsson Mobile Communications	South African GM (Delta SA and GM) DSW (Dead Sea Works) – VW

Adverse selection – common agency

Players

Lin and Germain (1998) concluded in their paper that cultural similarity stimulates a problem-solving approach to solve conflicts. Thus, 'the more IJV managers view the two partners at the organizational level as being culturally similar, the more likely they are to see their side as applying each of the following approaches when problems arise: entering into direct discussions, getting all concerns and relevant issues out into the open, openly telling the partner their ideas and asking the partner for theirs and providing the partner with the benefits of and logic behind, various courses of action' (p. 190). Another crucial variable was the length of time that an IJV has endured (or the age of the IJV). Therefore, the longer an IJV relationship has existed, the more likely it is that problem-solving behavior will be relied upon. IJV age results in familiarity, which not only produces an open, problem-solving approach to conflict resolution, but also a greater willingness to push for a partner's desired course of action. Another reason for positive effect of age according to the authors was that the longer an IJV has existed, the less likely partners are to rely on written agreements in conflict resolution. Though the paper gives some insights into the conflicts and problem-solving mechanism, the authors mentioned that limitations exist due to the selection of the countries (US-Chinese), the exclusion of failed IJVs and the inclusion of only on-site IJVs managers. The authors stated therefore an important characteristic of an IJV that there is a different picture drawn when observing on-site IJV managers and parent company managers. It is important to point out that at the beginning of an IJV, there is no knowledge about the compatibility of the players and the possible duration of the enterprise.

Like Lin and Germain (1998), Meschi (1997) explores in his article the extent to which the longevity of an international joint venture affects the intensity of its cultural differences (sample of 51 international joint venture set up in Hungary). In the centre of interest lies the cross-cultural issue of joint management. The chronic instability and a record level of failure can be related to the problems which trace back to cultural factors such as mutually incompatible social or organizational models. Since an IJV is an independent organization that federates the operations of two or more parents, individual and collective frictions can arise between the local professionals and expatriates working in the IJV. The success of the IJV is dependent on the congruence between the different cultures involved. Thus, the search for a culturally-compatible partner needs to be emphasized and can be shown by Meschi's statement 'When two or more companies start working together, their respective cultures come into contact: the local employee must deal with a different, sometimes unknown, foreign cultural environment, and likewise for the expatriate employee. The cultures represented in the international joint venture may collide and produce culture shock, disrupting the entire operation of the newly-formed company. Although relatively little is known about the means by which cultural differences actually influence international joint ventures, even less is known about the effectiveness of different managerial approaches used to handle cultural (national and organizational) issues in such ventures' (p. 214). Meschi emphasized in his study that the partners must develop a joint strategy of cultural integration. For culturally-incompatible partners to become compatible, the cultural transformation is a time-consuming, incremental and evolutionary process and therefore determined by time and learning. Compared to transferring large numbers of expatri- ate or local employees from existing operations of respective partners, the option to hire new employees offers an opportunity to facilitate the integration into another culture since the new recruits are less rooted in a given organizational culture. Meschi postulates that IJVs must create and develop a specific culture shared by the partners and referred to a set of conditions required for the ultimate success of the integration process. First, sufficient time to control and harmonize the entity's cultural differences must be granted and secondly during that period integration measures should be undertaken.

Besides the impact of partner characteristics on the success of an IJV, it is important to consider the quality of the IJV management as another source of the survival of an IJV. The difficulty to verify the ability of the management can be described as a hidden information or characteristics problem. Thus, incentive schemes should be designed such that the agent's dominant strategy is to reveal his type truthfully. Suppose there is a company in country A and another one in country B, the IJV will be set up in country B to provide market access for the foreign firm and technological know-how for local partner. Both parents contribute their expertise. The foreign firm does not know whether the local firm has market knowledge such as local knowledge, marketing know-how and skills in dealing with bureaucratic agendas. In the case of a low level of quality, the foreign firm might contribute expertise whereas the local firm free-rides on the partner's strength. Given the bad sales performance due to the lack of ability, the difficulty for the foreign firm will lead to negative effects on its own performance, besides problems in the acquisition of future partners in country B. How can we measure the ability of the parents and their representatives in the IJV management? The parents have an interest to offer incentive schemes which will lead to the revelation of the third player's type (ability). Depending on their own knowledge and the hidden information about each others' know-how, the parents will offer e.g. either sales or licensing contracts. In the case of the NUMMI joint venture between Toyota and General Motors, both parents offered licensing arrangements and Toyota got a percentage of the sales in addition to the licensing fee which made the IJV the residual claimant. Both parents contributed their expertise, Toyota provided the IJV with expertise in technology and management techniques, whereas General Motors was responsible for the market-access, production facilities and marketing of the joint product. Besides this famous case, there are many other IJVs dealing with hidden characteristics. Assuming that a firm in a developed country intends to form an IJV with an enterprise of a developing country without knowing the actual standing of the partner in the host country, the incentives should cover the type of the third player with respect to the local player's ability. The output of the joint product can be distinguished in the marketing and technological performance of the IJV. We can consider the adverse selection problem itself or in connection with moral hazard in the more complicated scenario.

Assuming that both parents send their representatives as board members to the IJV management, there is the joint player combining the special features of the two partners. Although different adverse selection models deal with the provision of quality, the application to the problem of hidden characteristics of an IJV management considers a new set of problems and perspectives. The incentive schemes comprise sales and cost factors, since marketing and technology can be modeled by using various contracts. The distinction between observable and verifiable quality occurs in connection with an appropriate mechanism design to get revelation. Since the IJV management can be seen as a collective body, the usual payment incentives are to be applied. In the case of an IJV as a self-organized system, the assumptions have to consider a third firm and its distinctive ability to maneuver between the parents, other competitors and consumers. The level of quality of the IJV management can vary and will be measured as a continuous function.

The pooling of complementary assets and skills owned by these firms is the main issue of the formation and management procedure. For this reason, the assumption that both firms have specific knowledge about either technology or marketing, in general, leads to asymmetries between the parents. However, the contracting stage needs to provide a mechanism for the third player to act truthfully towards both parents.

The third player called agent A_{IJV} is the (board of) management of the international joint venture since this separate unit is free to raise additional capital, enter into contracts, buy and sell goods and services, hire employees and the like (Balakrishnan and Koza, 1993). This management has special knowledge about the cost structure and other managerial details in the IJV itself. For this reason, the problem of asymmetric information between the parents and the IJV arises. Incentive schemes provided by the parents are designed to reveal the hidden information between the players. The number of players as a formal element is $N = 3$ and the set of players consists of three elements $N = \{P_{Loc}, P_{For}, A_{IJV}\}$.

Consider two competing hierarchies or companies (P_{Loc}, A_{Loc}) and (P_{For}, A_{For}), both agents A_{Loc} and A_{For} are representatives of the owners and constitute the IJV management, the third player called A_{IJV}. Thus,

$$A_{For} \subset A_{IJV}$$
$$A_{Loc} \subset A_{IJV}$$

Developing a joint agent on the basis of the two partners' features offers the possibility to design a common agency game to show the conflicting and the co-operative elements.

The adverse selection problem occurs because of the uncertainty about the quality of the management. It might be a source of one's own agent and the other parent's agent as well as the combination of both. For this reason, the incentive schemes offered by both partners consider the problem of hidden knowledge. In the common agency literature, the adverse selection problem was considered for the cases of different principals (Mezzetti, 1997) and identical principals (Martimort, 1992; Stole, 1991). Different equilibria can be derived because of the assumption of countervailing incentive schemes or co-operative incentives. Since the complementarity between tasks in an IJV is a general assumption to this work, the application of incentives offered by horizontally differentiated principals seems to be appropriate.

Under the assumption that the IJV has private information about the cost structure of the venture, the parents are interested to induce the agent to reveal his information about his ability by the contract he accepts. The two principals may offer their contracts independently or co-operatively. The representatives of the two principals are forming a coalition or the board of the IJV management. Thus, their private information about their costs (either marketing or technology) influences the IJV's cost structure of the endeavor, too. With respect to the cost function, the agent has private information about costs occurring in the production process and the sales of the product. Furthermore, the costs of putting two firms together in a joint enterprise are specified as the generic costs of the IJV. Thus, three parameters have to be taken into account costs local, costs foreign and IJV costs. In this respect, the costs developed by Buckley and Casson (1998) for the market entry as IJV are relevant costs considering trust building, technology transfer, marketing expertise and intermediate output flow. There are set-up costs (learning costs, adaptation costs and trust-building costs), the home location cost premium and the transaction costs. The costs are considered in the pay-off functions (see below in Table 5.4).

The double adverse selection problem is derived from the agent getting a contract offer from both parents and revealing different information to the parents. The agent has control over the message delivered to both principals. Therefore, the design of the contract needs to be appropriate.

The agent A_{IJV} is a special construction of both parents and therefore contains features of the complementary resources of the partners such as marketing knowledge, local expertise and technological know-how. The joint venture's value creating endeavor induces costs of production and sales. Thus, each representative knows about his own costs or those costs related to his task. Under the assumption that the agent's ability will be reflected in the costs, the particular agent will be offered a contract on the basis of his costs. This could be either discrete or continuous. Furthermore, we cannot only consider the task-related costs separately, but we also have to take into account the joint costs induced by putting together two business and national cultures.

Furthermore, the agent has private information about the homogeneity of the group (the team). We could introduce weights for the degree of homogeneity (0,1). In the case of a homogeneous group the costs would be lower than in an inhomogeneous group in which costs of training, translation and efforts to balance are higher. It could be taken into account that the agent's attempts to develop a successful team leads to costs which are difficult to be monitored by the parents.

Besides the consideration of costs as knowledge about the IJV management, the important knowledge in an IJV is derived from the contributions and the players' expertise. The homogeneity of the IJV is taken into account when both representatives contribute their knowledge in an appropriate way to perform well. The uncertainty about the other partner's quality of input into the IJV will lead to conflict. Thus, it is important to stress that the IJV's lemon problem occurs in the above-mentioned situation of an IJV, there is uncertainty about the agent's ability to manage the joint enterprise. Both parents are interested in extracting a high level of marketing, management or technological expertise. The simple case of incomplete information about the type of the agent leads to the set of types for IJV management. The elements of the agent's type set are high ability or low ability to manage the IJV.

As described in the theoretical part, the knowledge in an IJV can be distinguished in tacit and explicit knowledge which is related to the contribution of technology (explicit) and local expertise (tacit). This is connected to the measurement of the quality of the ability. It is easier to measure technological know-how than the contribution of local expertise.

$$T_{IJV} = \{\text{high ability; low ability}\} \text{ or } \{t_{IJVh}; t_{IJVl}\}$$

Specifying the combination of general managerial expertise in technological and marketing know-how, the types can be divided with respect to the parent's complementary resources. Furthermore, the following table shows the strategic configurations and the functional units with regards to their uncertainty about the knowledge input (divided already in tacit and explicit knowledge).

Table 5.3   Adverse Selection – Knowledge in IJVs

	Independent IJV	Shared IJV	Dominant IJV
Research Lab	Tacit knowledge (local, marketing, management), explicit knowledge (technology production), quality of contribution is uncertain such as knowledge	Local knowledge (tacit), technology, management uncertainty of quality of contribution (rivalry)	Local (host government) knowledge (tacit), knowledge (tacit), knowledge (explicit) uncertainty about contribution
Research Lab + Production Unit + Marketing in both countries separately	Knowledge of production, technology, management	Low quality of production facilities, tacit and explicit knowledge uncertainty	Technology and local knowledge uncertainty, quality of material and production facilities low
Research Lab + separate Production Unit + Marketing separate and joint	Technology, marketing – uncertainty of tacit knowledge and quality of technical know-how	Tacit and explicit knowledge uncertainty of quality	Uncertainty about technological, local and marketing skills
Research Lab + separate Production Units + joint Distribution	Market access knowledge (tacit) and technology know-how	Tacit and explicit knowledge uncertainty of quality	Uncertainty about technical and marketing skills
Research Lab + Production Unit + Marketing joint	Knowledge of production, marketing and technology uncertain	Low quality of production facilities, local and marketing knowledge (tacit) as well as technology uncertain	Uncertain quality of production facilities, technological, managerial and marketing skills

Ex ante the IJV partners do not know whether the counterpart will provide a high quality or low quality of the arranged contribution. This adverse selection problem is reflected in the type of the players. It can be a combination of the local and foreign parent as well as their representative. Thus, it is important to look at the possible contributions and the strategic implications for the structure and control in the IJV. Based on the three archetypes of strategic configuration between the parents and the IJV itself, the actual units (R&D, production, marketing and distribution) in the IJV are showing the contributions of the expertise to the joint enterprise. The typology of the IJVs can therefore indicate the uncertainties about the quality of the contribution. We have to distinguish between the different types of knowledge which have a stronger or weaker impact on the uncertainties. It is easier to monitor the quality of technological know-how than local expertise. In this respect, we can look at explicit and tacit knowledge in an IJV and the possibility to contribute 'lemons' and 'peaches'. The low or high quality of physical assets (production plants, estate and human resources) is another source of adverse selection problem and will be considered in the various cases, too.

In the case of the independent IJV, both parents are providing the IJV with staff of their own companies and maybe third country nationals. The expertise is with the IJV and the parents are interested in the returns of the IJV. Thus, it is useful to send representatives with technological know-how, marketing, local and managerial knowledge. Dependent on the configuration of the IJV, it is important to point out the independent R&D labs only need to look at the technological expertise. Since this is explicit knowledge the uncertainty about the quality will be detected during the duration. Nevertheless, it is important to notice that the representative might have a lower quality and this could jeopardize the returns of the IJV for the parent. The contributions for the production unit will be operational technological know-how and managerial knowledge which is a mixture of explicit and tacit knowledge. A higher degree of uncertainty has to be considered and additionally the (local) parent could provide a bad quality of production facilities which could endanger the outcome of the joint enterprise. Yet, since both parents are dependent on the returns, they have an interest in providing a higher quality of contributions. Finally, the marketing and distribution units (on their own or in combination with R&D and production units) need the contribution of the local parent which is in terms of expertise either local and marketing knowledge. As this is tacit knowledge it is much more difficult to monitor or control. The outcome of the IJV depends on this type of contribution and the lemon problem is much more severe in this setting.

Shared and dominant IJVs are dealing with the same uncertainties about technological, local, marketing and managerial knowledge. Nevertheless, the difference is that the IJV is directly related to the parents and their control since the managerial board and the production process are connected to the principals and their agents. In a shared management IJV, the parental roles are found in the IJV management itself and the difficulty about the compatibility of the agents has an impact on the ex ante specification of contracts and incentives. Like in the previous case, the provision of technological, managerial, marketing and local expertise can be crucial for the IJV configuration. Since there is a 50:50 split between the parents, the IJV is very much dependent on the fit of the two agents. Uncertainty about the quality of the contribution affects both sides. Thus, the explicit and tacit knowledge contribution are showing adverse selection cases for each configuration (R&D, production, marketing and distribution units on their own or in combinations).

The dominant IJV can be dealt with as the crucial case of uncertainty about the tacit knowledge provided. This is the strongest scenario of the possibility of low quality of local and marketing expertise. Especially, since this case occurs in transitional economies the risks for the foreign parent to lose the financial or technological contributions in the process is very high. The lemon problem is relevant, respectively. Thus, the configurations of IJVs in R&D, production, marketing and distribution units show the degree of growing uncertainty.

Actions

On an abstract level the three players have different sets of actions, since each player moves in the game according to the special assumption of asymmetric information. The local firm wants the joint agent to contribute a high level of technology and the foreign firm offers incentives to provide the joint enterprise with a high ability in marketing or management techniques. The principals offer their menus of contracts to the agents.

The space of actions can be designed for the players in the following way. In a simple game of adverse selection about the agent's skills, the agent offers his capability to run the business to the two principals, which offer contracts to encourage the revelation of his ability. With respect to the case of incomplete information about the agent's type, the dummy player has to draw the types of the agent in stage 0. We can assume that choosing a high or low type is the first set of actions C = {draw high type, draw low type}. In the first stage of the game, the agent learns his type. He has the action set C_{IJV} = {offers technological know-how, offers marketing know-how, doesn't offer know-how} and the principals have their action profiles C_{Loc} = {accepts; rejects} and C_{For} = {accepts; rejects}. Whereas the other possibility to play the game could be that the principals offer their contracts C_{Loc} = {offer contract for high ability, offer contract for low ability, don't offer} and C_{For} = {offer contract for high ability, offer contract for low ability}. The principals offer contracts with respect to their contribution and what type of revelation they want from the agent.

Pay-offs

The following table shows the pay-offs for the local and foreign parent, u_{Loc} and u_{For}, and the IJV itself, u_{IJV}. The pay-offs reflect the timing of the games and the strategic choices of the players. Since there is uncertainty about the quality of the contribution, the types t are considered to be important for the subgames played in the IJV. The principals' pay-offs comprise their value functions V which are dependent on the output of the IJV, of the local agent or of the foreign agent, q_{IJV}, q_{Loc} or q_{For} and the type of the players t, particularly of the agent t_{IJV} and the incentives paid to the agent I_{Loc} and I_{For}. The agent's pay-offs are dependent on sales R, costs C and profits π and the incentives I paid by the parents (I_{Loc} and I_{For}).

The independent IJV shows a particular case of offering incentives. Since both parents intend to be independent of the operations of the IJV, the selling-the-store contract could be an option for contractual arrangements. This type of contracts is for risk-neutral players. The agent IJV pays the parents incentives I_{Loc} and I_{For} and is the residual claimant of the IJVs performance. Thus, the parents receive flat fees which are a kind of returns (though ex ante paid) and the agent is fully responsible for the IJV and can claim the profits of the enterprise.

The shared IJV shows the pay-offs for the players which are dependent on their shared contributions and the shared incentives for the IJV. The configurations of the IJVs are considered in the output/performance of the players. The contracts offered are linear contracts which are sensitive to performance in the IJV.

Finally, the dominant IJV is distinguishing between the incentives from the local parent to the IJV and from the foreign parent to the IJV. The first-mentioned uses a linear contract, whereas the latter uses a flat fee contract.

Table 5.4 Adverse Selection – Pay-offs/Contracts

	Independent IJV	Shared IJV $\alpha \in [0, 1]$	Dominant IJV
Research Lab	$u_{Loc} = I_{Loc}$ $u_{For} = I_{For}$ $u_{IJV} = \pi(q_{IJV}) - I_{Loc} - I_{For}$	$u_{Loc} = V(q_{IJV}, t) - \alpha I(q_{IJV}, t)$ $u_{For} = V(q_{IJV}, t) - (1 - \alpha)I(q_{IJV}, t)$ $u_{IJV} = I(q_{IJV}, t) - C(q_{For}, t)$	$u_{Loc} = \pi(q_{IJV}, t) - I(q_{IJV})$ $u_{For} = \pi(q_{IJV}, t) - I_{For}$ $u_{IJV} = I_{Loc}(q_{IJV}, t) + I_{For} - C(q_{IJV}, t)$
Research Lab + Production Unit + Marketing in both countries separately	$u_{Loc} = R(q_{Loc}) + I_{Loc} - C(q_{Loc})$ $u_{For} = R(q_{Ror}) + I_{For} - C(q_{Loc})$ $u_{IJV} = \pi(q_{IJV}, t) - I_{Loc} - I_{For}$	$u_{Loc} = V(q_{IJV}, t) - \alpha I(q_{IJV}, t)$ $u_{For} = V(q_{IJV}, t) - (1 - \alpha)I(q_{IJV}, t)$ $u_{IJV} = I(q_{IJV}, t) - C(q_{IJV}, t)$ or $u_{Loc} = R(q_{Loc}) - \alpha I(q_{Loc})$ $u_{For} = R(q_{For}) - (1 - \alpha)I(q_{For})$ $u_{IJV} = I(q_{Loc}) + I(q_{For}) - C(q_{IJV}, t)$	$u_{Loc} = \pi(q_{IJV}, t) + R(q_{Loc}) - I(q_{IJV})$ $u_{For} = \pi(q_{IJV}, t) + R(q_{For}) - I_{For}$ $u_{IJV} = I(q_{IJV}, t) + I_{For} - C(q_{IJV}, t)$
Research Lab + separate Production Unit + Marketing separate and joint	$u_{Loc} = R(q_{Loc}) + I_{Loc} - C(q_{Loc})$ $u_{For} = R(q_{Ror}) + I_{For} - C(q_{Loc})$ $u_{IJV} = R(q_{IJV}) - C(q_{IJV}) - I_{Loc} - I_{For}$	$u_{Loc} = V(q_{IJV}, t) - \alpha I(q_{IJV}, t)$ $u_{For} = V(q_{IJV}, t) - (1 - \alpha)I(q_{IJV}, t)$ $u_{IJV} = V(q_{IJV}, t) - C(q_{IJV}, t)$ or $u_{Loc} = R(q_{Loc}) - C(q_{Loc}) - \alpha I(q_{IJV}, t)$	$u_{Loc} = \pi(q_{IJV}, t) + I(q_{IJV})$ $u_{For} = \pi(q_{IJV}, t) - I_{For}$ $u_{IJV} = I_{Loc}(q_{IJV}, t) + I_{For} - C(q_{IJV}, t)$ or $u_{Loc} = R(q_{Loc}) - (q_{IJV}, t) - C(q_{Loc})$

Table 5.4 Adverse Selection – Pay-offs/Contracts – *continued*

	Independent IJV	Shared IJV $\alpha \in [0, 1]$	Dominant IJV
		$u_{For} = R(q_{For}) - C(q_{For}) (1 - \alpha)I(q_{IJV}, t)$	$u_{For} = \pi(q_{IJV}, t) - I_{For}$
		$u_{IJV} = R(q_{IJV}, t) + I(q_{IJV}, t) - C(q_{IJV}, t)$	$u_{IJV} = R(q_{IJV}, t) - C(q_{IJV}, t) + I(q_{IJV}, t) + I_{For}$
Research Lab + separate Production Unit + joint Distribution	$u_{Loc} = R(q_{IJV}, t) + I_{Loc} - C(q_{Loc})$	$u_{Loc} = V(q_{IJV}, t) - \alpha I(q_{IJV}, t)$ $u_{For} = V(q_{IJV}, t) (1 - \alpha)I(q_{IJV}, t)$	$u_{Loc} = R(q_{IJV}, t) + I(q_{IJV}, t) - C(q_{Loc})$
	$u_{For} = R(q_{IJV}, t) + I_{For} - C(q_{For})$	$u_{IJV} = I(q_{IJV}, t) - C(q_{IJV}, t)$	$u_{For} = R(q_{IJV}, t) + I_{For} - C(q_{For})$
	$u_{IJV} = R(q_{IJV}) - C(q_{IJV}) - I_{Loc} - I_{For}$	or	$u_{IJV} = R(q_{IJV}) - C(q_{IJV}) - I_{Loc} - I_{For}$
		$u_{Loc} = R(q_{IJV}, t) - C(q_{Loc}) - \alpha I(q_{IJV}, t)$	
		$u_{For} = R(q_{IJV}, t) - C(q_{For}) (1 - \alpha)I(q_{IJV}, t)$	
		$u_{IJV} = R(q_{IJV}, t) + I(q_{IJV}, t) - C(q_{IJV}, t)$	
Research Lab + Production Unit + Marketing joint	$u_{Loc} = I_{Loc}$	$u_{Loc} = V(q_{IJV}, t) - \alpha I(q_{IJV}, t)$ $u_{For} = V(q_{IJV}, t) - (1 - \alpha)I(q_{IJV}, t)$	$u_{Loc} = \pi(q_{IJV}, t) + I(q_{IJV})$
	$u_{For} = I_{For}$		$u_{For} = \pi(q_{IJV}, t) + I_{For}$ $u_{IJV} = I_{Loc}(q_{IJV}, t) + I_{For} - C(q_{IJV}, t)$
	$u_{IJV} = \pi(q_{IJV}, t) - I_{Loc} - I_{For}$	$u_{IJV} = I(q_{IJV}, t) + R(q_{IJV}, t) - C(q_{IJV}, t)$	

Another important topic in relation to the pay-offs of the players is the attitude towards risks. In general, we have to consider the principals as independent firms which are risk-neutral. The difficulty occurs by judging the agent as risk-neutral or risk-averse. Principal-agent theory regards the agent in a manager-worker or shareholder-manager perspective as risk-averse. Whereas in the case of an IJV, we have to consider that the agent could be an independent enterprise or the board of directors or management board as well as a single manager. The assumption of a collective body of management may result in a risk-neutral agent, which can be reflected in the incentive scheme. The interesting questions arise with respect to a risk-averse agent, since the mechanism design takes the type of the agent into account. Finally, the distinction made with the three strategic archetypes applies the risk attitude to the independent, shared management and dominant parent IJV. The first mentioned shows a risk-neutral agent, whereas the other two archetypes have a risk-averse agent. The incentive schemes presented already consider the risk attitude.

The general adverse selection problem deals with the question of players lying to the mediator about their ability. Whereas the moral hazard case considers disobeying of the recommended actions.

Timing

Compared to the hidden action problem, the adverse selection situation in an IJV occurs because of incomplete information about the agent's ability. The game tree is transferred to the timing of a simple adverse selection problem which shows a four stage in which nature chooses the agent's ability to perform in the management process of the IJV. In the second step, the parent firms choose their actions by offering their contracts. In the third stage, the agent may accept or reject the contracts and finally in the forth stage he plays the mechanism provided by the contracts. Additionally, a signaling procedure might occur between stage one and two.

To apply this to the underlying situation, the structure of a dominant parent IJV shows the importance of providing a mediation plan for the agent which can be derived from two sources with different bargaining power. Firstly, the local firm does not know whether the agent has the ability to contribute to the value-adding process in a research laboratory, production plant or marketing distribution unit (Buckley and Casson, 1996). This means that depending on the local parent's contribution to the venture, the agent has knowledge about his own way of fulfilling the tasks. For this reason, the mechanism design should give the agent the appropriate incentive to work for the principals. As far as the local parent can take his own local knowledge into account and may offer a contract under this condition, the foreign parent has difficulties in judging the agent's ability. Besides different bargaining power and objective functions, the two principals will offer the agent two contracts according to their special needs.

Concerning the contracting situation in a shared management joint venture, both parents add complementary skills to the manufacturing process in the IJV. The agent's ability to contribute to the success of the enterprise can be seen as hidden knowledge. The solution may be to make the quality of the product contractible, testing and monitoring of the production process. Furthermore, special ways of signaling the capability of the management might be applied. Both principals offer a contract to the agent in order to get the revelation of his type which might be either accepted or rejected. The same situation will occur in an independent joint venture where both parents have only an interest in receiving returns of their investment.

Order of the play

(1) Nature chooses the ability of the agent as a type t_i of the set T_{IJV} = {high ability; low ability} according to a probability distribution $p(t_i)$,

(2) The agent A_{IJV} observes t_i and chooses the message from the set of feasible messages M which can be based on the amount of former contracts of the management, years of experience in IJVs or additional sales contracts with other companies.

(3) The principal P_{local} chooses from the set of action C_{local} which includes the actions don't offer, offer the agent one or more contracts (menu).

(4) The principal $P_{foreign}$ chooses from his set of actions $C_{foreign}$ which contains as well the elements don't offer, offer the agent one or more contracts (menu).

(5) The agent can now choose from his set of actions C_{IJV} = {accepts or rejects either one or all contracts}.

(6) Nature chooses a value for the state of the world according to the distribution $G(q)$

The contracting stage of the three-player model shows the terms of contracts as a 'lemon problem' with respect to the management's capability.

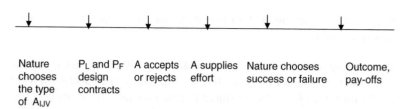

Figure 5.16   Timing of the double adverse selection game

Stage 1. Nature chooses the type of the agent. In this particular case the IJV management A_{IJV} could be either of low or high quality. Since this is a coalition of both partners, it is difficult to anticipate whether the combination of the two firms is successful or could lead to failure. The ability of the management is private information of the agent. It depends on various factors such as the ability of each parent's representative and the fit of the joint enterprise. The special nature of a double adverse selection problem occurs because of the information asymmetry between each parent and the agent. The principals do not know the agent's ability. They know the ability of their own representative, but not the skills of the partner's representative and of the conglomerate. Nature chooses the ability level of the agent.

Stage 2. The local firm P_{Loc} announces a contract, which they wish to sign with the agent. The contract specifies an incentive scheme I_{Loc} for the foreign representatives. Therefore, the production process and the technological know-how of the agent is concerned. The incentive scheme should depend on the cost function. The foreign firm P_{For} announces a contract, which they wish to sign with the agent. The cross-contracting idea should lead to an offer that induces the local part of the IJV management to reveal knowledge about its sales potential or ability. Therefore, the contract aims at the marketing skills of the agent and should be based on the sales or on the revenue function. The parents P_{Loc} and P_{For} design their contracts with respect to the signs they have got. Their contracts could be offered independently regarding whether the agent's knowledge of the local market or the technological know-how is affected. Furthermore, the principals could offer a joint contract. This incentive scheme might cover the costs of assimilation or the adaptation to another business or national culture.

Stage 3. The agent may either accept or reject the contract(s).

Stage 4. The agent supplies effort to the production process and the marketing of the product.

Stage 5. The outcome of the game depends on the nature's choice of success or failure.

The adverse selection game has the following timing for the independent, the shared and dominant IJV. In adapting to the special strategic configuration in IJVs, the timing of the independent IJV considers the risk attitude of the agent (risk-neutral) and the related selling-the-store contract in which the agent is the residual claimant and the parents receive a flat fee (contract).

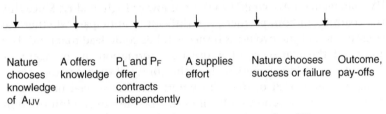

Nature	A offers	P_L and P_F	A supplies	Nature chooses	Outcome,
chooses	knowledge	offer	effort	success or failure	pay-offs
knowledge		contracts			
of A_{IJV}		independently			

Figure 5.17 Adverse Selection – Timing of the Independent IJV

The timing of the shared management IJV considers the parents offering a joint contract to the agent.

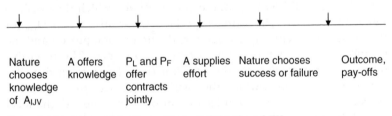

Nature	A offers	P_L and P_F	A supplies	Nature chooses	Outcome,
chooses	knowledge	offer	effort	success or failure	pay-offs
knowledge		contracts			
of A_{IJV}		jointly			

Figure 5.18 Adverse Selection – Timing of the Shared IJV

In the dominant parent IJV, the local principal only offers an incentive contract, whereas the foreign parent provides a flat fee.

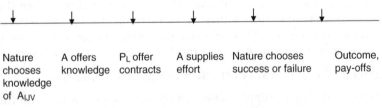

Nature	A offers	P_L offer	A supplies	Nature chooses	Outcome,
chooses	knowledge	contracts	effort	success or failure	pay-offs
knowledge					
of A_{IJV}					

Figure 5.19 Adverse Selection – Timing of Dominant IJV

The three strategic archetypes of IJVs have the differences in their timing in stage 3. In which the parents have different strategies in offering contracts according to their types. Furthermore, we can distinguish between the IJV configurations of research labs, production units, distribution and marketing units and their combinations. Thus, the following table shows the three archetypes in the columns and the configurations in the rows. The order of the play for an adverse selection game in IJVs offers fifteen combinations, respectively.

Table 5.5   Adverse Selection – Games (Order of the Plays)

	Independent IJV	Shared IJV	Dominant IJV
Research Lab	*Order of Play:* a) Nature chooses research/local knowledge of A_{IJV} b) A_{IJV} offers knowledge c) P_{Loc} and P_{For} offer contracts I_{Loc} and I_{For} d) A_{IJV} supply efforts Success or failure e) Pay-offs (Contracts)	*Order of Play:* a) Nature chooses research/local knowledge of A_{IJV} b) A_{IJV} offers knowledge c) P_{Loc} and P_{For} offer joint contract $I_{IJV,}$ or I_{Loc} and I_{For} d) A_{IJV} supply efforts Success or failure e) Pay-offs (Contracts)	*Order of Play:* a) Nature chooses research/local knowledge of A_{IJV} b) A_{IJV} offers knowledge c) P_{Loc} offers contracts d) A_{IJV} supply efforts Success or failure e) Pay-offs (Contracts)
Research Lab + Production Unit + Marketing in both countries separately	*Order of Play:* a) Nature chooses production/management technol. knowledge of A_{IJV} b) A_{IJV} offers knowledge c) P_{Loc} and P_{For} offer contracts I_{Loc} and I_{For} d) A_{IJV} supply efforts e) Success or failure f) Contracts/Pay-offs:	*Order of Play:* a) Nature chooses management knowledge and production facilities of A_{IJV} b) A_{IJV} offers knowledge c) P_{Loc} and P_{For} offer joint contract $I_{IJV,}$ or I_{Loc} and I_{For} d) A_{IJV} supply efforts e) Success or failure f) Pay-offs (contracts)	*Order of Play:* a) Nature chooses production/local/technol. know-how and production facilities of A_{IJV} b) A_{IJV} offers knowledge c) P_{Loc} offers contracts d) A_{IJV} supply efforts e) Success or failure
Research Lab + separate Production Unit + Marketing separate and joint	*Order of Play:* a) Nature chooses technology/marketing knowledge of A_{IJV} b) A_{IJV} offers knowledge c) P_{Loc} and P_{For} offer contracts I_{Loc} and I_{For}	*Order of Play:* a) Nature chooses technology/local/marketing knowledge of A_{IJV} b) A_{IJV} offers knowledge c) P_{Loc} and P_{For} offer joint contract $I_{IJV,}$	*Order of Play:* a) Nature chooses technology/local/marketing knowledge of A_{IJV} b) A_{IJV} offers knowledge c) P_{Loc} offers contracts d) A_{IJV} supply efforts e) Success or failure

Table 5.5 Adverse Selection – Games (Order of the Plays) – *continued*

	Independent IJV	Shared IJV	Dominant IJV
	d) A_{IJV} supply efforts e) Success or failure f) Contracts/Pay-offs:	or I_{Loc} and I_{For} d) A_{IJV} supply efforts e) Success or failure f) Contracts/Pay-offs:	f) Contracts/Pay-offs:
Research Lab + separate Production Units + joint Distribution	*Order of Play:* a) Nature chooses technology/market access knowledge of A_{IJV} b) A_{IJV} offers knowledge c) P_{Loc} and P_{For} offer contracts I_{Loc} and I_{For} d) A_{IJV} supply efforts e) Success or failure f) Contracts/Pay-offs:	*Order of Play:* a) Nature chooses technology/market access knowledge of A_{IJV} b) A_{IJV} offers knowledge c) P_{Loc} and P_{For} offer joint contract $I_{IJV,}$ or I_{Loc} and I_{For} d) A_{IJV} supply efforts e) Success or failure f) Pay-offs (contracts)	*Order of Play:* a) Nature chooses technology/market access knowledge of A_{IJV} b) A_{IJV} offers knowledge c) P_{Loc} offers contracts d) A_{IJV} supply efforts e) Success or failure f) Pay-offs (Contracts)
Research Lab + Production Unit + Marketing joint	*Order of Play:* a) Nature chooses production/technology/marketing/local knowledge of A_{IJV} b) A_{IJV} offers knowledge c) P_{Loc} and P_{For} offer contracts I_{Loc} and I_{For} d) A_{IJV} supply efforts e) Success or failure f) Contracts/Pay-offs:	*Order of Play:* a) Nature chooses production/technology/marketing/local knowledge of A_{IJV} b) A_{IJV} offers knowledge c) P_{Loc} and P_{For} offer joint contract $I_{IJV,}$ or I_{Loc} and I_{For} d) A_{IJV} supply efforts e) Success or failure f) Contracts/Pay-offs:	*Order of Play:* a) Nature chooses production/technology/marketing/local knowledge of A_{IJV} b) A_{IJV} offers knowledge c) P_{Loc} offers contracts d) A_{IJV} supply efforts e) Success or failure f) Contracts/Pay-offs:

Mechanism

The formal representation of the above-mentioned timings can be pointed out in the following objective function, participation and incentive compatibility constraints. Under the assumption that truth-telling is a dominant strategy, the revelation principle can be introduced for problems of adverse selection, signaling and moral hazard.

The maximization of the objective function of both principals shows the case of the incentive I_{IJV} offered for the high and low ability type I_{IJV}^{H} and I_{IJV}^{L} and the net benefit $V(e)$ dependent on the effort induced of the high and low type. The latter could also be dependent on the joint output or profit as well. The participation or individual rationality constraint deals with the agent's acceptance or rejection of the offer, which is dependent on his outside option or reservation utility. Thus, the contract must weakly dominate the reservation utility U. In the above-mentioned case, we used the utility function of the joint incentive payment for the low type $u(I_{ijv}^l)$ and considered the appropriate disutility of effort $k(_e^l)$ due to the fact that only the low type needs to be taken into account. The incentive compatibility constraint points out the problem that a low type could pretend to be a high type and vice versa. Thus, the incentives offered and accepted need to induce the agent's willingness to reveal his true type. The agent must be better off telling the truth.

Let the costs of the low quality management be higher than the costs of the high quality management $C(q_{ijv}^l) \geq C(q_{ijv}^H)$.

Individual rationality constraint (IR) is known as well as participation constraint which means that the agent will only accept the contract if it is higher than either the expected utility or 0. Furthermore, incentive compatibility constraint (IC) shows that the low and high types must be willing to reveal their true types given the contracts offered and that it does not pay off for them to lie about their true type. This is the revelation principal and it can be used to design the optimal contracts in this respect.

The optimal contract will include two different contracts for the agent. Since $e^H > e^{L'}$ it is not possible for both incentive constraints to bind simultaneously. The agent therefore will be offered an optimal contract menu with the following characteristics:

1. The participation constraint only binds for the agent with the highest costs (disutility of effort), while the other receives an informational rent of $(k - 1) v(e^L)$. The most efficient agent receives utility greater than his reservation level because of his private information.
2. The incentive constraint for high-efficiency agents bind in the solution.
3. The efficiency condition binds for the high-ability agent. Given an adverse selection problem, the only efficient contract is that designed for the agent with the 'high' characteristics. The outcome is different for risk-neutral and risk-averse agents.
4. The contract for the low-ability type is less attractive to high-ability types.

Thus, the assumption is that an optimal contract might avoid failure and could encourage co-operation. Hence, both parents could offer such an incentive scheme enforcing both agents to work well together which was shown in the previous tables (pay-off functions and timing).

The principals offer joint or independently incentive schemes with respect to the consolidated unit (IJV management) and its private information about its ability to work as a team which includes costs of adaptation, trust and learning. The homogeneity as a group involves communication between the representatives of each parent, therefore the creation of A_{IJV} means that the ability of the team has to be considered as a special stage in the set-up phase.

The agent has private information about the quality of his ability to manage the IJV. Each principal requires a single task be performed. Let (q_{For}) be the common agent's performance (e.g. output) on foreign principal's task and let (q_{Loc}) be the performance on principal local's task. Each principal observes the performance of the agent on her own task. The principals offer independently contracts consisting of a required output and a transfer. Let I be principal i's transfer to the agent. Assume that the net benefit of an additional unit of output by the agent is the same for both principals.

Under co-operation, the principals could offer a joint incentive contract to the agent. The two principal's joint pay-off and the agent's pay-off were shown in the shared management IJV columns.

Like in the exclusive dealing situations described in the common agency literature, the case of single-principal, single-agent benchmark develops the framework for each principal signing an exclusive contract with a separate agent. Going back to the set-up that two hierarchies are joint in an IJV, the foreign firm's agent performs only one task, such as contributing technology or management know-how, and the local firm's representative provides the enterprise with local knowledge, such as know-how about bureaucracies, marketing and market knowledge. Each agent is not affected by the other agent's output level, and has private information about his type. Based on the results in the appendix, we have:

a) Exclusive contracting

If each principal could offer exclusive contracts, there is no loss of generality in assuming that the incentive scheme selected by each principal is a direct mechanism that induces truth-telling.

The optimal incentive schemes have the familiar form of incentive schemes in the single-principal, single-agent adverse-selection model.

Only the best agent produces the optimal level of output (type $t_{IJV} = 0$ for principal local, type $t_{IJV} = 1$ for principal foreign). All other types produce less than the efficient level. Each principal distorts output below the optimal level so as to reduce her own agent's information rent.

b) Co-operation between the principals

The principals offer the agent the incentive scheme that maximizes their joint pay-off. Assuming that the incentive scheme selected by the principals is a direct mechanism which induces truth-telling, the principals choose output levels q_{Loc}, q_{For} and transfer I as functions of a single report t by the agent, subject to the incentive compatibility and participation constraints. An agent of type t_{IJV} that reports type t makes a profit Π (t, t_{IJV}), given the truth-telling direct mechanism (q_{Loc} (t), $q_{For}(t)$, $\tau(t)$),

The optimal incentive scheme under co-operation between principals exhibits pooling in an intermediate region, $t_{IJV} \in [1/4, 3/4]$, of the agent's type space. Types in this region have similar productivity in the two tasks. In equilibrium they receive a flat fee and produce the same output level for both principals. Outside the pooling region, types are offered an incentive pay and produce more for the principal, at whose task they are more productive; these are types with a significant advantage in one of the two tasks. Only types $t_{IJV} = 0$, $t_{IJV} = 1$ and $t_{IJV} = \frac{1}{2}$ choose the full-information output levels. Types in the interval $(0, \frac{1}{2})$ produce less than the optimal output level for principal local, $q_{Loca} < q_{Locf}$, and more than the optimal level of principal foreign, $q_{Fora} > q_{Forf}$. On the other hand, agent types in the interval $(\frac{1}{2}, 1)$ produce more than the optimal level of output for principal local, $q_{Loca} > q_{Locf}$, and less than the optimal level for principal foreign, $q_{Fora} < q_{Forf}$.

c) Independent contracting

Suppose the principals offer independently incentive packages to the agent. Each principal observes the agent's output only at her own task, and the incentive package offered cannot be made contingent on the output level in the other principal's task. Each principal selects a direct mechanism consisting of a pair of functions specifying, for any given reported type, the transfer to the agent and the level of output in the principal's own task. It is important to stress that the agent has to send a separate report to each principal; this is what differentiates independent contracting from co-operation. Under co-operation the principals act as a single entity (i.e. a single mechanism designer) and the agent sends a single report. Although the agent's reports to the two principals could differ, in equilibrium they coincide with the agent's true type. The two principals use continuous, piecewise-differentiable output and transfer functions.

Some problems in connection with the revelation principle occur since it concerns only the case of a single mechanism designer. Thus, it is an open question whether there is any loss of generality in assuming that the two principals use direct revelation mechanisms. Furthermore, the assumption of piecewise differentiable output and transfer functions involves some loss of generality. Under co-operation the simple revealed-preferences argument shows that these functions must be differentiable almost everywhere. Under independent contracting this argument fails, because the optimal report of the agent to a principal depends in a nontrivial way on the mechanism chosen by the other principal. If one principal's mechanism is not piecewise differentiable, the other's best response could also be nondifferentiable.

The individual rationality constraint binds in an interval $[t_{IJVcL}; t_{IJVcH}]$. For all t_{IJV} in such interval $q_{For}(t_{IJV}) = q_{Loc}(t_{IJV}) = $ constant.

The strategic revelation effects are induced by the presence of externalities between the contracting activities of the two principals. These externalities arise because the contract offered by one principal influence the other principal's contract by changing the marginal profit of the agent. This implies that the agent's report to a principal depends on the mechanism chosen by the other principal and thus that principal i is indirectly affected by the agent's report to principal j, because such a report determines the output level in task j. Recognizing this strategic interaction, when choosing a mechanism each principal views the agent's future optimal report to the other principal as a function of her own choice of a mechanism.

The optimal incentive mechanisms under independent contracting are similar to the ones under co-operation between principals. Because of the presence of countervailing incentives, there is pooling in an intermediate region of the agent's type space; that is, types with similar productivity at the two tasks produce the same output and are paid a flat fee by both principals. Compared with a full-information world, almost every agent produces less than the optimal level of output in the task at which he is more productive and more than the optimal level in the task at which he is less productive. Only the lowest, the middle, and the highest type select the full-information output levels for both tasks.

Outputs are closer to their full-information levels under independent contracting than under co-operation between principals. Thus, the power of the incentive schemes for types outside of the pooling region, as measured by the slope of the agent's rent (i.e. by the absolute value of the difference between outputs in the two tasks; is lower when principals co-operate than under independent contracting. Moreover, the pooling interval is smaller under independent contracting than under co-operation between principals. Note, however, that co-operation between principals reduces specialization and thus decrease efficiency, as measured by the total value of the parties' pay-offs. These observations are summarized in the mathematical appendix.

d) Welfare comparisons

If there is complete information, then the principals are indifferent between co-operation and independent contracting, and they prefer either of them to exclusive dealing. Clearly, under incomplete information the two principals attain a lower total expected pay-off than under full information. Due to the externality that one principal's incentive scheme imposes on the other principal, that under independent contracting distortions from the full-information output levels are smaller than under co-operation. As a result, each agent type's rent is higher, and the two principals' joint expected pay-off is lower, under independent contracting than under co-operation. Under exclusive dealing, output distortions are larger than under common agency, because each agent's temptation to understate his pay-off is not mitigated by the presence of countervailing incentives. Thus, to induce truth-telling the principals must give the agents higher information rents. Since common agency also allows principals to benefit from the complementarity between tasks, the principals' joint pay-off with either contractual arrangement under common agency is higher than under exclusive dealing. These results are summarized in the propositions in the mathematical appendix.

Under independent contracting there are smaller output distortions, and thus more surplus is available than under co-operation, but the agent receives more of it as information rent. The surplus effect dominates for types sufficiently close to the pooling interval. For these types the two principals' ex post welfare under independent contracting is higher than under co-operation between principals. On the contrary, for types near the endpoints of the type space, the 'information rent' effect prevails. On average, the information rent effect dominates, and thus the two principals' total expected pay-off is lower under independent contracting than under co-operation.

Moral hazard – common agency

The moral hazard problem occurs in IJVs because of the uncertainty to know the effort level induced for production, marketing, distribution and R&D units in IJVs. After signing the contract, the players could provide a low effort level for the joint enterprise. In moral hazard terms inducing a low effort is described as cheating. There are several forms of cheating, such as shirking, embezzling, sabotage.

Players

The newly formed enterprise contains resources from both parents. Let there be the two principals or parent firms P_{Loc} and P_{For}. The set of players consists of three elements $N = \{P_{Loc}, P_{For}, A_{IJV}\}$. The special efforts of both firms need to be combined in the management process of the IJV. The types of the players are determined by their effort based on their know-how. The representatives of both firms should be able to contribute to the IJV their own expertise and to learn about the other expertise.

The parents P_{Loc} and P_{For} have various options to offer contracts to the agent. Like in the adverse selection case, they could either look at countervailing incentive schemes, on co-operative incentives or exclusive contracting, dependent on their contribution to the enterprise and their strategic setting. Another contingency of incentives is trust contracts, incentive contracts and bonus contracts. Whatever the parents choose is a combination of various factors.

Under the assumption that the local parent contributes market knowledge, market entry and marketing channels, the local firm wants an optimal level of effort from his representative, but also from the other parent's agent. The foreign firm is supposed to provide technology, financial resources or, in general, management knowledge. Both partners have complementary skills and the outcome of the joint enterprise should be besides shares of the profit, returns on investment or equity as well a learning process with respect to the skills gained through the IJV. For this reason, the principals want the agent to extract an appropriate effort to the tasks involved. The local firm has to offer the IJV management a contract, which induces the agent to put into this project the optimal level of his technical skills. Vice versa, the foreign parent has to offer incentives with respect to the level of market knowledge or marketing skills. To enhance mutual truth-telling mechanisms, the contracts need to be incentive compatible and individually rational. Let the output q of the joint enterprise be either q_{Loc} (e) or q_{For} (e), which means the parents expect a techno-logical output and an output in sales terms dependent on the relevant efforts. The first-mentioned refers to the production process and the quality of the product, and the latter to the marketing of the new product. The agent can embezzle by using his own skills not to the optimal extent, since he is only interested in gaining the other player's capabilities. The agent contributing technological know-how is providing only a low level of effort, but trying to gain market access, knowledge or even marketing skills. The aim could be to derive a better position in the parent's enterprise after the termination of the IJV. Sometimes, the parents connect their representative's efforts to promotion in the firm after finishing the IJV, especially in projects with determined endgame cases.

On the other hand, the agent could only put a low effort into the sales of the product, since having already a good market potential or local knowledge. This case would be a combination of adverse selection and moral hazard. Focusing only on the moral hazard problem, the agent could learn the technological know-how or managerial skills of the partner by providing a low level of effort himself. This case of shirking could occur in situations in which monitoring is difficult. The hybrid of an IJV shows in those cases the difficulties to manage co-operation and conflict.

The agent has to report to the parents about managerial and techno-logical details of the project. Since 'hard' information can be controlled easily, the incentives should be targeted to cover truth-telling with regards to the soft information involved, too. In this case, 'soft' infor-mation can comprise information about quality of the production process and the product as well as the marketing efforts.

The three-player moral hazard problem in an IJV leads to the develop-ment of the information structure concerning the players. Assuming that the agent has more information about the actual management process, the type of the joint venture contains the effort level of the management board in a simple case. Both parents are interested in extracting a high level of effort concerning issues of management or technology.

$$T_{IJV} = \{\text{high effort; low effort}\} \text{ or } \{t_{IJVh}; t_{IJVl}\}$$

Having specified the agent as a combination of representatives of both parents, the mechanism design has to deal with the scenario of joint efforts but as well as with the coalitions of technology and marketing which leads to a double or even a triple moral hazard situation. For the

Table 5.6 Moral Hazard – Efforts in IJVs

	Independent IJV	Shared IJV	Dominant IJV
Research Lab	Effort of the players could be lower, since the intention to learn is an objective	Cheating (embezzling, sabotage, learning of competitors skills, shirking)	R&D effort low, local corruption payments, bribe, shirking, sabotage
Research Lab + Production Unit + Marketing in both countries separately	Cheating on low quality of contribution (production facilities, and technology)	Cheating (embezzling and shirking, possibility of sabotage)	Corruption, low effort in production and R&D, embezzling, shirking, sabotage
Research Lab + separate Production Unit + Marketing separate and joint	Cheating – embezzling, sabotage, low effort due to learning	Cheating (embezzling, shirking, sabotage, low effort of performance)	Corruption, embezzling, shirking, sabotage
Research Lab + separate Production Units + joint Distribution	Embezzling and shirking (material and skills)	Cheating (embezzling, shirking, sabotage, low effort of performance)	Corruption, embezzling, shirking, sabotage
Research Lab + Production Unit + Marketing joint	Embezzling and shirking (material and skills)	Cheating (embezzling, shirking, sabotage, low effort of performance)	Corruption, embezzling, shirking, sabotage

cases of the complex managerial scenarios of multiple moral hazard scenarios, the types of the players have the following elements:

T_{For} = {high effort in production process; low effort in production process} or {t_{fh}; t_{fl}}

T_{Loc} = {high effort of marketing personnel; low effort of marketing personnel} or {t_{lh}; t_{ll}}

The following table uses the typology of IJVs and the application of moral hazard problems to IJVs. In an independent IJV, the moral hazard problem has an impact on the parents' return and the selling-the-store contract could endanger the IJV per se. Though the agent has a lower incentive to cheat since he is the residual claimant of the contract.

In a shared IJV, the joint management could be jeopardized by the possibility that one player induces a lower effort in the joint endeavor (production process, marketing process, distribution or R&D unit). The games can be that one player has a lower effort with regards to the production process or to the sale of the product. Another possibility could be that the effort could be lower with regards to their own contribution, whereas the agent has the intention to learn from the other partner and puts a lot of the effort into learning. There could be intentional embezzling and shirking from local and foreign agents as well as deliberate cheating such as sabotage. In a joint management scenario, a low effort to perform (in technology, production, marketing and local knowledge contributions) could as well harm the IJV.

Furthermore, dominant IJVs have to deal with cheating of the local partner which could be that local corruption payments and bribes have an impact on the outcome of the IJV. The players could induce a low effort in production and R&D input. Shirking, embezzling and sabotage are also issues in this strategic archetype.

In general, the moral hazard problem can occur in terms of material and skills. Cheating will be considered in an IJV as having an influence on the success and failure of the joint enterprise.

Actions

Consider now the three-player situation of the above-mentioned cases, the two principals can choose their actions by offering a contract or incentive scheme to the agent independently. Since the principals contribute complementary skills to the joint venture, the agent gets two different contracts depending on each parent's contribution, interest and objectives. The agent may either accept or reject one of the contracts or both. Accepting both contracts may lead further either to reveal their type truthfully or to lie.

In the first stage of the game, the local principal P_{Loc} chooses his set of action C_{Loc} which is offering a menu of contracts to get the agent's real type and to prevent him from embezzling. The foreign principal P_{For} chooses his set of action C_{For} which is offering a range of contracts like the local principal. The incentives offered by both parents depend on the type of joint venture, the contributions to the joint venture and the strategic role of the players. In the second stage of the game the agent A_{IJV} may choose his action set C_{IJV} which is either accept both contracts, accept the contract of the local parent and reject the contract of the foreign parent, vice versa or reject both contracts. The latter could result in re-negotiations or the break-up of the joint venture. The third stage contains the agent's effort which can be either low or high given his knowledge about the potential of the area, the joint venture itself or the production process. Since the agent knows the real state of the nature, he may put either a high or a low effort into the business and shirk in order to benefit from the enterprise.

To solve the situation backwards, we start with the effort level of the agent and show the matrix of possibilities:

The foreign principal contributes technology and/or capital endowment to the joint venture and relies on the agent's efforts concerning marketing, production or other managerial issues. As long as the agent has knowledge about the area's sales potential, production capacities or the ability of the workforce, the agent may contribute as little effort as possible to maximize his own pay-off function and free ride on his hidden knowledge. The principal has to offer now an incentive scheme to encourage the agent in order to use his actual effort level for the joint enterprise. The incentive scheme has to consider the revelation of the effort in connection with market knowledge.

The local principal wants to get revelation about the true type of the agent concerning the effort level with regard to the production process and its technological know-how. The agent has the possibility to shirk by not contributing a high effort level to the joint enterprise. The incentive scheme has to get revelation about the true value of the costs, the technological know-how and the quality of the product.

The following strategy sets contain the elements of moves the various players can pursue:

$$C_{For} = \{\text{offer incentives } I_{For}; \text{ don't offer incentives}\}$$
$$C_{Foc} = \{\text{offer incentives } I_{Loc}; \text{ don't offer incentives}\}$$
$$C_{IJV} = \{\text{accept both contracts; accept } I_{For} \text{ and reject } I_{Loc}; \text{ accept } I_{Loc}$$
$$\text{and reject } I_{For}; \text{ reject both}\}$$
$$C_{IJV} = \{\text{choose high effort, choose low effort}\}$$

The incentive schemes for the local firm can be designed for low and high effort concerning the agent's revelation of technological know-how or production efforts, whereas the foreign firm's incentives are designed to get the disclosure about the agent's sales efforts.

According to the literature, the concept of the dominant parent joint venture shows the possibility to cheat in the following way. The local firm and the IJV board pursue the strategies c_{Loc} and c_{IJV} in the management of the joint enterprise. As far as the local partner contributes technological, production or marketing skills into the joint project, the problem occurs firstly in the possibility that the agent A_{IJV} may have an incentive to contribute low or high efforts in the value creating process. Since the local firm P_{Loc} has access to the joint venture through the board of directors and the actual opportunity to monitor the agent, the incentive scheme may have a different design than the contract of the foreign firm. The foreign firm P_{For} intends to contribute either capital endowment or technology and is interested in a more passive role in the IJV. Nevertheless, the parent firm wants to get returns on the investment. For this reason, the foreign firm will offer the agent a contract which prevents them to shirk. The effort level may be connected to the output of the joint venture or to a flat fee in the sense of a selling-the-store agreement. From the agent's perspective, different mechanisms concerning the reporting process and the revelation of his type may be appropriate. Especially, in connection with the different interests and contributions of the principals, the agent may accept or reject the offered contracts. The conflict bearing structure of this hybrid can be seen in the presence of various forms of agreements.

The shared management IJV comprises the complementary resources of the parents in the production process. Both partner firms have a strong bargaining power and offer the agent contracts to prevent him from embezzling. The incentive schemes may be related to the parent's contributions and particular interests. As far as there exists incomplete information about the effort of the agent, the principals can design their contracts in connection with the verified output. Royalties and bonuses in addition to a basic salary may help to create incentives to put the highest level of effort into the joint venture.

Finally, the third archetype called the independent IJV reflects a 'minor' interest of the parents in the actual manufacturing or value creating process in comparison with the other two forms. Nevertheless, both parents have an interest in getting a return out of the joint enterprise. For this reason, the principals offer contracts which guarantee that the agent avoids to embezzle. As far as this is a very rare form of IJVs, an equity-sharing contract might be appropriate.

Pay-offs

Given the different objectives of the reference groups mentioned above, we have to consider a moral hazard case for the managers. Suppose we have the crucial three-player (manager) setting, in which the manager of the local firm P_{Loc}, the manager of the foreign firm P_{For} and the manager of the IJV called A_{IJV} are related to each other in a multi-person decision-making scenario. Thus, we have to consider three different utility functions dependent on their attitudes towards risk and their informational asymmetries. We have to take into account that in an IJV, there is one CEO being sent from one parent and a deputy from the other parent. Additionally, it could be a newly hired person coming from a third country of origin. Thus, the incentives offered should consider the information asymmetries occurring because of the different background of corporate culture. We can use the table to show the focus of the IJV management based on the strength or background of the person in charge of the joint venture. The objectives would be different and the tension in the IJV could be strengthened or weakened. It might be therefore worthwhile to look at the contractual relationship between the principals and their joint agent in order to take these uncertainties into account.

Table 5.7   Performance Criteria of the Four Groups of Managers

Principal foreign P_{For}	Principal local P_{Loc}	Agent foreign A_{For}	Agent local A_{Loc}
Return on Investment Internal Rate of Return Sales and market shares,	Dividends Dividends plus taxes, Profits Productivity Technology Transfer	Firm output, such as costs, product scope Profits Transfer of management skills	Internal exchange process, such as sharing of culture, technology and management skills,

Source: Osland and Cavusgil (1998)

Incentive schemes can have fixed components as well as variable elements dependent on the output, profit, market share, and may either cover money rewards and punishment or even property rights (management buy-outs), promotion, royalties, salary increments. In the following chapters, the information economics approach leads to a framework for offering contracts in an IJV under moral hazard.

The utility functions for the three players are dependent on the actions and the types of the players in a Bayesian game with communication. Let u_i be the pay-off function of player i and in the special IJV game $u_{Loc}(c,t)$, $u_{For}(c,t)$ and $u_{IJV}(c,t)$.

The following table shows the pay-offs for the local and foreign parent, u_{Loc} and u_{For}, and the IJV itself, u_{IJV}. The pay-offs reflect the timing of the games and the strategic choices of the players. Since there is uncertainty about the quality of the contribution, the types t are considered to be important for the subgames played in the IJV. The principals' pay-offs comprise their value functions V which are dependent on the output of the IJV, of the local agent or of the foreign

Table 5.8 Moral Hazard – Pay-offs/Contracts: $q_{IJV}(e) = q_{Loc}(e_{Loc}) + q_{For}(e_{For})$

	Independent IJV	Shared IJV $\alpha \in [0, 1]$	Dominant IJV
Research Lab	$u_{Loc} = \pi_{Loc}(e_{Loc}) + I_{Loc}$ $u_{For} = \pi_{For}(e_{For}) + I_{For}$ $u_{IJV} = \pi(e_{IIV}) - I_{Loc} - I_{For}$	$u_{Loc} = V(q_{IJV}(e)) - \alpha I(q_{IJV}(e))$ $u_{For} = V(q_{IJV}(e)) - (1-\alpha)I(q_{IJV}(e))$ $u_{IJV} = I(q_{IJV}(e)) - C(q_{IJV}(e))$	$u_{Loc} = \pi(q_{IJV}(e)) - I(q_{IJV}(e))$ $u_{For} = \pi(q_{IJV}(e)) - I_{For}$ $u_{IJV} = I_{Loc}(q_{IJV}(e)) + I_{For} - C(q_{IJV}(e))$
Research Lab + Production Unit + Marketing in both countries separately	$u_{Loc} = R(q_{Loc}(e)) - C(q_{Loc}(e)) + I_{Loc}$ $u_{For} = R(q_{For}(e)) - C(q_{For}(e)) + I_{For}$ $u_{IJV} = \pi(q_{IJV}(e)) - I_{Loc} - I_{For}$	$u_{Loc} = V(q_{IJV}(e)) - \alpha I(q_{IJV}(e))$ $u_{For} = V(q_{IJV}(e)) - (1-\alpha)I(q_{IJV}(e))$ $u_{IJV} = I(q_{IJV}(e)) - C(q_{IJV}(e))$ or $u_{Loc} = R(q_{Loc}(e_{Loc})) - \alpha I(q_{Loc}(e_{Loc}))$ $u_{For} = R(q_{For}(e_{For})) - \alpha I(q_{For}(e_{For}))$ $u_{IJV} = I(q_{Loc}) + I(q_{For}) - C(q_{Loc}(e_{Loc}), q_{For}(e_{For}))$	$u_{Loc} = \pi(q_{IJV}(e)) - I(q_{IJV}(e))$ $u_{For} = \pi(q_{IJV}(e)) - I_{For}$ $u_{IJV} = I_{Loc}(q_{IJV}(e)) + I_{For} + R(q_{Loc}(e), q_{For}) - C(q_{IJV}(e))$

Table 5.8 Moral Hazard – Pay-offs/Contracts: $q_{IJV}(e) = q_{Loc}(e_{Loc}) + q_{For}(e_{For})$ – *continued*

	Independent IJV	Shared IJV $\alpha \in [0, 1]$	Dominant IJV
Research Lab + separate Production Unit + marketing separated and joint	$u_{Loc} = R(q_{Loc}(e)) - C(q_{Loc}(e)) + I_{Loc}$ $u_{For} = R(q_{For}(e)) - C(q_{For}(e)) + I_{For}$ $u_{IJV} = R(q_{IJV}) - C(q_{IJV}) - I_{Loc} - I_{For}$	$u_{Loc} = V(q_{IJV}, (e)) - \alpha I(q_{IJV}(e))$ $u_{For} = V(q_{IJV}, (e)) - (1-\alpha)I(q_{IJV}(e))$ $u_{IJV} = I(q_{IJV}) - C(q_{IJV}, (e))$ or $u_{Loc} = R(q_{Loc}(e_{Loc})) - C(q_{Loc}(e_{Loc})) - \alpha I(q_{Loc}(e_{Loc}))$ $u_{For} = I(q_{For}) + I(q_{For}) - C(q_{For}(e_{For}), q_{For}(e_{For}))$ $u_{IJV} = I(q_{Loc}) + I(q_{For}) - C(q_{Loc}(e_{Loc}), q_{For}(e_{For}))$	$u_{Loc} = \pi(q_{IJV}, (e)) - I(q_{IJV}(e))$ $u_{For} = \pi(q_{IJV}, (e)) - I_{For}$ $u_{IJV} = I_{Loc}q_{IJV}(e)) + I_{For} - C(q_{IJV}(e))$ or $u_{Loc} = R(q_{Loc}(e) - C(q_{Loc}(e)) - I(q_{IJV}, t)$ $u_{For} = \pi(q_{IJV}) - I_{For}$ $u_{IJV} = R(q_{IJV}(e)) - C(q_{IJV}(e)) + I(q_{IJV}(e)) + I_{For}$
Research Lab + separate Production Units + joint Distribution	$u_{Loc} = R(q_{IJV}(e)) - C(q_{IJV}(e)) + I_{Loc}$ $u_{For} = R(q_{IJV}(e)) - C(q_{IJV}(e)) + I_{For}$ $u_{IJV} = R(q_{IJV}(e)) - C(q_{IJV}(e)) - I_{Loc} - I_{For}$	$u_{Loc} = V(q_{IJV}(e)) - \alpha I(q_{IJV}(e))$ $u_{For} = V(q_{IJV}(e)) - (1-\alpha)I(q_{IJV}(e))$ $u_{IJV} = R(q_{IJV}(e)) C(q_{IJV}(e)) + I(q_{IJV}(e))$	$u_{Loc} = \pi(q_{IJV}(e)) - I(q_{IJV}(e))$ $u_{For} = \pi(q_{IJV}(e)) + I_{For}$ $u_{IJV} = I_{Loc}q_{IJV}(e)) + I_{For} - C(q_{IJV}(e))$ or

Table 5.8 Moral Hazard – Pay-offs/Contracts: $q_{IJV}(e) = qLoc(eLoc) + qFor(eFor)$ – *continued*

	Independent IJV	Shared IJV $\alpha \in [0, 1]$	Dominant IJV
			$u_{Loc} = R(q_{IJV}(e)) - C(q_{Loc}(e)) - I(q_{IJV}, t)$ $u_{For} = R(q_{IJV}(e)) - C(q_{For}(e)) - I_{For}$ $u_{IJV} = \pi(q_{IJV}(e)) + I_{Loc} + I_{For}$
Research Lab + Production Unit + Marketing joint	$u_{Loc} = \pi(q_{IJV}(e)) + I_{Loc}$ $u_{For} = \pi(q_{IJV}(e)) + I_{For}$ $u_{IJV} = \pi(q_{IJV}(e)) - I_{Loc} - I_{For}$	$u_{Loc} = V(q_{IJV}(e)) - \alpha I(q_{IJV}(e))$ $u_{For} = V(q_{IJV}(e)) - (1 - \alpha)I(q_{IJV}(e))$ $u_{IJV} = R(q_{IJV}(e)) - C(q_{IJV}(e)) + I(q_{IJV}(e))$	$u_{Loc} = \pi(q_{IJV}(e)) - I(q_{IJV}(e))$ $u_{For} = \pi(q_{IJV}, (e)) - I_{For}$ $u_{IJV} = I_{Loc}(q_{IJV}(e)) + I_{For} - C(q_{IJV}(e))$

agent, q_{IJV}, q_{Loc} or q_{For} and the type of the players t, particularly of the agent t_{IJV} and the incentives paid to the agent I_{Loc} and I_{For}. The agent's pay-offs are dependent on sales R, costs C and profits π and the incentives I paid by or to the parents (I_{Loc} and I_{For}).

The independent IJV shows a particular case of offering incentives. Since both parents intend to be independent of the operations of the IJV, the selling-the-store contract could be an option for contractual arrangements. This type of contracts is for risk-neutral players. The agent IJV pays the parents incentives I_{Loc} and I_{For} and is the residual claimant of the IJVs performance. Thus, the parents receive flat fees which are a kind of returns (though ex ante paid) and the agent is fully responsible for the IJV and can claim the profits of the enterprise.

The shared IJV shows the pay-offs for the players which are dependent on their shared contributions and the shared incentives for the IJV. The configurations of the IJVs are considered in the output/performance of the players. The contracts offered are linear contract which are sensitive to performance in the IJV.

Finally, the dominant IJV is distinguishing between the incentives from the local parent to the IJV and from the foreign parent to the IJV. The first-mentioned uses a linear contract, whereas the latter uses a flat fee contract.

Individual rationality constraint (IR) is known as well as participation constraint which means that the agent will only accept the contract if it is higher than either the expected utility or 0. Furthermore, incentive compatibility constraint (IC) shows that the low and high types must be willing to reveal their true types given the contracts offered and that it does not pay off for them to lie about their true type. This is the revelation principal and it can be used to design the optimal contracts in this respect.

Timing

The following order of the play shows the general game theoretical structure of the above-mentioned archetypes and it introduces the players, the plan of actions and the pay-offs on an abstract level. Since the different cases have special features, the conceptualization of the IJV common agency problem provides a tool of analysis.

Order of the play

(1) The principal P_{Loc} offers a menu of contracts to the agent.
(2) The principal P_{For} offers a menu of contracts to the agent.
(3) The agent may either accept or reject one of the contracts or both.
(4) The agent will choose his effort level as either shirk or do not shirk.
(5) Nature picks the state of the world to be successful or failure with a certain probability.

Consider now the management of an IJV as the agent, A_{IJV}, the parents will be called principals and get the notation P_{Loc} and P_{For} to distinguish between the foreign and local firm. The following order of the play shows the general game theoretical structure of the above-mentioned archetypes and it introduces the players, the plan of actions and the pay-offs on an abstract level. Since the different cases have special features, the conceptualization of the IJV common agency problem provides a tool of analysis.

In the moral hazard problem the players have the same information when the relationship is established, and the informational asymmetry arises from the fact that, once the contract has been signed, the principal cannot observe (or cannot verify) the action (or the effort) of the agent, or at least, the principal cannot perfectly control the action.

Stage 1. The parents or principals can either choose whether they want to offer a co-operative incentive scheme or individual contracts non-cooperatively. Since both principals pursue different objectives, we assume that they offer separately.

Stage 2. There exists an agent who is the management of the international joint venture with the notation A_{IJV}. This management has special knowledge about the cost structure and other managerial details in the IJV itself. Thus, the principals' offer should be either accepted or rejected. The agent can therefore accept or reject both contracts or accept one and reject the other.

Stage 3. The agent supplies the non-verifiable effort.

Stage 4. The game needs at that stage a dummy player to cover uncertainty about the failure and success. Thus, the game theoretical player 'Nature' is introduced which means that with a certain probability due to the agent's behavior the state of the world (joint venture) could either be success or failure. In the last stage the pay-offs will be determined.

Stage 5. The outcome and pay-offs of the players are determined. Since the timing reflects a game tree, the backward induction of the game starts with the final stage.

The game theoretical solution concepts are based on backward induction, which implies that the reasoning starts considering the last stage first and going backwards through the game tree (timing).

Some moral hazard problems arise when the agent, before carrying out the effort for which he has been contracted, observes the result of Nature's decision but the principal does not. All players have the same uncertainty when the contract is signed, but before the actual contracted

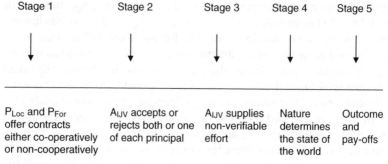

Figure 5.20   Moral Hazard Problems in the Common Agency of an IJV – the Agent's Action is not Verifiable

action is taken, the agent will have some sort of informational advantage by privately observing a relevant variable. This might occur as well in an IJV, especially when dealing in unknown local markets and the agent gets information which might alter the action profile. Stage 3 and 4 of the above-mentioned timing have to be exchanged in that case.

Dependent on the configuration of the IJV, the parents can offer their contracts in different ways. The following figures show the timing of the independent, shared and dominant IJV.

The timing for the independent IJV considers the option that either both parents offer their incentive schemes independently to an agent which is risk-averse and the selling-the-store contract already presented in the previous section in which the agent is risk-neutral. The difference can easily be seen, since the agent offers in the latter case the contracts to both principals and remains the residual claimant.

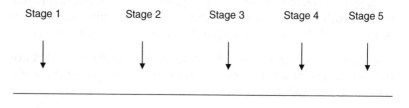

Figure 5.21   Moral Hazard – Timing of Independent IJV

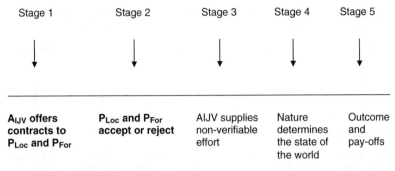

Figure 5.22 Selling-the-store Contracts in Independent IJV

In the shared management IJV, both parents offer co-operatively their contracts and the agent can either accept or reject. The parents form a coalition and have side payments.

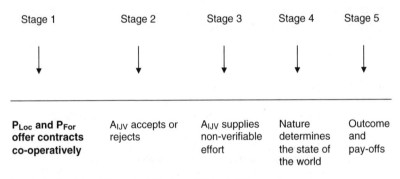

Figure 5.23 Moral Hazard – Timing of Shared IJV

The parents can offer their contracts independently which has an effect that the agent will report to both parents and their knowledge about the quality of effort is not correlated.

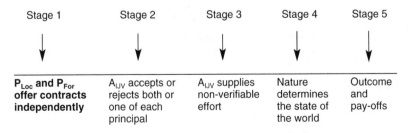

Finally, in the dominant parent IJV only the local parent offers a contract to the agent. The foreign parent is considered passive.

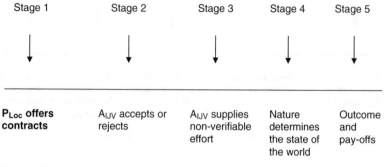

Stage 1	Stage 2	Stage 3	Stage 4	Stage 5
P_{Loc} **offers contracts**	A_{IJV} accepts or rejects	A_{IJV} supplies non-verifiable effort	Nature determines the state of the world	Outcome and pay-offs

Figure 5.24 Moral Hazard – Timing of Dominant IJV

The following table uses the timing of the independent, shared and dominant IJV and links the timing of the strategic types with the IJV configurations (units). Thus, we get a matrix with three columns for the three archetypes and five rows for the possible units represented in the IJV (research labs, production, distribution and marketing and its combinations).

Table 5.9 Moral Hazard – Games (Order of the Play)

	Independent IJV	Shared IJV	Dominant IJV
Research Lab	*Order of Play:* a) P_{Loc} and P_{For} offer contracts I_{Loc} and I_{For} b) A_{IJV} accepts or rejects c) A_{IJV} induces efforts (R&D, local, learning) d) Nature chooses success or failure e) Contracts/Pay-offs	*Order of Play:* a) P_{Loc} and P_{For} offer joint contract $I_{IJV,}$ or I_{Loc} and I_{For} b) A_{IJV} accepts or rejects $I_{IJV,}$ or I_{Loc} and I_{For} c) A_{IJV} induces efforts (R&D, local, learning) d) Nature chooses success or failure e) Contracts/ Pay-offs	*Order of Play:* a) P_{Loc} offers contracts I_{Loc} b) A_{IJV} accepts or rejects c) A_{IJV} induces efforts (R&D, local contribution, , learning bribe) d) Nature chooses success or failure e) Pay-offs (Contracts)
Research Lab + Production Unit + Marketing in both countries separately	*Order of Play:* a) P_{Loc} and P_{For} offer contracts I_{Loc} and I_{For} b) A_{IJV} accepts or rejects c) A_{IJV} induces efforts (R&D/production contribution) d) Nature chooses success or failure	*Order of Play:* a) P_{Loc} and P_{For} offer joint contract $I_{IJV,}$ or I_{Loc} and I_{For} b) A_{IJV} accepts or rejects $I_{IJV,}$ or I_{Loc} and I_{For} c) A_{IJV} induces efforts (R&D/production contribution)	*Order of Play:* a) P_{Loc} offers contracts I_{Loc} b) A_{IJV} accepts or rejects c) A_{IJV} induces efforts (R&D/production contribution) d) Nature chooses success or failure e) Contracts/Pay-offs:

Table 5.9 Moral Hazard – Games (Order of the Play) – *continued*

	Independent IJV	Shared IJV	Dominant IJV
	e) Pay-offs (Contracts)	d) Nature chooses success or failure e) Pay-offs (Contracts)	
Research Lab + separate Production Unit + Marketing separate and joint	*Order of Play:* a) P_{Loc} and P_{For} offer contracts I_{Loc} and I_{For} b) A_{IJV} accepts or rejects c) A_{IJV} induces efforts (R&D, marketing contributions) d) Nature chooses success or failure e) Pay-offs (Contracts)	*Order of Play:* a) P_{Loc} and P_{For} offer joint contract $I_{IJV,}$ or I_{Loc} and I_{For} b) A_{IJV} accepts or rejects $I_{IJV,}$ or I_{Loc} and I_{For} c) A_{IJV} induces efforts (R&D, marketing contributions) d) Nature chooses success or failure e) Pay-offs (Contracts)	*Order of Play:* a) P_{Loc} offers contracts I_{Loc} b) A_{IJV} accepts or rejects c) A_{IJV} induces efforts (R&D, marketing contributions) d) Nature chooses success or failure e) Pay-offs (Contracts)
Research Lab + separate Production Units + joint Distribution	*Order of Play:* a) P_{Loc} and P_{For} offer contracts I_{Loc} and I_{For} b) A_{IJV} accepts or rejects c) A_{IJV} induces efforts (R&D, market access, marketing) d) Nature chooses success or failure e) Pay-offs (Contracts)	*Order of Play:* a) P_{Loc} and P_{For} offer joint contract $I_{IJV,}$ or I_{Loc} and I_{For} b) A_{IJV} accepts or rejects $I_{IJV,}$ or I_{Loc} and I_{For} c) A_{IJV} induces efforts (R&D, market access, marketing) d) Nature chooses success or failure e) Pay-offs (Contracts)	*Order of Play:* a) P_{Loc} offers contracts I_{Loc} b) A_{IJV} accepts or rejects c) A_{IJV} induces efforts (R&D, market access, local know-how, marketing) d) Nature chooses success or failure e) Pay-offs (Contracts)
Research Lab + Production Unit + Marketing joint	*Order of Play:* a) P_{Loc} and P_{For} offer contracts I_{Loc} and I_{For} b) A_{IJV} accepts or rejects c) A_{IJV} induces efforts (production, R&D, marketing, market access, local) d) Nature chooses success or failure e) Pay-offs (Contracts)	*Order of Play:* a) P_{Loc} and P_{For} offer joint contract $I_{IJV,}$ or I_{Loc} and I_{For} b) A_{IJV} accepts or rejects $I_{IJV,}$ or I_{Loc} and I_{For} c) A_{IJV} induces efforts (production, R&D, marketing, market access, local) d) Nature chooses success or failure e) Pay-offs (Contracts)	*Order of Play:* a) P_{Loc} offers contracts I_{Loc} b) A_{IJV} accepts or rejects c) A_{IJV} induces efforts (production, R&D, marketing, market access, local) d) Nature chooses success or failure e) Pay-offs (Contracts)

The table shows the timings for the typology of IJVs in a moral hazard scenario. It is important to link the timing with the pay-offs of the previous section. This will lead to the solution of the problem. It is important to point out that the contracts should lead to a truth-telling mechanism based on the incentive compatibility constraints.

Mechanism

Consider two competing hierarchies or companies (P_{Loc}, A_{Loc}) and (P_{For}, A_{For}), both agents A_{Loc} and A_{For} are representatives of the owners and constitute the IJV management, third player called A_{IJV}. Distinguishing the moral hazard cases between these four players and the joint agent, we have the following options:

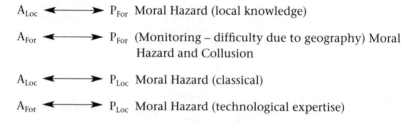

A_{Loc} ⟷ P_{For} Moral Hazard (local knowledge)

A_{For} ⟷ P_{For} (Monitoring – difficulty due to geography) Moral Hazard and Collusion

A_{Loc} ⟷ P_{Loc} Moral Hazard (classical)

A_{For} ⟷ P_{Loc} Moral Hazard (technological expertise)

The moral hazard problem occurs because of uncertainty about the effort level of the management which might be a source of one's own agent and the other parent's agent as well as the combination of both. For this reason, the incentive schemes offered by both partners consider the problem of hidden action. The parents offer contracts depending on their objective function and the private value in order to get revelation about the type of the agent. The costs of dishonesty have to be introduced into the model. There can be a combination of adverse selection and moral hazard.

Suppose that we have incentive schemes offered by both partners to the agent. The mediation plan may look like a Bayesian game with communication (see the previous chapter). We can use the structure of the above-mentioned timings and apply this mechanism to the particular form of an IJV management process.

Designing a mechanism for the special management process in an IJV, it is important to show the rules of this particular game in which at least two principals have one agent. The two principals shown above are the local and the foreign firm providing the international joint venture management with expertise through their appointed agents. The board of directors may consist of a representative of the local and/or the foreign firm.

Let us now look at the two ways of dealing with efforts (the decision in the above-mentioned abstract framework) in a moral hazard setting: discrete and continuous efforts. The former distinguishes between high and low efforts in general, whereas the latter considers efforts as values between 0 and 1 or $e \in [0. 1]$. Applying our framework to IJVs we could, furthermore, assume that the discrete types of effort are used for the relationship between the principals and the local representative and continuous types for the foreign expatriate's level of effort. This means that local knowledge and the efforts induced by the hosts can be seen as high or low and the foreign part's technological contribution as continuous, which might better reflect a real life setting. In abstract terms, we have disaggregated the joint agent in order to deal with hidden actions and tackle it by offering appropriate contracts.

The result implies that the participation constraint binds and the multiplier μ related to the incentive compatibility constraint must be non-negative.

Consider the following game with players $N = \{P_{For}, A_{IJV}\}$, in which the players have the set of actions (c_{For}, c_{IJV}). The actions were mentioned above by explaining the order of the play and showing the game theoretic reasoning. The foreign principal P_{For} offers a contract to the agent which can be seen as the action c_{For}, the local agent may either accept or reject this contract which is c_{IJV}. To choose the action accepted, the contract offered by the principal must cover the incentive to reveal the type (high or low effort) truthfully. This means it should not pay the agent to lie about his effort.

Now, consider the situation in an independent or dominant parent IJV in which a foreign principal who plays a passive role in an IJV and wants to ensure himself of getting the best out of this joint venture or encourage agent (A_{IJV}) to report his true type. The foreign principal is interested in offering an incentive scheme which gives the best return. For example, the selling-the-store contract (Rasmusen, 1994), P_{For} can offer a flat fee contract which might be accepted or rejected. This form of contract will give A_{IJV} the responsibility to connect his effort to the output he is expecting in the future. The principal will have her return and the agent has to invest the effort level which will be in connection with the expected utility. Thus, the pay-offs (u_{For}, u_{IJV}) for the players are shown in the value function V_{For} and V_{Loc}. This means that P_{For} gets his return as a flat fee F and withdraws from receiving a share of the joint profit, whereas A_{IJV} as the residual claimant has to add his expertise which makes the output dependent on his contributed effort e and offers him to keep every additional output. The intention to cheat (embezzle or shirk) will only harm himself. His pay-off is reflected in the value function depending on the output which is furthermore dependent on the contributed effort level. The value function contains the revenue R as a function of output dependent on e and the cost function on the basis of output q (e), additionally the flat fee has to be deducted from the profit too.

$$V_{For} = F \tag{1}$$
$$V_{IJV}(q(e)) = R(q(e)) - C(q(e)) - F \tag{2}$$

There might be the possibility that the producer or A_{IJV} cannot afford to pay the flat fee or he might be too risk-averse to bear the costs of this contract.

Consider the following game with N players and N = 2 or called P_{Loc} and A_{IJV}, in which the players have the set of actions (c_{Loc}, c_{IJV}). The actions were mentioned above by explaining the order of the play with the following reasoning. The local principal P_{local} offers a contract to the agent which can be seen as the action c_{Loc}, the foreign agent may either accept or reject this contract which is c_{IJV}. To choose the action accepted, the contract offered by the principal must cover the incentive to reveal the type (high or low effort) truthfully. This means it should not pay the agent to lie about his effort. The incentive scheme has to be chosen that the parameters satisfy firstly the condition that it does not pay to report a high type when there is low potential, and secondly that it does not pay to report low potential when the agent is a high type.

Consider now the case of a local principal P_{Loc} who contributes access to local markets or to production facilities in either a marketing joint venture or production joint venture. The agent provides the IJV with knowledge in technology, marketing or general management techniques. The problem for the principal occurs because of the lack of information about the agent's type which means whether A_{IJV} has a low or high effort potential. The incentive scheme offered by the principal has to focus on the high and the low type.

To find an incentive scheme for moral hazard problems between a local principal and an IJV agent, it is necessary to consider the participation constraint since A_{IJV} can opt out after being offered the contract. Furthermore, finding the incentive compatibility constraint is the next step in the revelation process. The participation constraint can be shown in the way that the offered contract has to be at least the reservation utility or should give him a net return which is not lower than elsewhere.

Suppose the output q is dependent on the effort e of the agent and on nature t which might be the territory's potential in marketing related knowledge, R&D potential or country and financial endowment for general management techniques. The agent knows the potential of his part and how much effort to put into the joint enterprise. To specify the output, q = 1 + e if the potential is good and q = e otherwise. The effort costs k(e) regardless of the potential. The agent will be paid a fixed rate f and a royalty rate r depending on the output q. Two different contracts are offered, one for each potential. If it is high

$$I_H = f_H + r_H q \tag{4}$$

and otherwise,

$$I_L = f_L + r_L q \tag{5}$$

If the potential is low and the corresponding contract is in force, the agent will get the net reward being dependent on the incentive scheme minus his costs of effort. The next step would be to specify the costs of the effort and by maximizing the net reward function we will get the effort level e*, which is the incentive compatibility constraint for the moral hazard problem.

The principal's problem is to maximize his pay-off function. The two models of moral hazard gave some idea about the bargaining power in an IJV and of the inherent double moral hazard problem which combines the perspectives of each player.

The parents P_{Loc} and P_{For} have various options to offer contracts to the agent. Dependent on their contribution to the enterprise and their strategic setting, they could either look at countervailing incentive schemes, on co-operative incentives or exclusive contracting. Another contingency of incentives is trust contracts, incentive contracts and bonus contracts. Whatever the parents chose is a combination of various factors (see pay-off table).

The static common agency framework for the strategic and functional configurations of IJVs showed that it is possible to offer contracts which are based on the ability and effort levels induced into the joint venture. It is important to develop the typology of IJVs first, then to show the knowledge and efforts in these IJV types and finally to come up with the timing and pay-off functions for the IJVs. This is considered for an ex ante perspective of looking forward and reasoning backward in a game theoretic sense.

The next chapter is based on the adverse selection problem and develops a signaling game for the typology of IJVs in the same way. It is important to point out that the dynamic approach is crucial in this respect.

6
Dynamic Common Agency

Signaling

Based on the uncertainties about the quality of the management, this chapter will look at the dynamic approach towards this problem. In general, skills are not observable ex ante. Thus, contracts have to be offered to get a true revelation of the quality of their skills. Several ways of moving are possible which might result in screening or signaling. Signaling takes place when the agent knows his ability and offers his skills first. In case the parents move first and offer their contracts, there we have a screening scenario.

Players

There are famous cases of IJVs and many other IJVs which deal with hidden characteristics. Assuming that a firm in a developed country intends to form an IJV with an enterprise of a developing country without knowing the actual standing of the partner in the host country, this has an impact on the quality of the joint management and its outcome. Thus, like in the previous chapter, incentives should cover the type of the third player with respect to the local player's ability and the quality of the joint venture. The output of the joint product can be distinguished in the marketing and technological performance of the IJV. As before, both parents may offer contracts jointly or independently.

With regards to ability, we have to consider uncertainty concerning the quality of the IJV management from the local and the foreign parent's perspective. Thus, the presence of uncertainty in the case of an IJV leads to the difficulty of designing efficient, incentive compatible contracts.

Since both parents send their representatives as board members to the IJV management, there is the joint player combining the special features of the two partners. Although different adverse selection models deal with the provision of quality, the application to the problem of hidden characteristics of an IJV management considers a new set of problems and perspectives. The distinction between observable and verifiable quality occurs in connection with an appropriate mechanism design to get revelation about the type of agent. What incentives can be offered and are there any signals of quality? Since the IJV management can be seen as a collective body, the usual payment incentives are to be applied. The level of quality of the IJV management can vary.

Besides the impact of partner characteristics on the success of an IJV, it is important to consider the quality of the IJV management as another source of the survival of an IJV. The difficulty to verify the ability of the management can be described as a problem of hidden information or characteristics. Thus, incentive schemes should be designed such that the agent's dominant strategy is to reveal his type truthfully. Up to this point it is relatively similar to the adverse selection process. The difference can be seen that there is an update in beliefs, since the agent is able to signal his ability to the principals.

Suppose there is a company in country A and another one in country B, the IJV will be set up in country B to provide market-access for the foreign firm and technological know-how for local partner. Both parents contribute their expertise. The foreign firm does not know whether the local firm has market knowledge such as local knowledge, marketing know-how and skills in dealing with bureaucratic agendas. In the case of a low level of quality, the foreign firm might contribute expertise whereas the local firm free-rides on the partner's strength. Given the bad sales performance due to the lack of ability, the difficulty for the foreign firm will lead to reputation problems. Besides negative effects on the own performance, low ability of the partner and the breakdown of the business relationship has an impact on the acquisition of future partners in country B. Developing a joint agent on the basis of the two partners' features offers the possibility to design a common agency game to show the conflicting and the co-operative elements. Shenkar and Zeira (1987) distinguished between three groups of employees in an IJV. Since the complexity of an IJV is derived because of the two distinguished groups of the parents, we would like to use the signaling case only for the two groups of agents.

The agent A_{IJV} will be offered both contracts I_{Loc} and I_{For} and may either accept both, reject one and accept the other or reject both. Under the assumption ($A_{loc} \subset A_{IJV}$ and $A_{for} \subset A_{IJV}$), the agent could have the following combinations of types T = {(H_{loc}, H_{for}), (H_{loc}, L_{for}), (L_{loc}, H_{for}), (L_{loc}, L_{for})}. Thus, the agent A_{IJV} can be seen as a coalition of both agents and could be the grand coalition. If we consider the parents offering incentives based on an experience signal separately according to previous contracts in MNEs or IJVs, we might constitute a mutual atmosphere of co-operation even under the non-cooperative game theoretical perspective. Since this is the ex ante stage of an IJV contractual setting, this special game could provide a solution to contractual uncertainties in the set-up phase.

It is important to mention that this tool for a double adverse selection scenario is only appropriate for the set-up period of an IJV between parents who doubt that their abilities do not fit together or the other partner or his representative could lie about the ability level.

P_{For} wants to encourage the agent to provide the enterprise with an optimal level of local knowledge or marketing skills. The payment may be based on numbers and sizes of sales contracts as signal of the agent's quality, ex ante. The local agent knows about the sales potential, which can be measured in the number of sales contracts (n_{SC}) acquired and managed by the local firm. Thus the sum or volume of it could be an indicator of the agent's marketing ability in this local environment. Another possibility to signal quality is to incidate the numbers/sizes of research contracts (n_{RC}) and production contracts (n_{PC}) which is relevant for the foreign agent.

To continue the combinations of incentive schemes, P_{Loc} considers the incentive scheme of the former case such as a payment based on the number/size of research contracts, which could be related to the agent's ability. P_{For} could offer an incentive scheme based on the number of sales contracts (n_{SC}). The difference between MNE experience and experience with international companies can be seen in the role of the player. The latter deals with the local firm's experience with other foreign firms as provider of local knowledge, whereas the MNE experience considers the foreign firms' knowledge in the international business setting internally and externally. Thus, P_{For} wants to reduce the marketing costs of the agent and the costs of learning in an international business setting. The sales, research and production contracts are used as a measure and determined by a critical value.

It can be stated that the uncertainty problem is dealt with in this chapter by using experience level as the signal which helps to update beliefs about the type of the agent. Thus, based on the experience and knowledge of the players, the signals are chosen as number/size of previous sales, research and/or production contracts in MNEs or IJVs.

These signals will be connected to a critical value which is determined by the principals. In the following table, the typology of the IJVs from the static common agency chapter is used again and the signals of experience as well as the timing and pay-off functions are applied to the various types of IJVs.

The independent IJV relies on the capability of the manager to perform in a risk-neutral setting. The management could be comprised by the representatives of each parent who have different expertise and experience levels. Suggesting that it might be a combination of two experience levels (both could be experienced or inexperienced and one or the other could be experienced or inexperienced). Dependent on the configuration of the IJV, the experience could be in managerial, technological or marketing terms.

In a shared IJV, the management needs to be selected carefully, since the compatibility of the agents will lead to success or failure. In terms of experience, the local and foreign agents are well endowed with technological, marketing or managerial expertise. Depending on the years or sales and research contracts, the management will signal their ability to perform.

Finally, the dominant IJV will be in the position to provide a local manager for leading the enterprise. This should be as well an expertise in technology, marketing and managerial terms. Therefore, the foreign part relies on the quality of the management and the foreign parent has an incentive to get experienced local managers to run the IJV.

Table 6.1   Signaling – Experience in IJVs

	Independent IJV	Shared IJV	Dominant IJV
Research Lab	{(e, e)} in order to manage an independent research IJV, the representatives need to have experience. It could be possible that there is the following combination {(e, u), (u, e)}. To find out the level of technological knowledge, there needs to be an ex ante contracting scenario.	{(e, u), (u, e)} Both players are experienced in their own expertise but lack the other's knowledge of the complementary skills.	{(e, u), (u, e)} Complementary expertise levels are important in this context.

Table 6.1 Signaling – Experience in IJVs – *continued*

	Independent IJV	Shared IJV	Dominant IJV
Research Lab + Production Unit + Marketing in both countries separately	{(e, e), (e, u), (u, e)}. The experience level in an IJV should be that both agents have enough experience to successfully manage the joint enterprise. In order to reveal whether one player is inexperienced, there needs to be a contracting stage in which the agents show the level of experience.	{(e, e), (e, u), (u, e)}, ideally both players have experience in their respective fields, it could be much more likely that the know-how is related to the complementary skills like above.	{(e, e), (e, u), (u, e)} The experience level refers to market knowledge and technological know-how. Both partners could have experience and either one could have experience in the field of complementary expertise.
Research Lab + separate Production Unit + Marketing separate and joint	{(e, e), (e, u), (u, e)} see (1)	{(e, e), (e, u), (u, e)} see (2)	{(e, e), (e, u), (u, e)} As in the previous cases, it is possible to have both players experienced regarding their expertise or one experienced and the other one inexperienced. In case both are inexperienced, this can be found out by offering appropriate incentive schemes.
Research Lab + separate Production Units + joint Distribution	{(e, e), (e, u), (u, e)} see (1)	{(e, e), (e, u), (u, e), (u, u)}	{(e, e), (e, u), (u, e)} Experience levels can vary dependent on the expertise (local knowledge, technological know-how) and can be distinguished in various ways according to complementary skills.
Research Lab + Production Unit + Marketing joint	{(e, e), (e, u), (u, e)} see (1)	{(e, e), (e, u), (u, e)} see (2)	{(e, e), (e, u), (u, e)} see above. If both are inexperienced, contracts need to be offered to reveal this situation in an appropriate way. Information asymmetries can occur

Strategies

The agent A_{IJV} will be offered both contracts I_{loc} and I_{for} and may either accept both, reject one and accept the other or reject both. Under the assumption ($A_{loc} \subset A_{IJV}$ and $A_{for} \subset A_{IJV}$), the agent could have the following combinations of types T = {(H_{loc}, H_{for}), (H_{loc}, L_{for}), (L_{loc}, H_{for}), (L_{loc}, L_{for})}. The agent performs an output q_{IJV} for both principals, either a new product or the development of a new production process, or even in the case of a joint task such as the marketing or research and its allocation to both parents q_{Loc} and q_{For}. Consider now the first case, both parents contribute complementary skills and receive a portion of the output or profit as return. Thus, the agent's actions are the contribution of their expertise a_I, where $a_{Loc} + a_{For}$ are the joint input. In case that the parents have no previous experience with each other, we have a *double adverse selection* problem. The agent's level of ability is reflected in the type of the players. Under the assumption that both parents offer incentive schemes to the agent of the other parent, double monitoring can be excluded. The agents may be kept and compensated independently with respect to their ability. The joint value creating process and assimilation procedure from the set-up to the actual management process needs co-operative or team incentives.

Pay-offs

The pay-offs of the players consider the utility function of the two principals and the agent. As in the previous chapters, the pay-offs for the two principals, u_{Loc} and u_{For}, consist of the value functions V, the profit functions π or revenues R and the incentive schemes I_{Loc} and I_{For} paid. The pay-offs for the agent are composed by the incentives received/paid and the costs C occurred as well as the profits made. The functions are dependent on the performance q and the types t of the players. Additionally, the agent can signal to the parents his type. This will lead to incentives offered on the basis of these signals. The signals can be the number of sales contracts n_{SC}, research contracts n_{RC} and production contracts n_{PC}. The following configurations of pay-offs are based on the strategic archetypes such as shared, dominant and independent IJVs. With regards to the installed units of the joint venture, the pay-offs are clearly based on the needs of expertise in these units.

The independent IJV shows a particular case of offering incentives. Since both parents intend to be independent of the operations of the IJV, the selling-the-store contract could be an option for contractual

Table 6.2 Signaling – Pay-offs/Contracts

	Independent IJV	Shared IJV $\alpha \in [0, 1]$	Dominant IJV
Research Lab	$u_{Loc} = \pi(q_{IJV}) + I_{Loc}(n_{RC})$ $u_{For} = \pi(q_{IJV}) + I_{For}(n_{RC})$ $u_{IJV} = I_{Loc}(n_{RC}) + I_{For}(n_{RC}) - C(q_{IIJV})$	$u_{Loc} = V(q_{IJV}, t) - \alpha I(n_{RC})$ $u_{For} = V(q_{IJV}, t) - (1-\alpha)I(n_{RC})$ $u_{IJV} = I(n_{RCLoc}, n_{RCFor}) - C(q_{IJV}, t)$	$u_{Loc} = \pi(q_{IJV}, t) - I(n_{RC})$ $u_{For} = \pi(q_{IJV}, t) - I_{For}$ $u_{IJV} = I_{For}(n_{RC}) + I_{For} - C(q_{IJV}, t)$
Research Lab + Production Unit Marketing in both countries separately	$u_{Loc} = \pi(q_{IJV}) + I_{Loc}(n_{PC})$ $u_{For} = \pi(q_{IJV}) + I_{For}(n_{RC})$ $u_{IJV} = I_{Loc}(n_{PC}) + I_{For}(n_{RC}) - C(q_{IJV})$	$u_{Loc} = V(q_{IJV}, t) - \alpha I(n_{PC})$ $u_{For} = V(q_{IJV}, t) - (1-\alpha)I(n_{RC})$ $u_{IJV} = I(n_{PC}, n_{RC}) - C(q_{IIV}, t)$ or $u_{Loc} = R(q_{Loc}) - \alpha I(n_{PC})$ $u_{For} = R(q_{For}) - (1-\alpha)I(n_{RC})$ $u_{IJV} = I(n_{RCLoc}, n_{RCFor}) - C(q_{IJV}, t)$	$u_{Loc} = \pi(q_{IJV}, t) + R(q_{Loc}) - I(n_{PC})$ $u_{For} = \pi(q_{IJV}, t) + R(q_{For}) - I_{For}(n_{RC})$ $u_{IJV} = I_{Loc}(n_{PC}, n_{RC}) + I_{For} = (n_{RC}) - C(q_{IJV}, t)$
Research Lab + separate Production Unit + Marketing separate and joint	$u_{Loc} = R(q_{Loc}) + I_{Loc}(n_{SC}) - C(q_{Loc})$	$u_{Loc} = V(q_{IJV}, t) + \alpha I(n_{SRC})$ $u_{For} = V(q_{IJV}, t) - (1-\alpha)I(n_{RC})$	$u_{Loc} = \pi(q_{IJV}, t) - I(n_{SRC})$ $u_{For} = \pi(q_{IJV}, t) - I_{For}$

Table 6.2 Signaling – Pay-offs/Contracts – *continued*

	Independent IJV	Shared IJV $\alpha \in [0, 1]$	Dominant IJV
	$u_{For} = R(q_{Ror}) + I_{For}(n_{RC}) - C(q_{For})$ $u_{IJV} = R(q_{IJV}) - C(q_{IJV}) - I_{Loc}(n_{SC}) - I_{For}(n_{RC})$	$u_{IJV} = I(n_{SRC}, n_{PRC}) - C(q_{IJV}, t)$ or $u_{Loc} = R(q_{Loc}) - C(q_{Loc}) - \alpha I(n_{SC})$ $u_{For} = R(q_{For}) - C(q_{For}) (1 - \alpha)I(n_{RC})$ $u_{IJV} = R(q_{IJV}, t) + I(n_{SRC}, n_{RC}) - C(q_{IJV}, t)$	$u_{IJV} = I_{Loc}(n_{SRC}) + I_{For} - C(q_{IJV}, t)$
Research Lab + separate Production Unit + joint Distribution	$u_{Loc} = R(q_{IJV}, t) + I_{Loc}(n_{SC}) - C(q_{Loc})$ $u_{For} = R(q_{IJV}, t) + I_{For}(n_{RC}) - C(q_{For})$ $u_{IJV} = R(q_{IJV}) - C(q_{IJV}) - I_{Loc}(n_{SC}) - I_{For}(n_{RC})$	$u_{Loc} = V(q_{IJV}, t) + \alpha I(n_{SC})$ $u_{For} = V(q_{IJV}, t) - (1 - \alpha)I(n_{PRC})$ $u_{IJV} = I(n_{SC}, n_{RC}) - C(q_{IJV}, t)$ or $u_{Loc} = R(q_{IJV}, t) - C(q_{Loc}) - \alpha I(n_{SC})$	$u_{Loc} = \pi(q_{IJV}, t) - I(n_{SRC})$ $u_{For} = \pi(q_{IJV}, t) - I_{For}$ $u_{IJV} = I_{Loc}(n_{SRC}) + I_{For} - C(q_{IJV}, t)$

Table 6.2 Signaling – Pay-offs/Contracts – *continued*

	Independent IJV	Shared IJV $\alpha \in [0, 1]$	Dominant IJV
		$u_{For} = R(q_{IJV}, t) - C(q_{For})$ $(1 - \alpha)I(n_{RC})$	
		$u_{IJV} = R(q_{IJV}, t) +$ $I(n_{SC}, n_{RC}) - C(q_{IJV}, t)$	
Research Lab + Production Unit + Marketing joint	$u_{Loc} = \pi(q_{IJV}, t) + I_{Loc}(n_{SRC})$ $u_{For} = \pi(q_{IJV}, t) + I_{Loc}(n_{PRC})$ $u_{IJV} = \pi(q_{IJV}) - I_{Loc}(n_{SRC})$ $- I_{For}(n_{PRC})$	$u_{Loc} = V(q_{IJV}, t) -$ $\alpha I(n_{SRC})$ $u_{For} = V(q_{IJV}, t) -$ $(1 - \alpha)I(n_{PRC})$ $u_{IJV} = I(n_{SRC}, n_{PRC}) +$ $R(q_{IJV}, t) - C(q_{IJV}, t)$	$u_{Loc} = \pi(q_{IJV}, t) - I(n_{SRC})$ $u_{For} = \pi(q_{IJV}, t) - I_{For}$ $u_{IJV} = I_{Loc}(n_{SRC}) + I_{For}$ $- C(q_{IJV}, t)$

arrangements. This type of contracts is for risk-neutral players. The agent IJV pays the parents incentives I_{Loc} and I_{For} and is the residual claimant of the IJVs performance. Thus, the parents receive flat fees which are a kind of returns (though ex ante paid) and the agent is fully responsible for the IJV and can claim the profits of the enterprise. Nevertheless, the parents' return is dependent on the ability of the agent. Thus, it is important to consider incentive schemes for this scenario, that they parents are offering incentive pay based on the experience level (meaning the ability). The contracts can be based on the sales, research and production expertise (volume of contracts managed before).

The shared IJV shows the pay-offs for the players which are dependent on their shared contributions and the shared incentives for the IJV. The configurations of the IJVs are considered in the output/performance of the players. The contracts offered are linear contract which are sensitive to performance in the IJV. In the same way as in the previous archetype the signal of expertise could be dependent on the functional contribution leading to the configuration.

Finally, the dominant IJV is distinguishing between the incentives from the local parent to the IJV and from the foreign parent to the IJV. The first-mentioned uses a linear contract, whereas the latter uses a flat fee contract. Therefore, it is only interesting to look at the local parent and her contracting.

Timing

Under the assumption that we have a signaling scenario, the timing of the game includes an additional move – the agent sends a signal about his ability. In the above-mentioned paragraph the contracts were based on the agent's experience or previous contracts dependent on the needed expertise (sales, production or research).

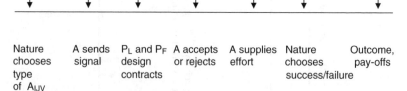

Nature chooses type of A_{IJV}	A sends signal	P_L and P_F design contracts	A accepts or rejects	A supplies effort	Nature chooses success/failure	Outcome, pay-offs

Figure 6.1   Timing of the Signaling Game

Stage 1. Like in the double adverse selection case, the principals do not know the agent's ability. They know the ability of their own representative, but not the skills of the partner's representative and of the conglomerate. Nature chooses the ability level of the agent.

Stage 2. The agent learns his ability and signals it to the principals. We assume that the agent might give a costly signal. This could be either number, size volume of previous research, production or sales contracts. The agent A_{IJV} might therefore signal to both parents.

Stage 3. The parents P_{Loc} and P_{For} design their contracts with respect to the signals they have got. Their contracts could be offered independently regarding whether the agent's knowledge of the local market or the technological know-how is affected. Furthermore, the principals could offer a joint contract. This incentive scheme might cover the costs of assimilation or the adaptation to another business or national culture.

Stage 4. The agent may either accept or reject the contract(s).

Stage 5. Like in the above-mentioned case the agent supplies effort.

Stage 6. The outcome of the game depends on the nature's choice of success or failure.

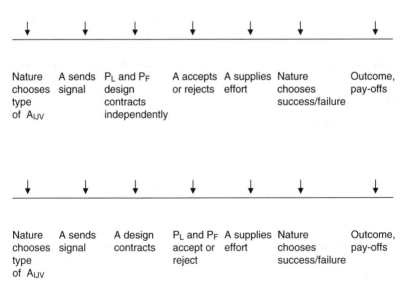

Figure 6.2   Signaling – Timing of Independent IJV

The timing of the signaling problem is adjusted to the strategic and control archetypes, since their way of offering contracts is different. For the sake of generality, the three archetypes are used to abstract the problem. Each stage shows the particular case of co-operatively or independently offered contracts applied to the needs of an IJV with a special unit structure.

As in the static common agency chapter, the timing of the games for independent IJVs considers the agent as offering contracts. Nevertheless, there is an additional timing for the case that the agent is risk-averse and the parents have to offer a signaling contract. It is important to notice, that the second stage is crucial for the dynamic approach, since the agent sends a signal which leads to the updating of beliefs.

Like in the previous chapter, it is important notice that the shared management IJV offers the possibility to have both parents offering a joint contract. The second stage is crucial when the agent sends a signal (research, production, sales contract, respectively).

In the case of a dominant parent IJV, the local principal offers an incentive contract, whereas the foreign parent can offer a flat fee.

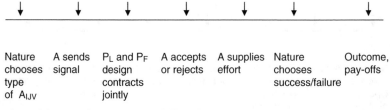

| Nature chooses type of A_{IJV} | A sends signal | P_L and P_F design contracts jointly | A accepts or rejects | A supplies effort | Nature chooses success/failure | Outcome, pay-offs |

Figure 6.3 Signaling – Timing of Shared IJV

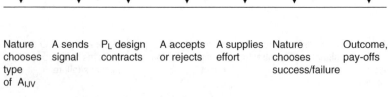

| Nature chooses type of A_{IJV} | A sends signal | P_L design contracts | A accepts or rejects | A supplies effort | Nature chooses success/failure | Outcome, pay-offs |

Figure 6.4 Signaling – Timing of Dominant IJV

Table 6.3 Signaling – Games (Order of the Play)

	Independent IJV	Shared IJV	Dominant IJV
Research Lab	*Order of Play:* a) Nature chooses experience of A_{IJV} b) A_{IJV} sends signal (research contracts) c) P_{Loc} and P_{For} offer contracts I_{Loc} and I_{For} d) A_{IJV} accepts or rejects e) A_{IJV} supplies efforts f) Success or failure	*Order of play:* a) Nature chooses experience of A_{IJV} b) A_{IJV} sends signal (research contracts) c) P_{Loc} and P_{For} offer joint contract I_{IJV}, or I_{Loc} and I_{For} d) A_{IJV} accepts or rejects e) A_{IJV} supplies efforts f) Success or failure	*Order of play:* a) Nature chooses experience of A_{IJV} b) A_{IJV} sends signal (research contracts) c) P_{Loc} offers contracts d) A_{IJV} accepts or rejects e) A_{IJV} supplies efforts f) Success or failure
Research Lab + Production Unit + Marketing in both countries separately	*Order of play:* a) Nature chooses experience of A_{IJV} b) A_{IJV} sends signal (research contracts, production contracts) c) P_{Loc} and P_{For} offer contracts I_{Loc} and I_{For} d) A_{IJV} accepts or rejects e) A_{IJV} supplies efforts f) Success or failure	*Order of play:* a) Nature chooses experience of A_{IJV} b) A_{IJV} sends signal (research contracts, production contracts) c) P_{Loc} and P_{For} offer joint contract I_{IJV}, or I_{Loc} and I_{For} d) A_{IJV} accepts or rejects e) A_{IJV} supplies efforts f) Success or failure	*Order of play:* a) Nature chooses experience of A_{IJV} b) A_{IJV} sends signal (research contracts, production) contracts c) P_{Loc} offers contracts d) A_{IJV} accepts or rejects e) A_{IJV} supplies efforts f) Success or failure
Research Lab + separate Production Unit + Marketing separate and joint	*Order of play:* a) Nature chooses experience of A_{IJV} b) A_{IJV} sends signal (research contracts, marketing contracts) c) P_{Loc} and P_{For} offer contracts I_{Loc} and I_{For} d) A_{IJV} accepts or rejects e) A_{IJV} supplies efforts f) Success or failure	*Order of play:* a) Nature chooses experience of A_{IJV} b) A_{IJV} sends signal (research contracts, marketing contracts) c) P_{Loc} and P_{For} offer joint contract I_{IJV}, or I_{Loc} and I_{For} d) A_{IJV} accepts or rejects e) A_{IJV} supplies efforts f) Success or failure	*Order of play:* a) Nature chooses experience of A_{IJV} b) A_{IJV} sends signal research contracts, (marketing) contracts c) P_{Loc} offers contracts d) A_{IJV} accepts or rejects e) A_{IJV} supplies efforts f) Success or failure
Research Lab + separate Production Units + joint Distribution	*Order of play:* a) Nature chooses experience of A_{IJV} b) A_{IJV} sends signal (research contracts, sales contracts) c) P_{Loc} and P_{For} offer contracts I_{Loc} and I_{For} d) A_{IJV} accepts or rejects e) A_{IJV} supplies efforts f) Success or failure	*Order of play:* a) Nature chooses experience of A_{IJV} b) A_{IJV} sends signal (research contracts, sales contracts) c) P_{Loc} and P_{For} offer joint contract I_{IJV}, or I_{Loc} and I_{For} d) A_{IJV} accepts or rejects e) A_{IJV} supplies efforts f) Success or failure	*Order of play:* a) Nature chooses experience of A_{IJV} b) A_{IJV} sends signal (research contracts, sales contracts) c) P_{Loc} offers contracts d) A_{IJV} accepts or rejects e) A_{IJV} supplies efforts f) Success or failure

Table 6.3   Signaling – Games (Order of the Play) – *continued*

	Independent IJV	Shared IJV	Dominant IJV
Research Lab + Production Unit + Marketing joint	*Order of play:* a) Nature chooses experience of A_{IJV} b) A_{IJV} sends signal (research, production, sales contracts) c) P_{Loc} and P_{For} offer contracts I_{Loc} and I_{For} d) A_{IJV} accepts or rejects e) A_{IJV} supplies efforts f) Success or failure	*Order of play:* a) Nature chooses experience of A_{IJV} b) A_{IJV} sends signal (research, production, sales contracts) c) P_{Loc} and P_{For} offer joint contract I_{IJV}, or I_{Loc} and I_{For} d) A_{IJV} accepts or rejects e) A_{IJV} supplies efforts f) Success or failure	*Order of play:* a) Nature chooses experience of A_{IJV} b) A_{IJV} sends signal (research, , production sales contracts) c) P_{Loc} offers contracts d) A_{IJV} accepts or rejects e) A_{IJV} supplies efforts f) Success or failure

Mechanism

Given the special nature of an IJV, we have to deal with a mixture of co-operative and non-cooperative game theory. Thus, the agent A_{IJV} can be seen as a coalition of both agents and could be the grand coalition. Since we assume that this conglomerate is a combination of both parents, the players can negotiate effectively or the grand coalition or all coalitions can negotiate effectively.

Suppose the agent is a coalition of both parents' representatives (or agents). Let $\gamma \in [0,1]$ be the fraction of local agents and $1 - \gamma$ be the one of foreign agents, or the equity shares of the local and foreign parent otherwise. To bind the hidden characteristics effectively to the opposite expertise, the principals offer their incentive to the counterpart's agent. Before turning to the actual signaling and contracting scenarios, several issues need to be considered. Firstly, there are two types of equilibria: the pooling and the separating equilibrium. Secondly, solutions under complete information are the first step and the asymmetric information scenario is the second step. Thirdly, both principals offer their contracts either independently or co-operatively. Thus, the principals' outcome and the agent's utility have to be considered.

All players have to offer something, either knowledge or contracts, which can be regarded as moves. We start with a situation in which the principals have to rely on ex ante known variables. The offered contracts may include a fixed payment, yet the agent could also choose whether a low or a high-ability contract is appropriate. In IJVs the parents can base their incentives on the experience level in multinationals such as measures in years or in the number of successful sales and/or production contracts and research projects. This could lead to independent contracts offered by the principals to enhance higher pay-offs with respect to their own firms.

Both principals offer flat fee contracts, though they distinguish between a low and a high ability type. Furthermore, these contracts are offered independently. Thus, the pay-offs for the three players consist of the following notation.

Principal local has the pay-off u_{Loc} which consists of the incentive scheme I_{Loc} offered to the foreign fraction of the agent and receive a net benefit dependent on the ability level of the agent. Similarly, the principal foreign's pay-off function is related to the net benefit derived from the joint venture and the costs the principal has to consider which is in this case I_{For}, the incentives offered to the local subset of the agent. Thus, the agent's pay-off is a combination of both principal's incentives and the costs of the ability.

Individual rationality constraints:

$$u_{IJV} \geq \bar{u}_{IJV}$$

The agent's utility pay-off needs to weakly dominate his reservation utility. The reservation utility can be zero. Thus, the agent is only willing to participate when his utility is greater or equal than zero or better than an outside option.

Both principals will also only participate in the game when their utility pay-offs are weakly dominating their reservation pay-off, such that

$$u_{Loc} \geq \bar{u}_{Loc} \text{ and}$$
$$u_{For} \geq \bar{u}_{For}$$

Incentive compatibility constraints:

$$I_{Loc}(n_{RC}, n_{SC}) - cq(n_{RC}, n_{SC}) \geq I_{Loc}(n_{RC}, n_{SC}) - cq(n_{RC}, n_{SC})$$
$$\forall n_{RC} \in \left[\underset{-RC}{n}, \bar{n}_{RC}\right] \forall n_{RC} \in \left[\underset{-RC}{n}, \bar{n}_{RC}\right]$$
$$I_{For}(n_{RC}, n_{SC}) - cq(n_{RC}, n_{SC}) \geq I_{For}(n_{RC}, n_{SC}) - cq(n_{RC}, n_{SC})$$
$$\forall n_{SC} \in \left[\underset{-SC}{n}, \bar{n}_{SC}\right] \forall n_{SC} \in \left[\underset{-SC}{n}, \bar{n}_{SC}\right]$$

Like in the previous cases, the mechanism is a truth-telling mechanism when low type is not better off lying and vice versa. Let be $I_{Loc}(n_{RC}, n_{SC})$ the transfer offered by the local principal, in which the foreign agent has the possibility to announce a different type than his real type. Thus, stands for the foreign agent's ability, or precisely for the signal of research contracts in multinational enterprises. It can be measured as low and high in the interval and therefore stands for a stochastic process. Similarly, the foreign principal can offer incentive schemes and the local agent has to accept this contract. It must pay the agent to contribute his ability level truly. Therefore, the compensation scheme is based on the number and volume of sales contracts. In the following paragraphs not only the research contracts of multinational experience serve as signal of the foreign partner's ability, but also the number and volume of production contracts are used for this purpose.

Given that the agent receives incentives from both parents, the agent could be lying about his ability to only one or both of them. Thus, the incentive compatibility constraints mean that the agent is better off by telling the truth to the local principal, which is shown in the first equation of the incentive compatibility constraint. Suppose that the principals restrict their attention to direct revelation mechanisms with the property that agreeing to participate and then truthfully revealing their type constitutes a Nash equilibrium for the agent in the corresponding game of incomplete information.

If participation and truth-telling are to be a Nash equilibrium for a given direct revelation mechanism, participation and incentive constraints are developed. In cases where flat fee contracts are used, the latter constraint is not necessary. Suppose we have flat fee payments for two types (low or high ability level), the incentive is independent of any kind of performance or other variable factor. Incentive schemes which are dependent on performance, in general, need to be incentive compatible and individual rational. Nevertheless, the agent might lie in both cases of compensation payment. Thus, the contracts should prevent the agent from hiding his true type. Incentive schemes can have fixed components as well as variable elements dependent on the output, profit, market share, and may either cover money rewards and punishment or even property rights (management buy-outs), promotion, royalties, salary increments.

A refinement of contracts and a method of taking into consideration the ex ante judgment of the agent's ability can be applied by offering incentives dependent on experience level. Another type of linear contract can be found in connection with royalties and fixed payments. The principal offers a high fixed payment plus a low royalty depending on the output or performance for the low ability agent and vice versa.

The agent has to give a revelation about his type by choosing a contract. Since it is possible to lie about the skills, the contracts have to be designed that they fulfill participation and incentive compatibility constraint such that it is difficult to accept a contract which is not appropriate for his type.

The sequence of events considers the hidden information of the agent and the offered contracts with respect to the evolved complexity. Given the particular situation of an IJV, in which both parents offer contracts, we have two schemes in an independent or co-operative setting. For reasons of simplicity, we only look at the contracts of each principal individually, since the parent firm offers a contract according to the signal he gets. Therefore, both parents should develop their critical values with respect to their needs.

The relationship between the local principal and his own agent can be based on a reward system, which aims at promotion after the successful return or termination of the IJV. Similarly, the foreign principal could offer his agent promotion.

7
Endgames – Termination Scenarios in the Last Stage of an IJV Life Cycle

Introduction

Suppose the situation of a three-player IJV-model (i = foreign firm, local firm and IJV), the impact of their different utility functions (u_i = u_{For}, u_{Loc}, u_{IJV}) on the management and the efforts of the IJV board of directors may lead to success or failure of the business endeavor. The actions (c_i = c_{For}, c_{Loc} and c_{IJV}) chosen to contribute to the success or failure of the IJV have to be considered too. Different strategic behavior occurs in the long run of an IJV. Developing a reputation over the special stages and considering learning of the players, the co-operative aspect of the joint enterprise in the beginning of the endgame scenario has to be taken as a prerequisite of the game. Apart from focusing on the several reasons, which may lead to the difficulties in managing the joint venture, the abstraction of the problem might provide solution concepts.

IJV termination scenarios

In Ott (2000b) an IJV was considered as a repeated game, the problem of the endgame occurs after several periods of co-operation and the game turns into another state. The termination of an IJV might be planned or unplanned. For this reason, the players may have a different time-horizon in choosing their actions. The liquidation of a joint venture can be on the one hand intended or on the other hand arise by the incompatibility of the partners during the duration of the IJV. Both termination possibilities could be designed in the contracting stage. Since the duration of the IJV contract (short-term and long-term) has an impact on the behavior of the players to co-operate and/or to cheat, the reputation of the players and their ability to learn has to be taken into consideration, too.

To look at the four major scenarios with the possible actions taken, we can distinguish between unplanned/friendly, unplanned/unfriendly, planned/friendly and planned/unfriendly termination of the IJV.

Unplanned terminations indicate an infinite horizon game from the first period perspective. The intention to end the joint enterprise was not considered in the game. Furthermore, the outcome may have a friendly or an unfriendly component which means that there are some hints about the behavior during the life cycle such as 'co-operating', cheating and shirking. We can assume that the unplanned and friendly termination is connected with learning of the players involved and the development into another state of business co-operation. The unplanned and unfriendly termination might occur in a situation of cheating during the various stages of the life cycle and the desire to exit because of an unbearable situation. There are two other scenarios which should be considered, the planned and friendly termination can be seen as the antipode of the last mentioned case (unplanned, unfriendly) in which all players know that the IJV is only founded for an ex ante specified period of time in order to gain knowledge, market access or avoid market entry risks. Secondly, the scenario of a planned but unfriendly termination may occur because of internal difficulties, a change of the player's goals and detected embezzling of a player.

Adding the actions in connection with the endgame to the four general scenarios will give the situation another two moves and for this reason eight termination possibilities have to be taken into account.

1) Unplanned friendly termination – co-operation in the last stage: both parents learned during the IJV's life cycle and decided to terminate their business endeavor due to reaching their objectives.

2) Unplanned friendly termination – cheating in the last stage: both parents have learned during the life cycle, the agent was cheating in the last stage and the termination of the IJV was decided.

3) Unplanned unfriendly termination – co-operation in the last stage: take-over of the IJV from the local partner being derived from host country regulations.

4) Unplanned unfriendly termination – cheating in the last stage: because of embezzling of the players the IJV was terminated, cheating was cause of break-up.

5) Planned friendly termination – co-operation in the last stage: the intention of the IJV was that both parents learn from each other, the IJV was successful and all players dissolve the enterprise.

6) Planned friendly termination – cheating in the last stage: the intention of creating the IJV was to gain knowledge and market access, in the meantime the parents knew that there was an endgame problem. According to game theoretical reasoning, the players cheat in the all stages of the game and thus have to cheat in the first periods, too.

7) Planned unfriendly termination – co-operation in the last stage: the termination is part of the IJV life cycle, the players anticipate the liquidation and co-operate to reach the set target, although the external players interfere and create a hostile environment between the parents and the IJV players.

8) Planned unfriendly termination – cheating in the last stage: since the termination was planned the players created a last mover game, in which they tried to get out the best outcomes for their own enterprises. Their self-interest was more important than co-operation.

Under the assumption that endgame scenarios could be categorized into the above-mentioned eight cases, the common agency situation of the previous chapter will be applied to these termination possibilities. Since the two principals and the agents have to deal with re-negotiation and reputation, the moral hazard problem can be enlarged to a dynamic common agency model. Figure 7.2 shows the timing of a common agency model considering cheating and co-operation of all players.

In order to develop an IJV endgame the different ways of termination have to be seen as outcome of the divorce scenario. Whether the players have to consider the takeover by one player, the bearing of losses, the sharing of the liquidation output or other pay-offs will depend on the outcome of the termination. The bargaining power of the players influence furthermore the acceptance and rejection of the contracts or incentive schemes of the IJV.

Having shown the different cases of termination, the next step is to specify the players and their actions in this setting in order to get the equilibrium and outcome of the underlying games. Since there are at least three players involved, a triangle symbolizing the local and the foreign firm and the IJV management connects the actions of the players and their behavior. The core problem reflects the agent's (IJV

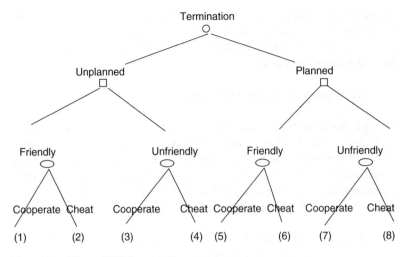

Figure 7.1 Ways of IJV Termination
Source: Ott (2000b)

management) possibility to either have hidden information about his ability in connection with the inherent potential of the endeavor or to pursue hidden actions in order to shirk and work for his own benefits. Since the parents have an interest in the truth-telling of the agent, they want to provide him with incentive schemes which may result in reporting the actual type as a dominant strategy.

Repeated games – repeated moral hazard

Players

Assume the two principals or parent firms from two different countries P_{Loc} and foreign player P_{For} continue their business project. Their agent A_{IJV} has special knowledge about the cost structure and other managerial details in the IJV itself. The problem of asymmetric information between the parents and the IJV arises. There should be an incentive scheme in order to reveal the hidden information. The principals need to get a report function from the management of the IJV and should know more about the efforts of the board.

The number of players as a formal element is $N = 3$ and the set of players consists of three elements $N = \{P_{Loc}, P_{For}, A_{IJV}\}$.

The three-player situation of a moral hazard problem in an IJV leads to the development of the information structure concerning the players. Assuming that the agent has more information about the actual management process, the type of the joint venture contains the effort level of the management board in a simple case. Both parents are interested in extracting a high level of effort concerning issues of management or technology.

$$T_{IJV} = \{\text{high effort; low effort}\} \text{ or } \{t_{IJVh}; t_{IJVl}\}$$

Having specified the agent as a combination of representatives of both parents, the mechanism design has to deal with the scenario of joint efforts but as well as with the coalitions of technology and marketing which leads to a double or even a triple moral hazard situation. For the cases of the complex managerial scenarios of multiple moral hazard scenarios, the types of the players have the following elements:

$T_{foreign}$ = {high effort in production process; low effort in production process} or $\{t_{fh}; t_{fl}\}$

T_{local} = {high effort of marketing personnel; low effort of marketing personnel} or $\{t_{lh}; t_{ll}\}$

The following table uses the typology of the previous chapter and the application of moral hazard problems to IJVs. In an independent IJV, the moral hazard problem has an impact on the parents' returns and the selling-the-store contract could endanger the IJV per se. Though the agent has a lower incentive to cheat since he is the residual claimant of the contract. In a repeated moral hazard scenario, it is assumed that the players will cheat in the last stage of the game and therefore it would not pay-off to co-operate throughout the life cycle. The incentives created need to prevent the players to cheat all along.

In a shared IJV, the joint management could be jeopardized by the possibility that one player induces a lower effort in the joint endeavor (production process, marketing process, distribution or R&D unit). The games can be that one player has a lower effort with regards to the production process or to the sale of the product. Another possibility could be that the effort could be lower with regards to the own contribution, whereas the agent has the intention to learn from the other partner and puts a lot of the effort into learning. There could be intentional embezzling and shirking from local and foreign agents as well as deliberate cheating such as sabotage. In a joint management scenario, a low effort to perform (in technology, production, marketing and local knowledge contributions) could as well harm the IJV. If the players in an IJV are contracting over a longer period, it is likely that cheating is the dominant strategy.

Furthermore, dominant IJVs have to deal with cheating of the local partner which could be that local corruption payments and bribe have an impact on the outcome of the IJV. The players could induce a low effort in production and R&D input. Shirking, embezzling and sabotage are also issues in this strategic archetype. The repeated moral hazard problem shows that over a period of time the players in an IJV have an incentive to cheat, since they are supposed to cheat in the last period.

In general, the repeated moral hazard problem can occur in terms of material and skills. Cheating will be considered in an IJV as having an influence on the success and failure of the joint enterprise. If the principals and agent in an IJV are considering short- and long-term contracts, then the possibility to cheat throughout the life cycle could be reduced.

Table 7.1 Repeated Moral Hazard – Efforts of Players in IJVs

	Independent IJV	Shared IJV	Dominant IJV
Research Lab	Effort of the players could be lower, since the intention to learn is an objective	Cheating (embezzling, sabotage, learning of competitors skills, shirking)	R&D effort low, local corruption payments, bribe, shirking, sabotage
Research Lab + Production Unit + Marketing in both countries separately	Cheating on low quality of contribution (production facilities, and technology)	Cheating (embezzling and shirking, possibility of sabotage)	Corruption, low effort in production and R&D, embezzling, shirking, sabotage
Research Lab + separate Production Unit + Marketing separate and joint	Cheating – embezzling, sabotage, low effort due to learning	Cheating (embezzling, shirking, sabotage, low effort of performance)	Corruption, embezzling, shirking, sabotage
Research Lab + separate Production Units + joint Distribution	Embezzling and shirking (material and skills)	Cheating (embezzling, shirking, sabotage, low effort of performance)	Corruption, embezzling, shirking, sabotage
Research Lab + Production Unit + Marketing joint	Embezzling and shirking (material and skills)	Cheating (embezzling, shirking, sabotage, low effort of performance)	Corruption, embezzling, shirking, sabotage

166 International Joint Ventures

Actions

Consider now the three-player situation of the above-mentioned cases, the two principals can choose their actions by offering a contract or incentive scheme to the agent independently. Since the principals contribute complementary skills to the joint venture, the agent gets two different contracts depending on each parent's contribution, interest and objectives. The agent may either accept or reject one of the contracts or both. Accepting both contracts may lead further to reveal either his type truthfully or lie.

In the first stage of the game, the local principal P_{Loc} chooses his set of action C_{Loc} which is offering a menue of contracts to get the agent's real type and to prevent him from embezzling. The foreign principal P_{For} chooses his set of action C_{For} which is offering a range of contracts like the local principal. The incentives offered by both parents depend on the type of joint venture, the contributions to the joint venture and the strategic role of the players. The second step of the game is that the agent A_{IJV} may choose his action set C_{IJV} which is either accept both contracts, accept the contract of the local parent and reject the contract of the foreign parent, vice versa or reject both contracts which may result in re-negotiation or break-up of the joint venture. The third stage contains the agent's effort which can be either low or high given his knowledge about the potential of the area, the joint venture itself or the production process. Since the agent knows the real state of the nature, he may either put a high or a low effort into the business and shirk in order to benefit from the enterprise.

The analysis of finite games in extensive form: each player's objective is to maximize the expected value of a utility pay-off that he gets at the end of the game. For repeated games, to allow an infinite time-horizon, this assumption must be dropped, and instead players get pay-offs at each round of the game. The pay-off outcome to a player is an infinite sequence of pay-offs. At each round k, each player recalls all the signals that he has got in rounds 1 through k. Assuring that he recalls his own past moves, it is sufficient to let one component of his signal in each round equal his own move from the preceding round. The set of all pure strategies C_i for player i in the general game is C_{Loc}, C_{For} and C_{IJV}.

The set of behavioral strategies B_i for player i is similarly. The IJV game is based on the common agency game of the previous chapter and uses the strategy sets of players.

Signals

The possibility of re-negotiation of contracts and the reputation of the players gained during the first stage leads to the repeated game and the need of signals to update the information each round of the game.

The signal in the common agency game can be the effort or the report of the agent. Since the agents have the possibility to create coalitions, their behavior during the management process will lead to co-operation and shirking towards the principals.

$S_{foreign}$ = {high effort in production process; low effort in production process} or $\{s_{fh}; s_{fl}\}$

S_{local} = {high effort of marketing personnel; low effort of marketing personnel} or $\{s_{lh}; s_{ll}\}$

S_{IJV} = {high effort of management board; low effort of management board} or $\{s_{IJVh}; s_{IJVl}\}$

Let Θ be a nonempty set of possible states of nature, and let the nonempty sets of Di and Si denote the set of moves that i can choose and the set of signals that i can receive, at each round of the game. Given these sets, the initial distribution q in $\Delta (S \times \Theta)$ and a transition function in p: $D \times \Theta \to \Delta (S \times \Theta)$ can be specified.

Pay-offs

Given these sets, we must specify an initial distribution q in $\Delta (S \times \Theta)$, a transition function p: $D \times \Theta \to \Delta (S \times \Theta)$ and for every player i a pay-off function u_i: $D \times \Theta \to R$. In the case of the repeated IJV game, the pay-off function of the players can be denoted as u_{local} (d, θ), $u_{foreign}$ (d, θ) and u_{IJV} (d, θ), since they are dependent on the moves and the state of nature.

The following table shows the pay-offs for the local and foreign parent, u_{Loc} and u_{For}, and the IJV itself, u_{IJV}. The pay-offs reflect the timing of the games and the strategic choices of the players. Since there is uncertainty about the quality of the contribution, the types t are considered to be important for the sub-games played in the IJV. The principals' pay-offs comprise their value functions V which are dependent on the output of the IJV, of the local agent or of the foreign agent, q_{IJV}, q_{Loc} or q_{For} and the type of the players t, particularly of the agent t_{IJV} and the incentives paid to the agent I_{Loc} and I_{For}. The agent's pay-offs are dependent on sales R, costs C and profits π and the incentives I paid by or to the parents (I_{Loc} and I_{For}).

The independent IJV shows a particular case of offering incentives. Since both parents intend to be independent of the operations of the

Table 7.2 Repeated Moral Hazard – Pay-offs/Contracts

	Independent IJV	Shared IJV $\alpha \in [0, 1]$	Dominant IJV
Research Lab	$u_{Loc} = \pi_{Loc}(e_{Loc}) + I_{Loc}$ $u_{For} = \pi_{For}(e_{For}) + I_{For}$ $u_{IJV} = \pi(e_{IJV}) - I_{Loc} - I_{For}$	$u_{Loc} = V(q_{IJV}(e)) - \alpha I(q_{IJV}(e))$ $u_{For} = V(q_{IJV}(e)) - (1 - \alpha)I(q_{IJV}(e))$ $u_{IJV} = I(q_{IJV}(e)) - C(q_{IJV}(e))$	$u_{Loc} = \pi(q_{IJV}(e)) - I(q_{IJV}(e))$ $u_{For} = \pi(q_{IJV}(e)) - I_{For}$ $u_{IJV} = I_{Loc}(q_{IJV}(e)) + I_{For} - C(q_{IJV}, t)$
Research Lab + Production Unit + Marketing in both countries separately	$u_{Loc} = R(q_{Loc}(e)) - C(q_{Loc}(e)) + I_{Loc}$ $u_{For} = R(q_{Loc}(e)) - C(q_{For}(e)) + I_{For}$ $u_{IJV} = \pi(q_{IJV}) - I_{Loc} - I_{For}$	$u_{Loc} = V(q_{IJV}(e)) - \alpha I(q_{IJV}(e))$ $u_{For} = V(q_{IJV}(e)) - (1 - \alpha)I(q_{IJV}(e))$ $u_{IJV} = I(q_{IJV}(e)) - C(q_{IJV}(e))$ or $u_{Loc} = R(q_{Loc}(e_{Loc})) - \alpha I(q_{Loc}(e_{Loc}))$ $u_{For} = R(q_{For}(e_{For})) - \alpha I(q_{For}(e_{For}))$ $u_{IJV} = I(q_{Loc}) + I(q_{For}) - C(q_{Loc}(e_{Loc}) + q_{For}(e_{For}))$	$u_{Loc} = \pi(q_{IJV}(e)) - I(q_{IJV}(e))$ $u_{For} = \pi(q_{IJV}(e)) - I_{For}$ $u_{IJV} = I_{Loc}(q_{IJV}(e)) + I_{For} + R(q_{Loc}(e), q_{For}) - C(q_{IJV}(e))$

Table 7.2 Repeated Moral Hazard – Pay-offs/Contracts – *continued*

	Independent IJV	Shared IJV $\alpha \in [0, 1]$	Dominant IJV
Research Lab + separate Production Unit + Marketing separate and joint	$u_{Loc} = R(q_{Loc}(e)) - C(q_{Loc}(e)) + I_{Loc}$ $u_{For} = R(q_{Ror}(e)) - C(q_{For}(e)) + I_{For}$ $u_{IJV} = R(q_{IIV}) - C(q_{IIV}) - I_{Loc} - I_{For}$	$u_{Loc} = V(q_{IJV}(e)) - \alpha I(q_{IJV}(e))$ $u_{For} = V(q_{IJV}(e)) - (1-\alpha)I(q_{IJV}(e))$ $u_{IJV} = I(q_{IJV}(e)) - C(q_{IJV}(e))$ or $u_{Loc} = R(q_{Loc}(e_{Loc})) - C(q_{Loc}(e_{Loc})) - \alpha I(q_{Loc}(e_{Loc}))$ $u_{For} = R(q_{For}(e_{For})) - C(q_{For}(e_{For})) - \alpha I(q_{For}(e_{For}))$ $u_{IJV} = I(q_{Loc}) + I(q_{For}) - C(q_{Loc}(e_{Loc})), q_{For}(e_{For})$	$u_{Loc} = \pi(q_{IJV}(e)) - I(q_{IJV}(e))$ $u_{For} = \pi(q_{IJV}(e)) - I_{For}$ $u_{IJV} = I_{Loc}(q_{IJV}(e)) + I_{For} - C(q_{IJV}(e))$ or $u_{Loc} = R(q_{Loc}(e)) - C(q_{Loc}(e)) - I(q_{IJV}, t)$ $u_{For} = \pi(q_{IJV}) - I_{For}$ $u_{IJV} = R(q_{IJV}(e)) - C(q_{IJV}(e)) + I(q_{IJV}(e)) + I_{For}$
Research Lab + separate Production Units + joint Distribution	$u_{Loc} = R(q_{IJV}(e)) - C(q_{IJV}(e)) + I_{Loc}$ $u_{For} = R(q_{IJV}(e)) - C(q_{IJV}(e)) + I_{For}$ $u_{IJV} = R(q_{IIV}(e)) - C(q_{IJV}(e)) - I_{Loc} - I_{For}$	$u_{Loc} = V(q_{IJV}(e)) - \alpha I(q_{IJV}(e))$ $u_{For} = V(q_{IJV}(e)) - (1-\alpha)I(q_{IJV}(e))$ $u_{IJV} = R(q_{IJV}(e)) - C(q_{IJV}(e)) + I(q_{IJV}(e))$	$u_{Loc} = \pi(q_{IJV}(e)) - I(q_{IJV}(e))$ $u_{For} = \pi(q_{IJV}(e)) - I_{For}$ $u_{IJV} = I_{Loc}(q_{IJV}(e)) + I_{For} - C(q_{IJV}(e))$ or

Table 7.2 Repeated Moral Hazard – Pay-offs/Contracts – *continued*

	Independent IJV	Shared IJV $\alpha \in [0, 1]$	Dominant IJV
Research Lab + Production Unit + Marketing joint	$u_{Loc} = \pi(q_{IJV}(e)) + I_{Loc}$ $u_{For} = \pi(q_{IJV}(e)) + I_{For}$ $u_{IJV} = \pi(q_{IJV}(e)) - I_{Loc} - I_{For}$	$u_{Loc} = V(q_{IJV}(e)) - \alpha I(q_{IJV}(e))$ $u_{For} = V(q_{IJV}(e)) - (1-\alpha)I(q_{IJV}(e))$ $u_{IJV} = R(q_{IJV}(e)) - C(q_{IJV}(e)) + I(q_{IJV}(e))$	$u_{Loc} = R(q_{IJV}(e)) - C(q_{Loc}(e)) - I(q_{IJV}, t)$ $u_{For} = R(q_{IJV}(e)) - C(q_{For}(e)) - I_{For}$ $u_{IJV} = \pi(q_{IJV}(e)) + I_{Loc} + I_{For}$ $u_{Loc} = \pi(q_{IJV}(e)) - I(q_{IJV}(e))$ $u_{For} = \pi(q_{IJV}(e)) - I_{For}$ $u_{IJV} = I_{Loc}(q_{IJV}(e)) + I_{For} - C(q_{IJV}(e))$

IJV, the selling-the-store contract could be an option for contractual arrangements. This type of contracts is for risk-neutral players. The agent IJV pays the parents incentives I_{Loc} and I_{For} and is the residual claimant of the IJV's performance. Thus, the parents receive flat fees which are a kind of returns (though ex ante paid) and the agent is fully responsible for the IJV and can claim the profits of the enterprise.

The shared IJV shows the pay-offs for the players which are dependent on their shared contributions and the shared incentives for the IJV. The configurations of the IJVs are considered in the output/performance of the players. The contracts offered are linear contract which are sensitive to performance in the IJV.

Finally, the dominant IJV is distinguishing between the incentives from the local parent to the IJV and from the foreign parent to the IJV. The first-mentioned uses a linear contract, whereas the latter uses a flat fee contract.

Timing

During several stages the players might have developed a reputation that they co-operate or cheat.

Considering repeated games in a three-player setting, there are three managers of the local, and foreign firms as well as the IJV itself in a strategic configuration. Thus, the uninformed players are the managers of the parent firm or the principals. The agent (manager of the IJV) knows about the private values in the management. Private information can be based on knowledge about the costs of operations, cultural composition and ability to co-operate, as well as performance and profits of the IJV. The principals want to induce the agent to reveal his type in the changing world of IJV transactions and interactions. The contracts in an IJV are relevant with respect to a dynamic setting of contracts offered.

Order of the play

(1) Nature chooses the ability of the agent to be high or low.
(2) Local parent offers a contract to the agent.
(3) Foreign parent offers a contract to the agent.
(4) The IJV management or agent either accepts both or one of them or rejects both.
(5) The agent reports his type to the local principal.
(6) The agent reports his type to the foreign principal.
(7) The game returns to (2) and repeats.

During several stages the players might have developed a reputation that they co-operate or cheat.

Considering planned and unplanned termination scenarios in terms of repeated games, the parents could offer either a long-term contract or a series of short-term contracts. Given the timing of the game we might take into account several rounds in both cases, which will lead to re-negotiation and reputational effects.

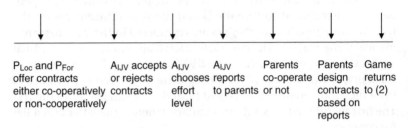

| P_{Loc} and P_{For} offer contracts either co-operatively or non-cooperatively | A_{IJV} accepts or rejects contracts | A_{IJV} chooses effort level | A_{IJV} reports to parents | Parents co-operate or not | Parents design contracts based on reports | Game returns to (2) |

Figure 7.2   The Timing of the Repeated Game (Moral Hazard)

A crucial stage in this timing is stage 5, which implies that the parents could either continue to co-operate, start to co-operate, continue to offer different incentive schemes (non-cooperatively) or even break-up based on the agents report. This involves the agent either co-operating or cheating with respect to the parents' firms and their objectives.

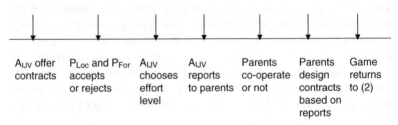

| A_{IJV} offer contracts | P_{Loc} and P_{For} accepts or rejects | A_{IJV} chooses effort level | A_{IJV} reports to parents | Parents co-operate or not | Parents design contracts based on reports | Game returns to (2) |

Figure 7.3   Repeated Moral Hazard-Timing – Independent IJV

As in the moral hazard case, the agent makes the first move in the Independent IJV and offers a contract to each parent. In the repeated moral hazard case, the parents can co-operate or not in the final stages of the IJV. Thus, there is still an opportunity for the parents to offer contracts in the later stages of an IJV. Finally, the repeated moral hazard has a stage in which the game returns to the first stage.

The timing of the shared management IJV starts with the principals offering contracts to the IJV. They can be jointly or independently

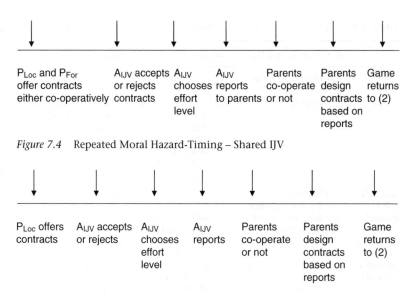

Figure 7.4 Repeated Moral Hazard-Timing – Shared IJV

Figure 7.5 Repeated Moral Hazard-Timing – Dominant IJV

offered. The contracts are dependent on the reports of the agent are designed on the basis of the reports. In stage 7 the game returns to the first stage. Finally, the timing of the dominant parent IJV starts with the local principal offering contracts. The rest of the stages is similar to the shared management IJV.

The relevant timings for the various combinations of units in these strategic archetypes are shown below. It is a way of showing the possible games being played in IJVs with different strategic and control structures as well as functional combinations. The outcome of the games lies in the combination of the timing and the pay-offs.

Table 7.3 Repeated Moral Hazard – Games (Order of the Plays)

	Independent IJV	Shared IJV	Dominant IJV
Research Lab	*Order of play:* a) P_{Loc} and P_{For} offer contracts I_{Loc} and I_{For} b) A_{IJV} accepts or rejects c) A_{IJV} induces efforts (R&D, local, learning) d) Parents co-operate or not	*Order of play:* a) P_{Loc} and P_{For} offer joint contract $I_{IJV,}$ or I_{Loc} and I_{For} b) A_{IJV} accepts or rejects $I_{IJV,}$ or I_{Loc} and I_{For} c) A_{IJV} induces efforts (R&D, local, learning)	*Order of play:* a) P_{Loc} offers contracts I_{Loc} b) A_{IJV} accepts or rejects c) A_{IJV} induces efforts (R&D, local , contribution learning, bribe) d) A_{IJV} reports to parents

Table 7.3 Repeated Moral Hazard – Games (Order of the Plays) – *continued*

	Independent IJV	Shared IJV	Dominant IJV
	e) Game returns to first stage parents	d) A_{IJV} reports to based on reports e) Parents co-operate or not f) Principals contracts based on reports g) Game returns to first stage	e) Parents co-operate or not f) Principals contracts g) Game returns to first stage
Research Lab + Production Unit + Marketing in both countries separately	*Order of play:* a) P_{Loc} and P_{For} offer contracts I_{Loc} and I_{For} b) A_{IJV} accepts or rejects c) A_{IJV} induces efforts (R&D/production contribution) d) Nature chooses success or failure e) Parents co-operate or not f) Game returns to first stage	*Order of play:* a) P_{Loc} and P_{For} offer joint contract $I_{IJV,}$ or I_{Loc} and I_{For} b) A_{IJV} accepts or rejects $I_{IJV,}$ or I_{Loc} and I_{For} c) A_{IJV} induces efforts (R&D/production contribution) d) A_{IJV} reports to parents e) Parents co-operate or not f) Principals contracts based on reports g) Game returns to first stage	*Order of play:* a) P_{Loc} offers contracts I_{Loc} b) A_{IJV} accepts or rejects c) A_{IJV} induces efforts (R&D/production contribution) d) A_{IJV} reports to parents e) Parents co-operate or not f) Principals contracts based on reports g) Game returns to first stage
Research Lab + separate Production Unit + Marketing separate and joint	*Order of play:* a) P_{Loc} and P_{For} offer contracts I_{Loc} and I_{For} b) A_{IJV} accepts or rejects c) A_{IJV} induces efforts (R&D, marketing contributions) d) Nature chooses success or failure e) Parents co-operate or not f) Game returns to first stage	*Order of play:* a) P_{Loc} and P_{For} offer joint contract $I_{IJV,}$ or I_{Loc} and I_{For} b) A_{IJV} accepts or rejects $I_{IJV,}$ or I_{Loc} and I_{For} c) A_{IJV} induces efforts (R&D, marketing contributions) d) A_{IJV} reports to parents e) Parents co-operate or not f) Principals contracts based on reports g) Game returns to first stage	*Order of play:* a) P_{Loc} offers contracts I_{Loc} b) A_{IJV} accepts or rejects c) A_{IJV} induces efforts (R&D, marketing contributions) d) A_{IJV} reports to parents e) Parents co-operate or not f) Principals contracts based on reports g) Game returns to first stage
Research Lab + separate Production Units + joint Distribution	*Order of play:* a) P_{Loc} and P_{For} offer contracts I_{Loc} and I_{For} b) A_{IJV} accepts or rejects	*Order of play:* a) P_{Loc} and P_{For} offer joint contract $I_{IJV,}$ or I_{Loc} and I_{For} b) A_{IJV} accepts or	*Order of play:* a) P_{Loc} offers contracts I_{Loc} b) A_{IJV} accepts or rejects c) A_{IJV} induces efforts

Table 7.3 Repeated Moral Hazard – Games (Order of the Plays) – *continued*

	Independent IJV	Shared IJV	Dominant IJV
	c) A_{IJV} induces efforts (R&D, market access, marketing) d) Nature chooses success or failure e) Parents co-operate or not f) Game returns to first stage	rejects I_{IJV}, or I_{Loc} and I_{For} c) A_{IJV} induces efforts (R&D, market access, parents marketing) d) A_{IJV} reports to parents e) Parents co-operate or not f) Principals contracts based on reports g) Game returns to first stage	(R&D, market access, local know-how, marketing) d) A_{IJV} reports to e) Parents co-operate or not f) Principals contracts based on reports g) Game returns to first stage
Research Lab + Production Unit + Marketing joint	*Order of play:* P_{Loc} and P_{For} offer contracts I_{Loc} and I_{For} A_{IJV} accepts or rejects A_{IJV} induces efforts (production, R&D, marketing, market access, local) Nature chooses success or failure Parents co-operate or not Game returns to first stage	*Order of play:* P_{Loc} and P_{For} offer joint contract I_{IJV}, or I_{Loc} and I_{For} A_{IJV} accepts or rejects I_{IJV}, or I_{Loc} and I_{For} A_{IJV} induces efforts (production, R&D, marketing, market access, local) A_{IJV} reports to parents Parents co-operate or not Principals contracts based on reports Game returns to first stage	*Order of play:* P_{Loc} offers contracts I_{Loc} A_{IJV} accepts or rejects A_{IJV} induces efforts (production, R&D, marketing, market access, local) A_{IJV} reports to parents Parents co-operate or not Principals contracts based on reports Game returns to first stage

Repeated mechanism design

In long-term relationships, the players perceive that their current behavior will have an impact on each other's future behavior. They may rationally become more co-operative (as in the getting-even equilibrium) or more aggressive, depending on the kind of linkage between present and future behavior (Myerson, 1991, p. 332).

Many real life situations consider individuals' beliefs about each other as being derived from long past experience interacting with each other. Concerning the information structure, there might be some things about himself that a player tends to reveal to others who are involved in long-term relationships with him, and other things that he tends to conceal. In general, a player would try to let others know about his strengths, but would try to maintain uncertainty about his weaknesses. The study of repeated games with incomplete information provides a framework of formalizing and studying hypotheses like this.

A general conceptual structure that can include models of repeated games as special cases is provided by the following game (Mertens, Sorin and Zamir, 1994)

$$\Gamma^r = (N, \Theta, ((D_i, S_i, u_i)_{i \in N}, q, p) \tag{1}$$

Let N be the nonempty set of players and Θ be a nonempty set denoting the set of possible states of nature. For each i in N, let the nonempty sets D_i and S_i denote respectively the set of moves that i can choose and the signals that player i may receive, at each round of the game. Given these sets, we must specify an initial distribution q in $\Delta (S \times \Theta)$, a transition function p: $D \times \Theta \rightarrow \Delta (S \times \Theta)$ and for every player i a pay-off function u_i: $D \times \Theta \rightarrow \mathbf{R}$.

The interpretation of the above-mentioned concept is as follows: the game is played in an infinite sequence of rounds. At each round, some state in Θ is the current state of nature. Each player i's new information about the state of nature is summarized by a signal in Si that he receives at the beginning of the round. As a function of the signals that he has received in the current round and all previous rounds, each player must choose a move in D_i. The probability that θ^1 is the state of nature in the first round and that each player i receives the signal s_i^1 at the beginning of the first round is q (s^1, θ^1). At any round k, if the current state of nature is q^k and the moves of the players are $d^k = (d_i^k)_{i \in N}$ in D, then u_i (d^k, θ^k) is the round-k pay-off to each player, and p $(s^{k+1}, \theta^{k+1} \mid d^k, \theta^k)$ is the conditional probability that the signals and the state of nature at round k+1 will be (s^{k+1}, θ^{k+1}).

Given the common agency moral hazard setting, the players in an IJV have the possibility to co-operate and to cheat during the management process. The incentives offered by the two principals (P_{local} and $P_{foreign}$) should have lead to truth-telling as a dominant strategy. Since many IJVs fail in the course of time or have a limited time-horizon per se, the question is whether the implicit free-rider situation might have the implication that the players act for their own benefit and embezzling occurs in an IJV enterprise. The assumption of a dynamic moral-hazard model, that the involved parties develop a different behavior during the life cycle of an IJV, has to focus on a re-negotiation of incentives and an updating of the beliefs on the basis of the experiences gained while managing the IJV.

The underlying model of a repeated game with the refinement of a common agency moral-hazard problem should lead to the development of different termination scenarios due to the various options in an IJV management process.

Intertemporal common agency

In a mechanism design problem of common agency for IJVs, we have to consider that this particular problem arises when there are contract complements, which is when an increase in activity for principal I raises the marginal utility of contracting with principal j. This occurs when the agent's technology possesses economies of scope or if there are other kinds of positive externalities in production and consumption (Olsen and Torsvik, 1995). In the special case of IJVs contract complements arise when putting together complementary resources such as marketing and technology. Regarding the strategic configurations of an IJV several options may be applied.

The intertemporal problem looks at decentralizing provision of incentives and mitigation of the ratchet effect. The ratchet effect occurs when the agent realizes that any information revealed about his productivity at the first stage, will be exploited by the principals in the future. Olsen and Torsvik (1995) consider this in incomplete contract situations in the sense that full long-term commitments are infeasible.

Given that contracts will be offered repeatedly, Olsen and Torsvik (1995) argued that in their case it may be better to operate non-cooperatively rather than co-operatively.

Planned termination

Planned termination occurs in IJVs in several well-known settings especially for projects, which have a time limit due to host country legal implications. Furthermore, the competitive side of two rivals matching up in a joint venture to introduce a new product or production process in order to access new markets triggered in some cases a planned time-horizon. Thus, we have to consider friendly and unfriendly termination for the case of planned termination. The two models dealing with this are two dynamic signaling models in a long-term relationship. Therefore, reputation will be important.

Friendly (co-operation, cheating)

Planned friendly termination – *Co-operation*: the IJV was set up to create a learning process for both parents. Since the target was reached and the IJV was successful, all players dissolve the enterprise. The agent was contributing to the success of the IJV by co-operation.

Planned friendly termination – *Cheating*: Host government regulations or regulations from antitrust bodies limited the duration of the IJV to a specified period of time. Gaining technological knowledge and market access were major reasons for the set-up of the IJV. Anticipating the end of the game, the agent might have an interest to cheat in the last stage of the game. According to game theoretical reasoning (backward induction), the players may cheat in the last stage of the game and thus have to cheat in the first periods, too (see theoretical section).

Unfriendly (co-operation, cheating)

Planned unfriendly termination – *Co-operation*: Like above, the IJV was limited to a certain period of time either to learn or because of regulations, the unfriendly scenario occurs because of the substantial learning process of only one parent or the interference of an external player. Thus, the termination is part of the IJV life cycle, the agent co-operates to reach the set target, although the external players (host country, antitrust bodies) interfere and create a hostile environment between the parents and the IJV players.

Planned unfriendly termination – *Cheating*: Since the termination was planned the players created a last mover game, all players tried to free-ride on the other's expertise. Their self-interest was more important than co-operation. The reputation developed during the life cycle was not in favor of the players.

Unplanned termination

Under the assumption that unplanned termination could be dealt with by focusing on a series of short-term contracts, the following problems of friendly and unfriendly termination with their implications on cheating and co-operating might be tackled in two models of dynamic double moral hazard. The incentive schemes are offered in a sequence and regarded as short-term. In this case re-negotiation matters.

Friendly (co-operation, cheating)

Unplanned friendly termination – *Co-operation*: both parents have learned the skills which they need for their own enterprises and decided to terminate their business endeavor due to reaching their objectives. The agent has co-operated and reported his true type to the parents. The successful joint venture was derived from the co-operative behavior of all players involved.

Unplanned friendly termination – *Cheating*: both parents have learned during the life cycle, the agent (IJV management) was cheating (embezzling, shirking) in the last stage and the termination of the IJV was decided.

Unfriendly (co-operation, cheating)

Unplanned unfriendly termination – *Co-operation*: take-over of the IJV from the local partner being derived from host country regulations, the substantial learning of one parent and the devaluation of the other's expertise or the acquisition of an outsider were reasons of an unfriendly termination between the parents. The agent was co-operating during the life-cycle.

Unplanned unfriendly termination – *Cheating*: See the parent's behavior in 3) and the agent's actions were determined by cheating. The agent could have embezzled or shirked due to anticipating the other players' moves in the last stage.

This chapter studied the applicability of repeated games to the termination scenarios in an IJV. As far as the mechanism of a common agency situation is concerned, there exists a combination of a multi-principal agent model with repetition in a contracting game. This means that there are a variety of options to offer incentives in IJVs on the basis of a common agency game.

The application of formal repeated game models to the problems in IJVs could be developed on the basis of short-term and long-term perspectives which are again related to the unplanned and planned termination scenarios. It could be shown that in an IJV it is important to anticipate re-negotiation of contracts in the various stages in order to get revelation about the private information of the agent (IJV management). Appropriate incentives can be based on performance, profits and factors which are detrimental to the nature of the IJV. Thus, the choice between short-term and long-term contracts is dependent on the ex ante perspective of the players and their perceived objectives of the IJV. In case of a planned time-horizon, the players will fix an agreement for the duration with the option to re-negotiate. However, the sequence of short-term contracts and the unplanned termination option might be useful in order to update information gained, reputation and even co-operation between the principals.

Thus, the conclusion of this chapter offers the possibility to develop a new type of endgame problem for the IJV common agency case and its application to real-life scenarios as a supergame of re-negotiation of incentive schemes in IJVs.

8
Conclusion

Theoretical contributions

Introduction

The research monograph has dealt with an important theoretical application to International joint ventures. The subtitle of the book 'an interplay of co-operative and non-cooperative games under incomplete information' was chosen to indicate the nature of IJV's and the difficulties due to the hybrid structure. The introduction of the monograph showed in a sequential manner the development of game theory and its applicability to the IJV problem. In the same way, it was important to show the theoretical concepts of game theory and its application in information economics, contract theory, principal-agent theory and common agency theory. Otherwise, it will always be linked to Prisoner's Dilemma which is only a facet of the power the theoretical tool game theory offers. Thus, it is important to point out that we have game theoretical reasoning in the above-mentioned theoretical concepts in economic theory and the various directions of economics. Particular for management and international business, the robust theoretical models of economic theory can contribute to strengthen a discipline which would otherwise struggle with empirical work without having a firm and rigorous analytical basis to apply empirical methods.

The *co-operative and non-cooperative games* are therefore analyzed in the common agency games which are like the IJVs a hybrid between non-cooperative and co-operative game theory. The two parents are considered as two principals and the joint management is the agent. The games between these players can be non-cooperative and co-operative.

Since IJVs have several problems of uncertainties over their life cycle to tackle, this monograph focused on the various stages with *incomplete information* issues. This led to the focus on information economics with adverse selection, moral hazard and signaling as well as finally the repeated moral hazard solution concepts. The structure of the book used these concepts and showed the static and dynamic nature of incomplete information problems in IJVs.

On the other hand, there are the IJVs and their theoretical literature. The positioning as hybrid was always an important feature in this stream of literature. The strategic and control structure of three archetypes was used to show the relationship between the parents and the IJV management. It can be distinguished into shared management, dominant parent and independent IJVs. This structure fitted nicely together with the general common agency structure on an abstract information economics and contract-theory level. To use the useful economic explanations of IJVs created by Buckley and Casson (1996), the IJV configurations into research units, production units, marketing and distribution units as well as their combinations were developed. This led to a focus on IJV units and the parents' contributions, skills and information asymmetries. The typology for IJVs (strategic and unit based) was used throughout the monograph. It helped to focus on the IJVs and the players' information asymmetries as well as the solution concepts.

Based on the rules of the game, each chapter was divided in sections relating to the players, the types (ability, efforts and experience), the strategies, the pay-offs and the timing of the games. This finally led to a very structured approach to disaggregate the problems faced in an IJV. It showed that the games which are played in IJVs are based on uncertainties about the other players and their strategic moves. It was important to show these strategic moves as information asymmetries and the best way to solve this was in revelations of the types and offering of contracts.

The research monograph can be seen as a very structured approach to real life IJVs and their information asymmetries. The author wanted to achieve a compact, rigorous and structured approach towards solving information problems in IJVs. It is only possible to tackle real life issues when the problem becomes clear on an abstract level.

Adverse selection

The adverse selection problem in an IJV arises because of the uncertainty about the quality of the management. Several reasons for the information asymmetry between the parents and the IJV management could exist. The monograph traces it back to the different contributions in terms of knowledge (explicit and tacit). Although the explicit knowledge, provided by the parent who contributes technology, can be easier measured or seen, it is still a source of uncertainty whether the player is willing to contribute. This is particularly important in IJVs, since the players gain by the contributions of the other player. Thus, there could be an interest to provide less of one's own expertise and free-ride on the partner's expertise.

The chapter of the adverse selection problem in IJVs is structured in the way that it continues with the overall rules of the game structure: the players, the types (uncertainty about quality of contributions – particularly knowledge), the strategies, the pay-offs and the timing of the games. Especially, the part of the uncertainties of the players about the other's type and its IJV applications to IJVs are a compact way of dealing with the difficulties in the set-up stage. Therefore, the two levels of uncertainty are shown in the type of the agent (low or high ability of IJV management). The ability in this case was the contribution of explicit or tacit knowledge which was either seen as technological and production know-how or as market or local knowledge. This was tackled in the typology of IJVs in a strategic and configurative combination. The strategic part was the choice of actions of the players which was either offering contracts for the principals or revelation of the types for the agent. The pay-offs were developed for all three players (two principals – local and foreign – and the agent). Though it was designed in a mathematical way, the logic of these functions was explained and it showed the moves of the players. The timing of the game was finally important to show how the players will play their games. The order of the play was applied to the adverse selection case and the three archetypes first and then it was transferred into the typologies.

Moral hazard

The moral hazard problem in an IJV is related to its inherent complex structure as a hybrid of at least two firms in two countries. Like in the adverse selection problem, the uncertainty about the quality of the joint enterprise leads to the development of contractual arrangements to avoid failure. In the moral hazard case, the cheating of the players after signing the contract is the crucial problem. Thus, in the first section of the chapter the possibilities of different effort levels were considered. This means that cheating in an IJV can occur in various ways, such as shirking, embezzling or even sabotage. Dependent on the parent-IJV strategic archetypes, the contracts were designed and the IJV configuration was taken into account, too.

The chapter of the moral hazard problem in IJVs deals with the players, the types of the agent, the strategies, the pay-offs and the timing of the games. As in the previous chapters, the structure of the rules of the games provides a consistent and compact approach towards the conceptualization of a complex subject. The fifteen options of IJV's strategic configurations are tackled in the effort level, the pay-off and the timing of the games sections. The starting point is the analysis of the effort level as type of the agent. The effort level could be low which implies that the agent is cheating. Several reasons for cheating might be possible, reaching from shirking and embezzling to sabotage. It is, therefore, important to point out that this possibility occurs after signing the contract. Thus, the backward induction of game theoretical reasoning should help to offer the right incentive scheme to get the revelation of the type. Low efforts induced can be source of dissatisfaction between the parents, their representatives and the IJV management as a whole. It was shown what kind of low efforts could be found in the underlying typology of IJVs. The low effort levels were possible in terms of cheating in the research, production and distribution process. The intention to learn from the other party could have led to a lower effort for its own performance and a high effort to acquire expertise from the other side. The pay-off functions show the profits, value functions and incentives for the players and what costs they have in the venture process. Furthermore, order of the play for each combination of strategic interaction helped to show the design of the games being played.

Signaling

The signaling problem in an IJV is connected to the adverse selection problem, yet it deals with a dynamic approach. The quality of the IJV management is again the important focus of this part. In case of the lemon problem, it was the uncertainty about the quality of the IJV management in terms of knowledge provided. In a signaling scenario, the agent can send a signal to the principal(s). The principals can use this signal to design appropriate contracts. Thus, the signal must be easy to measure, otherwise it will be difficult to offer incentive schemes. In an IJV, there are several ways to look at the signaling problem of the management. Under the assumption that the quality of an IJV management is determined by the experience of the representatives of the parents which make up the joint enterprise. It is useful to develop signals based on experience. The chapter, therefore, starts with the experience level in the various IJV types (strategic archetypes in combination with IJV configurations). The analysis showed that it will be difficult to have a totally inexperienced IJV team, nevertheless both parents could send someone with less experience and someone with more experience. Thus, the typology used three different combinations of experience levels to show the quality of the IJV reaching from less to a lot of experience. Needless to mention, that the IJV could benefit from two experienced teams. The experience levels were important to be measurable and it was necessary to choose experience based on the IJV configurations (research lab, production unit, marketing and distribution units). Therefore, the experience was chosen as number/volume of research, production and sales contracts. The IJV managers should, therefore, signal to the principals their previous number/volume of (research, production, sales) contracts as a basis for their incentive schemes.

The signaling chapter continued with the overall structure and was based on the experience levels. The pay-off function of the players showed the importance of taking the signal into account by offering contracts. This dynamic mechanism helped to solve a pre-contractual uncertainty about the ability of the IJV management. Besides, the pay off functions, the timing of the games dealt with the mechanism of looking forward and reasoning backwards. This strategic approach puts the problems of uncertainty about the quality of the IJV on an abstract level which helps to prescribe an optimal way of solving the problems.

Endgames

Finally, the endgame problems in IJVs occur due to its nature as a means to enter foreign markets with clear termination date or the failure of the venture based on the inability to work together. The starting point of this chapter was embedded in the various ways IJV could terminate their operations. This means that the strategic implications of the special triangle form between the parents and the IJV management could lead to planned and unplanned termination, friendly or unfriendly termination or it could even be based on the cheating and co-operating of the agent. Eight possibilities of endgames were developed and this super-game (repeated game theory) had a moral hazard problem as source game. Since reputation and re-negotiation are part of the endgame problem, the re-negotiation of contracts was a general issue tackled in this section. Therefore, the dynamic approach of the moral hazard problem was used in this chapter. In theory, if it pays off to cheat in the last stage of the game, it should be considered all along. This determines the behavior of agents and could mean that the repeated moral hazard problem is used in an IJV setting and leads to its failure. Under this assumption, the literature on IJVs which in the majority only assumes the co-operative side of the IJV endeavors (motives, partner similarities, risk reduction etc.) can be updated by a much more dismal side to the IJVs and an explanation to its proneness to failure.

The endgame chapter picks up the dynamic perspective in the form of a repeated game of moral hazard. Besides the repeated moral hazard, this chapter focuses on the endgame scenarios for IJVs. There are eight scenarios which have the structure of planned and unplanned, friendly and unfriendly termination under cheating and co-operative behavior of the agent. Therefore, the players determine the contingencies of endgames. Though the overall cheating approach of rational agents should be regarded as one possibility, since the reputational effects in this context could lead to the loss of potential future partners. It does not mean that there will always be co-operative behavior. It only points out that in the course of the life cycle, there is not a clear cut strategic route to follow. The repetition of actions will lead to an updating of beliefs. The shirking, embezzling and sabotaging of previous periods will be taken into account. The players need to report and the parents can choose whether they want to co-operate or deviate (end the contract, cheat on the partner or take over). The pay-offs of the repeated moral hazard are considered under the time-perspective (discounting). The timing of the games shows the game theoretical reasoning in a dynamic framework.

Embedded in the previous chapters, the final chapter combines the ex-ante uncertainty about the quality of the IJV management and the uncertainty about the induced effort levels during the managerial period with the actual outcome of an IJV over its life cycle. During its life an IJV and its players has various options to play co-operatively and non-cooperatively. The termination of an IJV can happen in a number of ways (at least these eight contingencies of the last chapter). The solution to an uncertain environment lies in a sequential approach to each stage and an anticipation of problems in the next stage. The human nature to cheat and co-operate has its impact on the artificial constructs of co-operative business ventures and mirrors behavior in its positive and negative ways.

Managerial implications for IJVs

Having created a theoretical framework for the IJV problems of uncertainty, it is now important to transfer these propositions into the prescriptive approach of managerial implications for IJVs.

Ex-ante uncertainties about the quality of the management

The monograph has dealt with the pre-contractual uncertainties of the set-up period, in particular the uncertainty about the quality of the management. There were two ways of dealing with this: the adverse selection problem (uncertainty about the ability) and signaling problem (uncertainty about the experience). It was found that the incentive schemes offered need to consider the technological and market knowledge as well as the research, production and sales contracts into account. In particular, it will be important to use linear contracts in which the experience level is productive to get revelation about the type of the player.

Ex-post uncertainties about cheating of the players

The uncertainty about the proneness of cheating in an IJV was dealt with in the particular chapter of moral hazard. The principals offer contracts which are useful to get truth-telling about the agent's type (IJV management). The shirking, embezzling and sabotage should be reduced by contracts which are jointly or independently offered by the principals.

Reputation of the players in the life cycle of an IJV

As with the development of a life cycle theory for IJVs, it is important to consider the changes over several periods. The static part of the monograph dealt with the adverse selection problem and the moral hazard problem. If the signaling chapter can be seen as the dynamic solution concept for adverse selection problems, then the final chapter should be seen as dynamic solution to moral hazard problems. Co-operative behavior and cheating will occur in any joint venture, though it was rarely tackled in an overall theoretical sense. The possibility to react to cheating can lead to co-operative behavior in the next period or to cheating again. Compared to the chainstore paradox, the strategic implications in an IJV could be circumvented by offering incentive schemes which induce the players to truth-telling. Additionally, there is an incentive to co-operate since the reputation in a particular country could be ruined by cheating and therefore the possibility to set-up a new joint venture might suffer from reputational effects. Thus, the players might choose a well-balanced strategic profile of cheating and co-operating over the duration of the IJV.

Re-negotiation of the contracts in an IJV

Finally, the most important managerial implications are the creation of short-term contracts which are linked to the stages of an IJV and the types of the agent in these stages. The re-negotiation of contracts should avoid ex-ante lying about the ability to work in research, pro-duction, marketing and/or distribution units of IJVs and cheating after signing the contract. Since the incentive schemes are linked to the experience level in the pre-contractual stage, the contribution of knowledge (technological and marketing/local) and the appropriate effort levels over time, the players should be able and willing to contribute to the success of the joint venture.

Mathematical Appendix

This appendix contains formal models for the problems raised in the main body. The papers of these results were published in established economics journals to provide a robust grounding of theory. The application to IJVs is logical and shows the rigorous background of the problems raised and solved in the chapters of the books. Thus, this part is only for the mathematically interested reader.

Based on Mezzetti (1997) the common agency problem in IJVs is tackled in a formal model. The appendix shows the proofs for common agency problems (two principals and one agent) which can be applied to the IJVs.

Complete information

For all contractual arrangements, the agent's pay-off must be higher than his reservation pay-off which is

$$U_{IJV}(t_{IJV}) \geq 0 \text{ for all } t_{IJV}. \tag{9}$$

Consider now three cases under full information: independent contracting, co-operation and exclusive contracting. Firstly, for any incentive scheme chosen by for instance the local principal, principal foreign P_{For} fixes τ_{For} so that the participation constraint (9) binds and induces the agent to choose the output level that maximizes U_{For}. The principals' first-order conditions are

$$v - 2\sigma t_{IJV} - \alpha q_{Loc} + \beta q_{For} = 0 \tag{10}$$
$$v - 2\sigma (1 - t_{IJV}) - \alpha q_{For} + \beta q_{Loc} = 0 \tag{11}$$

from which we can solve for the full-information output levels as functions of the agent's type, $q_{Loc}(t_{IJV})$ and $q_{For}(t_{IJV})$.

$$Q_{Loc}(t_{IJV}) = \frac{v}{\alpha - \beta} - \frac{2\sigma\beta}{\alpha^2 - \beta^2} - \frac{2\sigma t_{IJV}}{\alpha + \beta} \tag{12}$$

$$Q_{For}(t_{IJV}) = \frac{v}{\alpha - \beta} - \frac{2\sigma\alpha}{\alpha^2 - \beta^2} + \frac{2\sigma t_{IJV}}{\alpha + \beta} \tag{13}$$

The case of co-operation considers that the principals choose τ such that the participation constraint (9) binds. The principals' choice of output functions are to induce the agent's selection of output levels that maximize $U_{Loc} + U_{For}$. The output levels chosen by the principals in the case of independent contracting coincides with the levels that maximize their joint pay-off.

Exclusive 'contracting': Each principal selects τ_i so that her own agent's individual rationality constraint binds, $U_{IJVi}(t_{IJV}) = 0$, and chooses the output function that maximizes U_i. The first-order conditions for the two principals are

$$v - 2\sigma\, t_{IJV} - \alpha q_{local} = 0 \tag{14}$$
$$v - 2\sigma\,(1 - t_{IJV}) - \alpha q_{For} = 0 \tag{15}$$

from which we can solve for the output levels $q_{Locec}(t_{IJV})$ and $q_{Forec}(t_{IJV})$

$$q_{Locfec}\left(t_{IJV}\right) = \frac{v - 2\sigma t_{IJV}}{\alpha}$$

$$q_{Locfec}\left(t_{IJV}\right) = \frac{v - 2\sigma\left(1 - t_{IJV}\right)}{\alpha}$$

Since $v > 4\sigma$, $q_{Locec}(t_{IJV})$, $q_{Forec}(t_{IJV})$, $q_{Locl}(t_{IJV})$ and $q_{For}(t_{IJV})$ are positive for all t_{IJV}. The following full-information results derived in this section.

Proposition I: If the principals have full information about the agent's type, the independent contracting and co-operation have output levels, $q_{Loc}(t_{IJV})$ and $q_{For}(t_{IJV})$. The optimal output levels under exclusive contracting are $q_{Locec}(t_{IJV})$ and $q_{Forec}(t_{IJV})$.

Under independent contracting and under co-operation, the output levels are quite the same with full information and hold with pay-off functions of $U_{Loc} = U_{Loc}(q_{Loc}, \tau_{Loc})$, $U_{For} = U_{For}(q_{For}, \tau_{For})$ and $U_{IJV} = U_{IJV} (\tau_{Loc} + \tau_{For}, q_{Loc}, q_{For}, t_{IJV})$. The complementarity between tasks, $\beta > 0$, leads to the result that the full-information output levels and the joint principal's pay-off are higher under common agency than under exclusive contracting.

Exclusive contracting

If each principal could offer exclusive contracts, there is no loss of generality in assuming that the incentive scheme selected by each principal is a direct mechanism that induces truth-telling. Consider principal local: She chooses q_{Loc} and τ_{Loc} as functions of her agent's report θ so as to maximize the expected value of $v q_{Loc}(t_{IJV}) - \tau_{Loc}(t_{IJV})$, subject to the incentive compatibility and participation constraints. Principal foreign's maximization problem takes on a similar form. Let $q_{Locec}(t_{IJV})$ and $q_{Forec}(t_{IJV})$ be the output functions. The assumption $v > 4\sigma$ guarantees that the output levels are strictly positive for all t_{IJV}.

Proposition 2: Under exclusive contracting, the output functions are

$$Q_{Locec}\left(t_{IJV}\right) = \frac{v - 4\sigma t_{IJN}}{\alpha} = q_{Locfec}(0) - \frac{4\sigma t_{IJN}}{\alpha}$$

$$Q_{Forec}\left(t_{IJV}\right) = \frac{v - 4\sigma t(1 - t_{IJV})}{\alpha} = q_{Locfec}(1) - \frac{4\sigma(1 - t_{IJV})}{\alpha}$$

The optimal incentive schemes have the familiar form of incentive schemes in the single-principal, single-agent adverse-selection model. Only the best agent produces the optimal level of output (type $t_{IJV} = 0$ for principal local, type $t_{IJV} = 1$ for principal foreign). All other types produce less than the efficient level. Each principal distorts output below the optimal level so as to reduce her own agent's information rent.

Co-operation between the principals

The principals offer the agent the incentive scheme that maximizes their joint pay-off. Assuming that the incentive scheme selected by the principals is a direct mechanism which induces truth-telling, the principals choose output levels q_{Loc}, q_{For} and transfer τ as functions of a single report θ by the agent, subject to the incentive compatibility and participation constraints. An agent of type t_{IJV} that reports type θ makes a profit $\Pi\,(\theta, t_{IJV})$, given the truth-telling direct mechanism $(q_{Loc}\,(\theta), q_{For}(\theta), \tau(\theta))$,

$$U_{IJV}\big(\theta, t_{IJV}\big) = \tau(\theta) - \frac{\alpha}{2}\Big(q_{Loc}(\theta)^2 + q_{For}(\theta)^2\Big) + \beta\, q_{Loc}(\theta) q_{For}(\theta) -$$
$$2\,\sigma\big[t_{IJV}\, q_{Loc}(\theta) + \big(1 - t_{IJV}\big) q_{For}(\theta)\big] \tag{5}$$

The principal's maximization problem can be written in the following way:

$$\max\nolimits_{q_{Loc}(\theta),\, q_{For}(\theta),\, \tau(\theta)} \int_0^1 \big\{v\big[q_{Loc}\big(t_{IJV}\big) + q_{For}\big(t_{IJV}\big)\big] - \tau\big(t_{IJV}\big)\big\}\, d\big(t_{IJV}\big) \quad \text{subject to}$$

$$U_{IJV}\big(t_{IJV}, t_{IJV}\big) \geq U_{IJV}\big(\theta, t_{IJV}\big) \qquad \text{for all } \theta,\, t_{IJV}$$

$$U_{IJV}\big(t_{IJV}, t_{IJV}\big) \geq 0 \qquad \text{for all } t_{IJV}$$

The incentive compatibility constraint requires that $\theta = t_{IJV}$ maximizes $U_{IJV}(\theta, t_{IJV})$. According to the revealed preferences argument, $q_{For}(t_{IJV}) - q_{Loc}(t_{IJV})$ must be increasing and differentiable almost everywhere, and the indirect profit function $U_{IJV}(t_{IJV}) \equiv U_{IJV}(t_{IJV},\, t_{IJV})$, which is the net profit or information rent, made by the agent t_{IJV} when reporting truthfully, must be differentiable almost everywhere. Let $t_{IJV} > \theta$, the incentive compatibility constraint implies that

$$2\sigma\,[t_{IJV} - \theta][q_{For}(t_{IJV}) - q_{Loc}(t_{IJV})] \geq U_{IJV}(t_{IJV}) - U_{IJV}(\theta) \geq 2\sigma\,[t_{IJV} - \theta][q_{For}(\theta) - q_{Loc}(\theta)].$$

Without loss of generality, the analysis can be restricted to piecewise differentiable functions $q_{For}(t_{IJV})$, $q_{Loc}(t_{IJV})$ and $\tau(t_{IJV})$.

$$U_{IJV}\theta\,(\theta, t_{IJV}) \quad = \quad \tau'(\theta) - \alpha\,(q_{Loc}\,(\theta) q_{Loc}'(\theta) + q_{For}'(\theta) q_{For}'(\theta)) + \beta\,[q_{Loc}(\theta) q_{For}'(\theta) +$$
$$q_{For}(\theta) q_{Loc}'(\theta)] - 2\sigma\,[t_{IJV} - q_{Loc}'(\theta) + (1 - t_{IJV}) q_{For}'(\theta)]$$

$$U_{IJV}\,\theta_\theta\,(\theta, t_{IJV}) \quad = \quad -\,U_{IJV}\theta\theta\,(\theta, t_{IJV}) = 2\sigma\,[q_{For}'(\theta) - q_{Loc}'(\theta)] \geq 0 \text{ for } \theta = t_{IJV},$$

where subscripts indicate the partial derivatives of $U_{IJV}(\theta, t_{IJV})$. For the second-order condition $q_{Loc}' \geq 0$ and $q_{For}' \geq 0$ are sufficient to be satisfied. By the envelope theorem

$$[U_{IJV}'(t_{IJV}) = 2\sigma\,[q_{For}(t_{IJV}) - q_{Loc}(t_{IJV})].$$

The second-order condition implies that the agent's net profit $U_{IJV}(t_{IJV})$ is minimized when $q_{Loc} = q_{For}$, and that there can be at most one interval $[t_{IJVL}, t_{IJVH}]$ where $q_{local} = q_{For}$. If this interval is nondegenerate (i.e. if $t_{IJVL} \neq t_{IJVH}$), then it is optimal for the principals to choose a transfer scheme such that $U_{IJV}(t_{IJV}) = 0$

for all $t_{IJV} \in [t_{IJVL}, t_{IJVH}]$; that is, the participation constraint (6) binds in the interval $[t_{IJV}, t_{IJV}]$. Let $q_{Fora}(t_{IJV})$ and $q_{Loca}(t_{IJV})$ be the output functions that solve the principals' maximization program.

Proposition: Under co-operation between the principals, the optimal output functions are

$$\frac{v}{\alpha - \beta} - \frac{2\sigma\beta}{\alpha^2 - \beta^2} - \frac{4\sigma t_{IJV}}{\alpha + \beta} = q_{Locf}(0) - \frac{4\sigma t_{IJV}}{\alpha + \beta} \qquad \text{for } t_{IJV} \leq t_{IJVaL}$$

$$q_{Loca}(t_{IJV}) = \frac{v - \sigma}{\alpha - \beta} \qquad \text{for } t_{IJV} \in [t_{IJVaL}, t_{IJVaH}]$$

$$\frac{v}{\alpha - \beta} - \frac{2\sigma\beta}{\alpha^2 - \beta^2} - \frac{2\sigma(2t_{IJV} - 1)}{\alpha + \beta} = q_{Locf}(1) - \frac{4\sigma(t_{IJV} - 1)}{\alpha + \beta} \qquad \text{for } t_{IJV} \leq t_{IJVaL}$$

$$\frac{v}{\alpha - \beta} - \frac{2\sigma\alpha}{\alpha^2 - \beta^2} + \frac{4\sigma t_{IJV}}{\alpha + \beta} = q_{Forf}(0) + \frac{4\sigma t_{IJV}}{\alpha + \beta} \qquad \text{for } t_{IJV} \in [t_{IJVaL}, t_{IJVaH}]$$

$$q_{Fora}(t_{IJV}) = \frac{v - \sigma}{\alpha - \beta} \qquad \text{for } t_{IJV} \in [t_{IJVaL}, t_{IJVaH}]$$

$$\frac{v}{\alpha - \beta} - \frac{2\sigma\alpha}{\alpha^2 - \beta^2} + \frac{2\sigma(2t_{IJV} - 1)}{\alpha + \beta} = q_{Forf}(1) + \frac{4\sigma(t_{IJV} - 1)}{\alpha + \beta} \qquad \text{for } t_{IJV} \geq t_{IJVaH}$$

where

$$t_{IJVaH} = \frac{1}{4}$$

$$t_{IJVaH} = \frac{3}{4}$$

The optimal incentive scheme under co-operation between principals exhibits pooling in an intermediate region, $t_{IJV} \in [\frac{1}{4}, \frac{3}{4}]$, of the agent's type space. Types in this region have similar productivity in the two tasks. In equilibrium they receive a flat fee and produce the same output level for both principals. Outside the pooling region, types are offered an incentive pay and produce more for the principal, at whose task they are more productive; these are types with a significant advantage in one of the two tasks. Only types $t_{IJV} = 0$, $t_{IJV} = 1$ and $t_{IJV} = \frac{1}{2}$ choose the full-information output levels. Types in the interval $(0, \frac{1}{2})$ produce less than the optimal output level for principal local, $q_{Loca} < q_{Locf}$, and more than the optimal level of principal foreign, $q_{Fora} > q_{Forf}$. On the other hand, agent types in the interval $(\frac{1}{2}, 1)$ produce more than the optimal level of output for principal local, $q_{Loca} > q_{Locf}$, and less than the optimal level for principal foreign, $q_{Fora} < q_{Forf}$.

If the principals offered the full-information contract, the agent would not reveal his true type. Under the full-information contract, the transfer schedule $\tau(\theta)$ is such that $U_{IJV}(\theta, \theta) = 0$ for all θ; the agent would be facing countervailing incentives. If output for principal local, q_{Loc} were the only concern, the agent would want to overstate his type. If, on the contrary, the only concern were q_{For}, the agent would want to understate his type. Since it is $q_{Loc} > q_{For}$ for $t_{IJV} < \frac{1}{2}$, in such a case the incentive to overstate prevails, while for $t_{IJV} > \frac{1}{2}$ it is $q_{Loc} < q_{For}$ and the incentive to understate dominates. Thus, to induce truthful revelation the principal must reduce q_{Loc} below and increase q_{For} above the full-information levels for $t_{IJV} < \frac{1}{2}$, and they must increase q_{Loc} above and reduce q_{For} below the full-information levels for $t_{IJV} > \frac{1}{2}$. Thus the functions $q_{For}(t_{IJV})$, $q_{Loc}(t_{IJV})$ either have an upward (respectively downward) jump discontinuity at some intermediate value of t_{IJV} and are not monotone, or they are constant in an intermediate region of the type space. The second-order condition for the agent's reporting problem does not force $q_{Loc}(t_{IJV})$ and $q_{For}(t_{IJV})$ to be monotone, but it requires that $q_{Loc}(t_{IJV}) - q_{For}(t_{IJV})$ be increasing, which would be violated by the described discontinuous functions. There must be a pooling in an intermediate region of the type space.

Independent contracting

Suppose the principals offer independently incentive packages to the agent. Each principal observes the agent's output only at her own task, and the incentive package offered cannot be made contingent on the output level in the other principal's task. Each principal selects a direct mechanism consisting of a pair of functions specifying, for any given reported type, the transfer to the agent and the level of output in the principal's own task. It is important to stress that the agent has to send a separate report to each principal; this is what differentiates independent contracting from co-operation. Under co-operation the principals act as a single entity (i.e. a single mechanism designer) and the agent sends a single report. Although the agent's reports to the two principals could differ, in equilibrium they coincide with the agent's true type. The two principals use continuous, piecewise-differentiable output and transfer functions.

Some problems in connection with the revelation principle occur since it concerns only the case of a single mechanism designer. Thus, it is an open question whether there is any loss of generality in assuming that the two principals use direct revelation mechanisms. Furthermore, the assumption of piecewise differentiable output and transfer functions involves some loss of generality. Under co-operation the simple revealed-preferences argument shows that these functions must be differentiable almost everywhere. Under independent contracting this argument fails, because the optimal report of the agent to a principal depends in a nontrivial way on the mechanism chosen by the other principal. If one principal's mechanism is not piecewise differentiable, the other's best response could also be nondifferentiable.

Let θ_{Loc} be the type reported to the principal local and θ_{For} the one reported to principal foreign. Given the mechanisms $(q_{Loc}(\theta_{Loc}), {}_{Loc}(\theta_{Loc}))$ and $(q_{For}(\theta_{For}), \tau_{For}(\theta_{For}))$, chosen by the principals local and foreign respectively, an agent of type t_{IJV} that reports type $_i$ to principal i makes a profit $U_{IJV}(\theta_{Loc}, \theta_{For}, t_{IJV})$, where

$$U_{IJV}(\theta_{Loc}, \theta_{For}, t_{IJV}) = \tau_{For}(\theta_{Loc}) + \tau_{For}(\theta_{For}) - \frac{\alpha}{2}\left(q_{Loc}(\theta_{Loc})^2 + q_{For}(\theta_{For})^2\right) +$$

$$\beta\, q_{Loc}(\theta_{Loc}) q_{For}(\theta_{For}) - 2\sigma\left[t_{IJV} q_{Loc}(\theta_{Loc}) + (1 - t_{IJV})\right.$$

$$\left. q_{For}(\theta_{For})\right]$$

Let $U_{IJV}(t_{IJV})$ be the indirect profit function or information rent, by the envelope theorem we have

$$U_{IJV}{}'(t_{IJV}) = 2\sigma\left[q_{For}(t_{IJV}) - q_{Loc}(t_{IJV})\right].$$

This is analogous to the incentive compatibility constraint under co-operation. The next lemma shows that the agent's information rent is minimized in an interval of the type space as in the case of co-operation between principals.

Lemma 1: The optimal output functions must satisfy
(i) $[\beta q_{For}'(t_{IJV}) = 2\sigma] q_{Loc}'(t_{IJV}) \geq 0$;
(ii) $[\beta q_{For}'(t_{IJV}) + 2\sigma] q_{Loc}'(t_{IJV}) \geq 0$;
(iii) $q_{For}'(t_{IJV}) - q_{Loc}'(t_{IJV}) \geq 0$

The individual-rationality constraint binds in an interval $[t_{IJVcL}; t_{IJVcH}]$. For all t_{IJV} in such interval $q_{For}(t_{IJV}) = q_{Loc}(t_{IJV}) = $ constant.

The strategic revelation effects induced by the presence of externalities between the contracting activities of the two principals. These externalities arise because the contract offered by one principal influence the other principal's contract by changing the marginal profit of the agent. This implies that the agent's report to a principal depends on the mechanism chosen by the other principal and thus that principal i is indirectly affected by the agent's report to principal j, because such a report determines the output level in task j. Recognizing this strategic interaction, when choosing a mechanism each principal views the agent's future optimal report to the other principal as a function of her own choice of a mechanism. Formally, given foreign principal's choice of a mechanism, principal local recognizes that the agent's optimal report to principal foreign, θ_{For}, is a function of her own choice of output and transfer functions: $\theta_{For}*(q_{Loc}(\theta_{Loc}), \tau_{Loc}(\theta_{Loc}))$.

Similarly, principal foreign recognizes that θ_{local} is a function of $(q_{For}(\theta_{For})$ and $\tau_{For}(\theta_{For})$: $\theta_{Loc}*((q_{For}(\theta_{For}), \tau_{For}(\theta_{For}))$. The following lemma characterizes the local impact of a change in a principal's mechanism on the agent's optimal report to the other principal.

Lemma 2: In equilibrium, for all $t_{IJV} \in [0,1]$:
$\partial \theta_{For}*/\partial q_{Loc} (2\sigma + \beta q_{Loc}'(t_{IJV})) q_{For}'(t_{IJV}) = \beta q_{For}'(t_{IJV})$,
$\partial \theta_{Loc}*/\partial q_{For} (2\sigma - \beta q_{For}'(t_{IJV})) q_{Loc}'(t_{IJV}) = -\beta q_{Loc}'(t_{IJV})$,
$\partial \theta_{For}*/\partial \tau_{Loc} = 0 = \partial \theta_{Loc}*/\partial \tau_{For}$

Furthermore,
(i) if $q_{For}'(t_{IJV}) = 0$, then $\partial \theta_{For}*/\partial q_{local} = 0$;
(ii) if $q_{Loc}'(t_{IJV}) = -2\sigma/\beta$, then $q_{For}'(t_{IJV}) = 0$;
(iii) if $q_{Los}'(t_{IJV}) = 0$, then $\partial \theta_{Loc}*/\partial q_{For} = 0$ and
(iv) if $q_{For}'(t_{IJV}) = -2\sigma/\beta$, then $q_{Loc}'(t_{IJV}) = 0$.

Note that, by Lemma 1, if $q_{For}' > 0$, then $\partial \theta_{For}*/\partial q_{Loc} > 0$, and if $q_{Loc}' < 0$, then $\partial \theta_{Loc}*/\partial q_{For} = 0$. Thus, an increase in q_{Loc} will induce q_{For} to increase by pushing up $_{For}$. Similarly, an increase in q_{For} will push up q_{Loc} by reducing θ_{Loc}. This is due to q_{Loc} and q_{For} being complements; an increase in output in a task increases the agent's marginal pay-off in the other task, $\partial U_{IJV} /\partial q_{Loc} \partial q_{For} > 0$. Since the quasi-linearity of the agent's pay-off function rules out wealth effects, changes in a principal's transfer schedule have no impact on the agent's report to the other principal. We can thus suppress τ_i as an argument of θ_i^*. We can then write principal local's maximization problem as follows:

$$\max\nolimits_{q_{Loc}(\theta),\ \tau_{Loc}(\theta)} \int_0^1 \{v\, q_{Loc}(t_{IJV}) - \tau_{Loc}(t_{IJV})\}\, d(t_{IJV}) \text{ subject to}$$

$$U_{IJV}\left(t_{IJV}, \theta_{For}{}^*(q_{Loc}(t_{IJV})), t_{IJV}\right) \ge U_{IJV}\left(\theta_{Loc}, \theta_{For}{}^*(q_{Loc}(\theta_{Loc})), t_{IJV}\right) \text{ for all}$$

$$t_{IJV}, \theta_{Loc}$$

$$U_{IJV}\left(t_{IJV}, t_{IJV}, t_{IJV}\right) \ge 0 \hspace{4cm} \text{for all } t_{IJV}$$

The incentive constraint says that it must be optimal for the agent to report his true type to principal local. The foreign principal's maximization problem is analogous.

Lemma 3: Under independent contracting, the optimal incentive mechanisms of the two principals must satisfy the following conditions:

$$\alpha[q_{Locf}(0) - q_{Locc}(t_{IJV})] - \beta[q_{Forf}(0) - q_{Forc}(t_{IJV})] - 2\sigma t_{IJV} - 2\sigma t_{IJV}\,[1 - q_{Forc}'(t_{IJV})\,\partial\,\theta_{For}{}^*/\partial\,q_{Loc}] = 0$$

for $t_{IJV} < t_{IJVcL}$

$$\alpha[q_{Locf}(1) - q_{Locc}(t_{IJV})] - \beta[q_{Forf}(1) - q_{Forc}(t_{IJV})] + 2\sigma\,(1 - t_{IJV}) + 2\sigma\,(1 - t_{IJV})\,[1 - q_{Forc}'(t_{IJV})\,\partial\,\theta_{For}{}^*/\partial\,q_{Loc}] = 0$$

for $t_{IJV} < t_{IJVcH}$

$$\alpha[q_{Forf}(0) - q_{Forc}(t_{IJV})] - \beta[q_{Locf}(0) - q_{Locc}(t_{IJV})] + 2\sigma\, t_{IJV} + 2\sigma\, t_{IJV}\,[1 - q_{Locc}'(t_{IJV})\,\partial\,\theta_{For}{}^*/\partial\,q_{For}] = 0$$

for $t_{IJV} < t_{IJVcL}$

$$\alpha[q_{Forf}(1) - q_{Forc}(t_{IJV})] - \beta[q_{Locf}(1) - q_{Locc}(t_{IJV})] - 2\sigma\,(1 - t_{IJV}) - 2\sigma\,(1 - t_{IJV})\,[1 - q_{Locc}'(t_{IJV})\,\partial\,\theta_{Loc}{}^*/\partial\,q_{For}] = 0$$

for $t_{IJV} > t_{IJVcH}$

$$q_{Locc}(t_{IJV}) = q_{Forc}(t_{IJV}) = \text{constant} \hspace{3cm} \text{for } t_{IJV} \in [t_{IJVcL}, t_{IJVcH}]$$

Finding the equilibrium output functions under independent contracting is more complicated than under co-operation between principals; it involves solving a system of differential equations rather than just a system of equations. Note that the value of q_{Loc} and q_{For} in the pooling interval $[t_{IJVcL}, t_{IJVcH}]$ cannot be determined before solving the system of differential equations.

Lemma 3 implies that $q_{Locf}(0) = q_{Locc}(0)$, $q_{Locf}(1) = q_{Locc}(1)$, $q_{Forf}(0) = q_{Forc}(0)$, $q_{Forf}(1) = q_{Forc}(1)$. Under independent contracting, as well as under co-operation between principals, the highest and lowest type of agent choose the full-information output levels in both tasks. Thus, for t_{IJV} close to one we can approximate $q_{Locc}(t_{IJV})$ with $q_{Locf}(1) - (1 - t_{IJV})\, q_{Locc}'(t_{IJV})$ and $q_{Forc}(t_{IJV})$ with $q_{Forf}(1) - (1 - t_{IJV})\, q_{Forc}'(t_{IJV})$. Similarly, for t_{IJV} close to zero we can approximate $q_{Locc}(t_{IJV})$ with $q_{Locf}(0) + t_{IJV}\, q_{Locc}'(t_{IJV})$ and $q_{Forc}(t_{IJV})$ with $q_{Forff}(0) + t_{IJV}\, q_{Forc}'(t_{IJV})$. Hence, for t_{IJV} close to one, (18) and (20) become

$$2\sigma + \alpha q_{Locc}'(t_{IJV}) - \beta q_{Loc}'(t_{IJV}) + 2\sigma\,[1 - q_{Forc}'(t_{IJV})\,\partial\,\theta_{For}{}^*/\partial\,q_{Loc} = 0$$
$$-2\sigma + \alpha q_{Forc}'(t_{IJV}) - \beta q_{Locc}'(t_{IJV}) + 2\sigma\,[1 - q_{Locc}'(t_{IJV})\,\partial\,\theta_{Loc}{}^*/\partial\,q_{For} = 0$$

Note that for t_{IJV} close to zero, (17) and (19) also reduce to (22) and (23). This means that each output function has the same slope at the two endpoints of the agent's type space. Let m_{For} be the slope of q_{For} and m_{Loc} be the slope of q_{Loc} at $t_{IJV} = 0$ and $t_{IJV} = 1$. Adding up (22) and (23) yields

$$(\alpha - \beta)[m_{Loc} + m_{For}] - 2\sigma [m_{For} \partial \theta_{For}^*/\partial q_{Loc} - m_{Loc} \partial \theta_{Loc}^*/\partial q_{For}] = 0.$$

Lemma 4 shows that if $\alpha \neq 2\sigma$, then in any equilibrium the slope of the output functions

$$q_{Forc}{}'(0) = q_{Forc}{}'(1) = -q_{Locc}{}'(0) = -q_{Locc}{}'(1) = \frac{\sigma}{\beta} + \frac{3\sigma\beta - \sigma\sqrt{\alpha^2 + 8\beta^2}}{\beta(\alpha + \beta)} = m_{For}{}^*$$

Lemma 3 provides first-order conditions that an equilibrium must satisfy. Lemma 4 shows that at the endpoints of the agent's type space the slope of any output functions q_{Loc} and q_{For} satisfying the first-order conditions is uniquely determined. However, this does not necessarily imply that equilibrium is unique. In fact, there could be a continuum of equilibria. This is so because equations (17) and (19), respectively, (18) and (20), reduce to a differential equation that has a singular point at the endpoint $t_{IJV} = 0$ and $t_{IJV} = 1$. The topological nature of the singularity determines whether the first-order conditions are satisfied by a unique pair of by a continuum of pairs of output functions. The proof of the next proposition establishes first that the output functions satisfying the conditions in Lemma 3 are uniquely determined, and then that the second-order conditions for the two principals' maximization programs are satisfied.

Proposition 4: Under independent contracting, there exists a unique piecewise-differentiable equilibrium. The optimal output functions for the two principals are the following:

$$\frac{\upsilon}{\alpha - \beta} - \frac{2\sigma\beta}{\alpha^2 - \beta^2} - m_{For}{}^* t_{IJV} = q_{Locf}(0) - m_{For}{}^* t_{IJV} \qquad \text{for } t_{IJV} \leq t_{IJVcL}$$

$$q_{Locc}(t_{IJV}) = \frac{\upsilon - \sigma}{\alpha - \beta} \qquad \text{for } t_{IJV} \in [t_{IJVcl}, t_{IJVcH}]$$

$$\frac{\upsilon}{\alpha - \beta} - \frac{2\sigma\beta}{\alpha^2 - \beta^2} - \frac{2\sigma}{\alpha + \beta} - m_{For}{}^* (t_{IJV} - 1) = q_{Locf}(1) - m_{For}{}^* (t_{IJV} - 1) \qquad \text{for } t_{IJV} \geq t_{IJVcH}$$

$$\frac{\upsilon}{\alpha - \beta} - \frac{2\sigma\alpha}{\alpha^2 - \beta^2} + m_{For}{}^* t_{IJV} = q_{Forf}(0) + m_{For}{}^* t_{IJV} \qquad \text{for } t_{IJV} \leq t_{IJVcL}$$

$$q_{Forc}(t_{IJV}) = \frac{\upsilon - \sigma}{\alpha - \beta} \qquad \text{for } t_{IJV} \in [t_{IJVcL}, t_{IJVcH}]$$

$$\frac{\upsilon}{\alpha - \beta} - \frac{2\sigma\alpha}{\alpha^2 - \beta^2} + \frac{2\sigma}{\alpha + \beta} + m_{For}{}^* (t_{IJV} - 1) = q_{Forf}(1) + m_{For}{}^* (t_{IJV} - 1) \qquad \text{for } t_{IJV} \geq t_{IJV\,cH}$$

$$t_{IJVcL} = \frac{\sigma}{(\alpha + \beta)m_{For}^*}$$

$$t_{IJV\,cH} = 1 - \frac{\sigma}{(\alpha + \beta)m_{for}^*}$$

The optimal incentive mechanisms under independent contracting are similar to the ones under co-operation between principals. Because of the presence of countervailing incentives, there is pooling in an intermediate region of the agent's type space; that is, types with similar productivity at the two tasks produce the same output and are paid a flat fee by both principals. Compared with a full-information world, almost every agent produces less than the optimal level of output in the task at which he is more productive and more than the optimal level in the task at which he is less productive. Only the lowest, the middle, and the highest type select the full-information output levels for both tasks.

Note that $m_{For}^* < \frac{4\sigma}{\quad}$; the slope of q_{Locc} and q_{Forc} is less than the slope of q_{Loca} and q_{Fora}. Outputs are closer to their full-information levels under independent contracting than under co-operation between principals. Thus, the power of the incentive schemes for types outside of the pooling region, as measured by the slope of the agent's rent (i.e. by the absolute value of the difference between outputs in the two tasks; see equation (16)), is lower when principals co-operate than under independent contracting. Moreover, the pooling interval is smaller under independent contracting than under co-operation between principals. *Think of co-operation between principals as the formation of a joint venture with the agent as an employee, and of independent contracting as the contractual relationships between two principals and an independent contractor.* Then, our results are consistent with the Williamsonian view that incentives should be lower powered within an organization than in the marketplace. Note, however, that co-operation between principals reduces specialization and thus decrease efficiency, as measured by the total value of the parties' pay-offs. These observations are summarized in the following corollary.

Corollary 1: Output specialization is higher with full information than with incomplete information . If there is incomplete information, then there is more output specialization under independent contracting than under co-operation between principals. The region of types that produce the same output level for both principals and are paid a flat fee is higher under co-operation.

To see why output specialization is higher under independent contracting, recall that distortions from the full-information output levels are introduced to decrease the agent's information rent. Consider the case when $t_{IJV} < \frac{1}{2}$. The absolute value of the agent's marginal information rent is $|U_{IJV}'| = 2\sigma|q_{For} - q_{Loc}| = 2\sigma(q_{For} - q_{Loc})$. Thus, because of the externality between the contracting activities, under independent contracting a unit increase in q_{For} reduces $|U_{IJV}'|$ by $2\sigma(1 - q_{Loc}'(\partial \theta_{Loc}^*/\partial q_{For}))$, which is less than 2σ, the reduction under co-operation between the principals. Principal foreign has a smaller incentive to raise q_{For} above its full-information level, and as a result $q_{Fora}(t_{IJV}) > q_{Forc}(t_{IJV}) > q_{Forf}(t_{IJV})$ for $t_{IJV} < \frac{1}{2}$. Similarly, a unit decrease in q_{Loc} has a smaller impact on $|U_{IJV}'|$ under independent contracting – it reduces it by $2\sigma(1 - q_{For}'(\partial \theta_{For}^*/\partial q_{Loc}))$ – than under co-operation between principals, when it reduces it by 2σ. Principal local has a smaller incentive to lower q_{Loc} below its full-information level, and thus $q_{Loca}(t_{IJV}) < q_{Locc}(t_{IJV}) < q_{Locf}(t_{IJV})$. A similar argument can be made for the case when $t_{IJV} > \frac{1}{2}$.

Welfare comparisons

If there is complete information, then the principals are indifferent between co-operation and independent contracting, and they prefer either of them to exclusive dealing. Clearly, under incomplete information the two principals attain a lower total expected pay-off than under full information. Recall, due to the externality that one principal's incentive scheme imposes on the other principal, that under independent contracting distortions from the full-information output levels are smaller than under co-operation. As a result, each agent type's rent is higher, and the two principals' joint expected pay-off is lower, under independent contracting than under co-operation. Under exclusive dealing, output distortions are larger than under common agency, because each agent's temptation to understate his pay-off is not mitigated by the presence of countervailing incentives. Thus, to induce truth-telling the principals must give the agents higher information rents. Since common agency also allows principals to benefit from the complementarity between tasks, the principals' joint pay-off with either contractual arrangement under common agency is higher than under exclusive dealing. These results are summarized in the following proposition.

Proposition 5:
(i)   With complete information, the agent earns no rent, and the sum of the principals' pay-offs under independent contracting and under co-operation between principals is the same and higher than under exclusive dealing.
(ii) With incomplete information, the sum of the principals' expected pay-off is higher under co-operation between the principals than under independent contracting, and it is lowest under exclusive dealing; the agent's information rent is higher under independent contracting than under co-operation between the principals for all values of t_{IJV}, and is highest under exclusive dealing.

Under independent contracting there are smaller output distortions, and thus more surplus is available than under co-operation, but the agent receives more of it as information rent. The 'surplus' effect dominates for types sufficiently close to the pooling interval. For these types the two principals' ex post welfare under independent contracting is higher than under co-operation between principals. On the contrary, for types near the endpoints of the type space, the 'information rent' effect prevails. On average, the information rent effect dominates, and thus the two principals' total expected pay-off is lower under independent contracting than under co-operation.

Bibliography

Afriyie, K., A technology-transfer methodology for developing joint production strategies in varying technological systems. In F. Contractor & P. Lorange (eds), *Cooperative Strategies in International Business – Joint Ventures and Technology Partnerships between Firms* (New York: Lexington Books 1988), 81–95.

Akerlof, George A., 'The Market for "Lemons": Qualitative Uncertainty and the Market Mechanism', *Quarterly Journal of Economics*, 84(3) (1970) 488–500.

Anderson, E., 'Two firms, one frontier: On assessing joint venture performance', *Sloan Management Review*, 1 (1990) 19–29.

Balakrishnan, S. and M.P. Koza, 'Information asymmetry, adverse selection and joint ventures theory and evidence', *Journal of Economic Behaviour & Organization*, 20(1) (1993) 99–117.

Barden, J.Q., H.K. Steensma and M.A. Lyles, 'The influence of parent control structure on parent conflict in Vietnamese international joint ventures: an organizational justice-based contingency approach,' *Journal of International Business Studies*, 36(2) (2005) 156–174.

Beamish, P.W., J.P. Killing, D.J. Lecraw and A.J. Morrison, *International Management – Text and Cases* (Illinois: Irwin 1994).

Berg, S.V. and Ph. Friedman, 'Causes and effects of joint venture activity: knowledge acquisition versus parent horizontality', *The Antitrust Bulletin*, 25 (1980) 143–68.

Berg, S.V. and J.M. Hoekman, Entrepreneurship over the product life cycle: joint venture strategies in the Netherlands. In F. Contractor & P. Lorange (eds), *Cooperative Strategies in International Business – Joint Ventures and Technology Partnerships between Firms* (New York: Lexington Books 1988) 145–67.

Bergemann, D. and J. Valimaki, 'Dynamic Common Agency', *Working Paper*, Yale University 1998.

Bernheim, B.D. and M.D. Whinston, 'Common Marketing Agency as a Device for Facilitating Collusion', *RAND Journal of Economics*, 16(2) (1985) 269–81.

Bernheim, B.D. and M.D. Whinston, 'Common Agency', *Econometrica*, 54(4) (1986) 923–42.

Bhattacharya, S., J. Glazer and D.E.M. Sappington, 'Licensing and the sharing of knowledge in research joint ventures', *Journal of Economic Theory*, 56(1) (1992) 43–69.

Blodgett, L.L., 'Partner contributions as predictors of equity share in international joint ventures', *Journal of International Business Studies*, 22 (1991) 63–78.

Brouthers, K.D. and G.J. Bamossy, 'The role of key stakeholders in international joint venture negotiations: case studies from Eastern Europe', *Journal of International Business Studies*, 28 (1997) 285–308.

Buckley, P.J. and M.C. Casson, 'An economic model of international joint venture strategy', *Journal of International Business Studies*, Special Issue (1996) 849–903.

Buckley, P.J. and M.C. Casson, 'Analyzing foreign market entry strategies: extending the internalization approach', *Journal of International Business Studies*, 29(3) (1998) 539–62.

Buckley, P.J. and M.C. Casson, 'Models of the Multinational Enterprise', *Journal of International Business Studies*, 29(1) (1998) 21–44.

Buckley, P.J. and M.C. Casson, International Joint Ventures, in M.C. Casson, *Economics of International Business – A New Research Agenda* (Cheltenham, UK: Edward Elgar Publishing 2000) 161–188.

Burton, F.N. and F.H. Saelens, 'Partner choice and linkage characteristics of international joint ventures in Japan – an exploratory analysis of the inorganic chemicals sector', *Management International Review*, 22 (1982) 20–9.

Campbell, D.E., *Incentives – Motivation and the Economics of Information* (Cambridge: Cambridge University Press 1997).

Casson, M.C. *Enterprise and competitiveness: a systems view of international business* (Oxford: Clarendon Press 1990).

Chi, T., 'Performance verifiability and output sharing in collaborative ventures', *Management Science*, 42 (1996) 93–109.

Choi, C.-B. and P.W. Beamish, 'Split management control and international joint venture performance', *Journal of International Business Studies*, 35(3) (2004) 201–15.

Chiappori, P.-A., I. Macho, P. Rey and B. Salanie, 'Repeated moral hazard: The role of memory, commitment and the access to credit markets', *European Economic Review*, 38 (1994) 1527–53.

Contractor, F.J. and P. Lorange, Why should firms cooperate? The strategy and economics basis for cooperative ventures. In F. Contractor & P. Lorange (eds), *Cooperative Strategies in International Business – Joint Ventures and Technology Partnerships between Firms* (New York: Lexington Books 1988) 3–28.

Dasgupta, A. and N. Siddharthan, 'Industrial distribution of Indian exports and joint ventures abroad', *Development and Change*, 16(1) (1985) 159–74.

Daspupta, S. and Z. Tao, 'Contractual Incompleteness and the Optimality of Equity Joint Ventures', *Journal of Economic Behaviour & Organisation*, 37 (1999) 391–413.

Datta, D.K., 'International joint ventures: a framework for analysis', *Journal of General Management*, 14(2) (1988) 78–91.

Dhanaraj, C., M.A. Lyles, H.K. Steensma and L. Tihanyi, 'Managing tacit and explicit knowledge transfer in IJVs: the role of relational embeddedness and the impact on performance', *Journal of International Business Studies*, 35(5) (2004) 428–42.

Doz, Y.L., Technology partnerships between larger and smaller firms: some critical issues. In F. Contractor & P. Lorange (eds), *Cooperative Strategies in International Business – Joint Ventures and Technology Partnerships between Firms* (New York: Lexington Books 1988) 317–38.

Dussauge, P. and B. Garrette, 'Determinants of success in international strategic alliances – evidence from the global aerospace industry', *Journal of International Business Studies*, 26(3) (1995) 505–30.

Eisele, J., *Erfolgsfaktoren des Joint Venture Managements* (Wiesbaden: Gabler 1995).

Fudenberg, D. and J. Tirole, 'Moral hazard and renegotiation in agency contracts', *Game Theory* (Cambridge, MA: MIT Press 1991).

Fudenberg, D., B. Holmstrom and P. Milgrom, 'Short-term Contracts and Long-term Agency Relationships', *Journal of Economic Theory*, 51 (1990) 1–31.

Fudenberg, D. and J. Tirole, Moral Hazard and Renegotiation in Agency Contracts, *Econometrica*, 58(6): (1990) 1279–1319.

Gal-Or, E., 'A Common Agency with Incomplete Information', *RAND Journal of Economics*, 22(2) (1991) 274–86.

Gardner, R., *Games for business and economics* (New York: Wiley 1995).

Garvey, G.T., 'Why reputation favors joint ventures over vertical and horizontal integration – A simple model', *Journal of Economic Behavior and Organization*, 28 (1995) 387–97.

Geringer, J.M., 'Strategic determinants of partner selection criteria in international joint ventures', *Journal of International Business Studies*, 22 (1991) 41–62.

Geringer, J.M. and L. Hebert, 'Control and performance of international joint ventures', *Journal of International Business Studies*, 20 (1989) 235–55.

Geringer, J.M. and L. Hebert, 'Measuring performance of international joint ventures', *Journal of International Business Studies*, 22 (1991) 249–63.

Geringer, J.M. and C.P. Woodcock, 'Agency Costs and the Structure and Performance of International Joint Ventures', *Group Decision and Negotiation*, 4 (1995) 453–67.

Ghemawat, P., *Games Businesses Play* (Cambridge, MA: The MIT Press 1997).

Gibbons, R., *A primer in game theory* (Hemel Hemstead: Harvester-Wheatsheaf 1992).

Gomes-Casseres, B., Joint Venture Cycles: The evolution of ownership strategies of US MNEs, 1945–75. In F. Contractor & P. Lorange (eds), *Cooperative Strategies in International Business – Joint Ventures and Technology Partnerships between Firms* (New York: Lexington Books 1988) 111–28.

Guesnerie, R. and J.-J. Laffont, 'A complete solution to a class of principal-agent problems with an application to the control of a self-managed firm', *Journal of Public Economics*, 25 (1984) 329–69.

Harrigan, K.R., Strategic alliances and partner asymmetries. In F. Contractor & P. Lorange (eds), *Cooperative Strategies in International Business – Joint Ventures and Technology Partnerships between Firms* (New York: Lexington Books 1988) 205–26.

Harsanyi, J., 'Games with incomplete information played by Bayesian players', *Management Science*, 14 (1967–8) 159–82, 320–34, 486–502.

Hennart, J.-F. 'A transaction costs theory of equity joint ventures', *Strategic Management Journal*, 9 (1988) 361–74.

Hennart, J.-F., 'The transaction costs theory of joint ventures: An empirical study of Japanese subsidiaries in the United States', *Management Science*, 37 (1991) 483–97.

Holler, M.J. and G. Illing, *Einführung in die Spieltheorie* (Berlin: Springer 1996).

Holmstrom, B., 'Moral Hazard and Observability', *Bell Journal of Economics*, 10 (1979) 74–91.

Holmstrom, B., 'Managerial Incentive Problems: A Dynamic Perspective', *Review of Economic Studies*, 66 (1999) 169–82.

Inkpen, A., *The management of international joint ventures – an organizational learning perspective* (London and New York: Routledge 1995).

Inkpen, A. and P.W. Beamish, 'Knowledge, bargaining power and the instability of international joint ventures', *Academy of Management Review*, 22(1) (1997) 177–202.

Jensen, M. and W. Meckling, 'Theory of the firm: managerial behavior, agency costs and ownership structure', *Journal of Financial Economics*, 3 (1976) 305–60.

Killing, J.P., 'How to make a global joint venture work', *Harvard Business Review*, 61(3) (1982) 120–27.

Kogut, B. and H. Singh, Entering the United States by Joint Ventures: Competitive Rivalry and Industry Structure. In F. Contractor & P. Lorange (eds), *Cooperative Strategies in International Business – Joint Ventures and Technology Partnerships between Firms* (New York: Lexington Books 1988) 241–51.

Kogut, B., A study of the life cycle of joint ventures. In F. Contractor and P. Lorange (eds), *Cooperative Strategies in International Business – Joint Ventures and Technology Partnerships between Firms* (New York: Lexington Books 1988a) 169–85.

Kogut, B., 'Joint ventures: theoretical and empirical perspectives', *Strategic Management Journal*, 9(4) (1988b) 319–32.

Lin, Xiaohua and R. Germain, 'Sustaining Satisfactory Joint Venture Relationships: The Role of Conflict Resolution Strategy', *Journal of International Business Studies*, 29(1) (1998) 179–96.

Lorange, P. and G.J.B. Probst, 'Joint ventures as self-organizing systems: A key to successful joint venture design and implementation', *Columbia Journal of World Business*, 22 (1987) 71–7.

Luo, Y., *Co-opetition in International Business* (Copenhagen: Copenhagen Business School Press 2004).

Luo, Y. and S.H. Park, 'Multiparty cooperation and performance in international equity joint ventures', *Journal of International Business Studies*, 35(2) (2004) 142–60.

Lyles, M.A. and J.E. Salk, 'Knowledge acquisition from foreign parents in international joint ventures: an empirical examination in the Hungarian context', *Journal of International Business Studies*, Special Issue (1996) 877–903.

Macho-Stadler, I. and J.D. Perez-Castrillo, *An Introduction to the Economics of Information – Incentives and Contracts* (Oxford: Oxford University Press 2001).

Martimort, D., *Multiprincipaux en Economie de l'Information*, Ph.D. diss, EHEss (Toulouse 1992).

Martimort, D., 'Multiprincipal Regulatory Charter as a Safeguard against Opportunism', *Working Paper* (Toulouse 1995a).

Martimort, D., 'The Multiprincipal Nature of Government', *Working Paper* (Toulouse 1995b).

Martimort, D., 'Exclusive dealing, common agency, and multiprincipal incentive theory', *RAND Journal of Economics*, 27(1) (1996) 1–31.

McConnell, J.J. and T.J. Nantell, 'Corporate combinations and common-stock returns – The case of joint ventures', *Journal of Finance*, 40(2) (1985) 519–36.

McGee, J.E., M.J. Dowling and W.L. Megginson, 'Cooperative strategy and new venture performance: the role of business strategy and management experience', *Strategic Management Journal*, 16 (1995) 565–80.

McMillan, J., *Games, strategies and managers* (New York: Oxford University Press 1992).

Mertens, J.F., S. Sorin and S. Zamir, 'Repeated Games. Part A-C', *CORE Discussion Paper* 9420-2 (1994).

Meschi, P.X., 'Longevity and cultural differences of international joint ventures: toward time-based cultural management', *Human Relations*, 50(2) (1997) 211–27.

Mezzetti, Claudio, 'Common Agency with Horizontally Differentiated Principals', *Rand Journal of Economics*, 28(2) (1997) 323–45.

Miller, R.R., J.D. Glen, F.Z. Jaspersen and Y. Karmokolias, 'International joint ventures in developing countries', *The World Bank and International Finance Corporation*, Discussion Paper 29 (1996).

Mirrlees, J., 'An Exploration in the Theory of Optimum Income Taxation', *Review of Economic Studies*, 38(2) (1971) 175–208.

Myerson, R.B., *Game Theory: Analysis of Conflict* (Cambridge, MA: Harvard University Press 1991).

Myerson, R.B., 'Optimal Coordination Mechanisms in Generalized Principal-Agent Problems', *Journal of Mathematical Economics*, 10 (1982) 67–81.

Nash, J., 'The Bargaining Problem', *Econometrica*, 18(1) (1950) 155–62.

Nash, J., 'Noncooperative Games', *Annals of Mathematics*, 54 (1951) 289–95.

Nash, J., 'Co-operative Games', *Econometrica*, 21 (1953) 128–40.

Olsen, T.E. and G. Torsvik, 'Intertemporal common agency and organizational design: How much decentralization?' *European Economic Review*, 39 (1995) 1405–28.

Osborne, M.J. and A. Rubinstein, *A Course in Game Theory* (Cambridge, MA: MIT Press 1994).

Osland, G.E. and S.T. Cavusgil, Performance issues in US-China joint ventures, *California Management Review*, 38 (1996) 106–30.

Osland, G.E. and S.T. Cavusgil, The use of multiple-party perspectives in international joint venture research. *Management International Review*, 38 (1998) 191–202.

Ott, U.F., 'International Joint Ventures: A Common Agency Problem', *Global Business & Economics Review*, 2(1) (2000a) 67–84.

Ott, U.F., 'Termination and Endgame Scenarios in International Joint Ventures', *Global Business & Economics Review*, 2(2) (2000b) 172–84.

Ott, U.F., 'Games International Joint Ventures Play during Their Life Cycle: Key Factors for Co-operation and Conflict', *Journal of International Business Studies, www.jibs.net*, 2 (2003) 1–16.

Pan, Y., 'Influences on foreign equity ownership level in joint ventures in China', *Journal of International Business Studies*, 27(1) (1996) 1–27.

Parkhe, A., 'Messy research, methodological predispositions and theory development in international joint ventures', *Academy of Management Review*, 18(2) (1993a) 227–68.

Parkhe, A., 'Partner nationality and the structure-performance relationship in strategic alliances', *Organization Science*, 4(2) (1993b) 301–24.

Parkhe, A., International joint ventures. In B.J. Punnett & O. Shenkar (eds), *Handbook for International Management Research* (Cambridge, MA: Blackwell 1996).

Rasmusen, E. *Games and information – an introduction to game theory* (Cambridge, MA: Blackwell 1994).

Reuer, J.J. and M.P. Koza, 'Asymmetric information and joint venture performance: Theory and evidence for domestic and international joint ventures', *Strategic Management Journal*, 21 (2000a) 81–8.

Reuer, J.J. and M.P. Koza, 'On lemons and indigestibility: resource assembly through joint ventures', *Strategic Management Journal*, 21 (2000b) 195–97.

Richter, F.J. and K. Vettel, 'Successful joint ventures in Japan: Transfering knowledge through organisational learning', *International Journal of Strategic Management*, 28 (1995) 37–45.

Riley, J., 'Silver Signals: Twenty-Five Years of Screening and Signaling', *Journal of Economic Literature*, 39 (2001) 432–78.

Rogerson, W.P., 'Repeated Moral Hazard', *Econometrica*, 53(1) (1985) 69–76.

Rumelt, R.P., D. Schendel and D. Teece, Strategic Management and Economics. *Strategic Management Journal*, 12 (1991) 5–29.

Schaan, J.-L. and P.W. Beamish, Joint Venture General Managers in less developed countries. In F. Contractor & P. Lorange (eds), *Cooperative Strategies in International Business – Joint Ventures and Technology Partnerships between Firms* (New York: Lexington Books 1988) 279–99.

Schelling, T.C., *The Strategy of Conflict* (Cambridge: Harvard University Press 1960).

Selten, R., 'Spieltheoretische Behandlung eines Oligopolmodells mit Nachfragetragheit', *Zeitschrift fur die gesamte Staatswissenschaft* 121 (1965) 301–24 and 667–89.

Selten, R., 'Chain Store Paradox', *Theory and Decision*, 9 (1978) 127–59.

Serapio, M.G. and W.F. Cascio, 'End-games in International Alliance', *Academy of Management Executive*, 10(1) (1996) 62–73.

Shenkar, O., 'International joint ventures problems in China – risks and remedies', *Long Range Planning*, 23(3) (1990) 82–90.

Shenkar, O. and Y. Zeira, 'Human resource management in international joint ventures: directions for research', *Academy of Management Review*, 12(3) (1987) 546–57.

Shenkar, O. and Y. Zeira, 'Role-conflict and role ambiguity of chief executive officers in international joint ventures', *Journal of International Business Studies*, 23 (1992) 55–75.

Sheridan, D., 'International joint ventures – Soviet and Western perspectives', *Journal of Management Studies*, Book Review, 30(5) (1993) 839–41.

Spence, M., 'Job Market Signaling', *Quarterly Journal of Economics*, 87(3) (1973) 355–79.

Stole, L., 'Mechanism design under common agency', *Working Paper* (MIT 1990).

Stole, L., 'Mechanism design under common agency', *Discussion Paper*, No. 100 (Harvard Law School 1991).

Svejnar, J. and S.C. Smith, 'The economics of joint ventures in Less Developed Countries', *Quarterly Journal of Economics*, 99(1) (1984) 149–67.

Terpstra, V. and B.L. Simonin, Strategic alliances in the triad: an exploratory study. *Journal of International Marketing*, 1 (1993) 4–20.

Turpin, D., 'Strategic alliances with Japanese firms: myths and realities', *Long Range Planning*, 26(4) (1993) 4–15.

Valdes Llaneza, A. and E. Garcia-Canal, 'Distinctive features of domestic and international joint ventures', *Management International Review*, 38 (1998) 49–66.

Veugelers, R. and K. Kesteloot, 'On the design of stable joint ventures', *European Economic Review*, 38 (1994) 1799–1815.

Vickrey, W. 'Counterspeculation auctions and competitive sealed tenders', *Journal of Finance*, 16(1) (1961) 41–50.

Von Neumann, J. and O. Morgenstern, *The Theory of Games and Economic Behavior* (Princeton, NJ: Princeton University Press 1944).

Webster, D.R., 'International joint ventures with Pacific Rim partners,' *Business Horizons*, March–April (1989) 65–71.

Weiss, S.E., 'Creating the GM-Toyota joint venture: a case in complex negotiation', *Columbia Journal of World Business*, 22(2) (1987) 23–37.

Winfrey, F.L. and A.L. Austin, 'Reciprocal agency: Toward a theory of international joint ventures', in Woodside A.G. and R.E. Pitts (eds), *Creating and managing international joint ventures* (Westport, CN: Quorum Books, Greenwood Publishing Group, Inc. 1996) 21–32.

Yan, A. and M. Zeng, 'International joint venture instability: a critique of previous research, a reconceptualization, and direction for future research', *Journal of International Business Studies*, 30(3) (1999) 397–414.

Yan, A.M. and B. Gray, 'Bargaining power, management control, and performance in United-States China joint ventures – a comparative case study', *Academy of Management Journal*, 37(6) (1994) 1478–1517.

Zhang, Y. and N. Rajagopalan, 'Inter-partner credible threat in international joint ventures: an infinitely repeated prisoner's dilemma model', *Journal of International Business Studies*, 33(3) (2002) 457–78.

Author Index

Afriyie, K., 44
Akerlof, G.A., 14, 16, 17, 23
Anderson, E., 50, 51
Austin, A.L., 20

Balakrishnan, S., 17, 18, 33, 54, 55
Bamossy, G.J., 43
Barden, J.Q., 45, 46
Beamish, P.W., 3, 4, 32, 38, 39, 40, 48
Berg, S.V., 36
Bergemann, D., 29
Bernheim, B.D., 14, 15, 29
Bhattacharya, S., 55
Blodgett, L.L., 36, 38
Brouthers, K.D., 42
Buckley, P.J., 33, 38, 39, 44, 45, 48, 71, 181
Burton, F.N., 36, 38

Campbell, D.E., 19, 23, 27
Cascio, W.F., 25, 55
Casson, M.C., 33, 38, 39, 44, 45, 48, 71, 181
Cavusgil, S.T., 20, 50
Chi, T., 20, 33, 50, 52
Chiappori, P.-A., 29
Choi, C.-B., 48
Contractor, F.J., 45, 69

Dasgupta, A., 20
Daspupta, S., 38
Datta, D.K., 32, 42, 45, 47, 69, 70
Dhanaraj, C., 53
Dowling, M.J., 51
Doz, Y.L., 38
Dussauge, P., 50

Eisele, J., 55

Fudenberg, D., 4, 12, 28, 29, 34

Gal-Or, E., 14, 15, 16, 19, 29
Garcia-Canal, E., 2

Gardner, R., 4, 11, 34
Garrette, B., 50
Garvey, G.T., 56
Germain, R., 57, 99
Geringer, J.M., 14, 19, 20, 33, 36, 37, 49, 50
Ghemawat, P., 5
Gibbons, R., 4, 11, 34
Glazer, J., 55
Glen, J.D., 38
Gomes-Casseres, B., 38, 44
Gray, B., 26, 38, 46, 56
Guesnerie, R., 14, 49

Harrigan, K.R., 36, 38, 54
Harsanyi, J., 11, 12
Hebert, L., 33, 50
Hennart, J.-F., 33
Hoekman, J.M., 36
Holler, M.J., 12
Holmstrom, B.,14, 28, 29, 49

Inkpen, A., 32, 33
Illing, G., 12

Jaspersen, F.Z., 38
Jensen, M., 14, 15, 49

Karmokolias, Y., 38
Kesteloot, K., 33
Killing, J.P., 3, 4, 17, 39, 45, 69
Kogut, B., 3, 4, 33, 38, 50. 55
Koza, M.P., 17, 18, 32, 33, 54, 55

Laffont, J.J., 14, 49
Lecraw, D.J., 3, 4, 39
Lin, X., 57, 99
Lorange, P., 45, 46, 47, 69, 70
Luo, Y., 7, 49, 53, 73
Lyles, M.A., 36, 45, 46, 53

Macho-Stadler, I., 19, 23, 29
Martimort, D., 14,15, 16, 19, 29

Subject Index